Down-Home Wholesome

Down-Home Wholesome

300 Low-Fat Recipes from a New Soul Kitchen

Danella Carter

A DUTTON BOOK

DUTTON
Published by the Penguin Group
Penguin Books USA Inc., 375 Hudson Street, New York, New York 10014, U.S.A.
Penguin Books Ltd, 27 Wrights Lane, London W8 5TZ, England
Penguin Books Australia Ltd, Ringwood, Victoria, Australia
Penguin Books Canada Ltd, 10 Alcorn Avenue, Toronto, Ontario, Canada M4V 3B2
Penguin Books (N.Z.) Ltd, 182–190 Wairau Road, Auckland 10, New Zealand

Penguin Books Ltd, Registered Offices: Harmondsworth, Middlesex, England

First published by Dutton, an imprint of Dutton Signet,
a division of Penguin Books USA Inc.
Distributed in Canada by McClelland & Stewart Inc.

First Printing, November, 1995
10 9 8 7 6 5 4 3 2 1

 REGISTERED TRADEMARK—MARCA REGISTRADA

LIBRARY OF CONGRESS CATALOGING-IN-PUBLICATION DATA

Carter, Danella.
Down-home wholesome : 300 low-fat recipes from a new soul kitchen / by Danella Carter.
p.   cm.
Includes bibliographical references and index.
ISBN 0-525-93909-1 (acid-free paper)
1. Afro-American cookery.   2. Cookery, American—Southern style.
3. Low-fat diet—Recipes.   I. Title.
TX715.C313   1995
641.59'296073—dc20   95-19240
                                                    CIP

Printed in the United States of America
Set in Garamond Light
Designed by Eve Kirch

To Mom, Grandpop Cothran, and Eli.

In Memory of

Emma Roundtree Taylor (1900–1990)
Louise Carey Cothran (1918–1982)
Kimberly Ross (1968–1993)
Claudia Outlaw Bowman (1934–1995)

Acknowledgments

In the beginning there was food. No manuscript, no publisher, no idea to write a cookbook. Then came the title. From there, a chain of synchronistic events led me to the writing of this book, and I am indebted to every kind soul who helped it along, beginning with the invaluable handful of people who initially inspired and/or encouraged me: Alfreda Carter, Anderson Cothran, Lisa Bradley, Nevine Michaan, Kinnari Panikar, Linda Villarosa, and Esther Gottlieb. Taking it from there was my agent, Nicole Aragi, who, with her wit, practicality, and buoyant good humor, helped carry my idea forth to Julia Moskin, my trusted editor. Julia's insight, patience, and dedication provided crucial comfort at every stage of the process. Of equal importance were those who helped me with research in the planning stages: Emory S. Campbell and his assistant, Juanita Taylor, of the Penn Center in St. Helena's Island; Marvin Dulaney and his assistant, Karen Thrower, of the Avery Research Center for African-American History and Culture at the College of Charleston; and John J. Vander Velde, Rare Books Librarian of the cookery collection at Kansas State University.

I am also thankful for the friends who took time from their harried schedules to test and/or taste the recipes, providing me with key commentary: Kim

Carter, Jackie Woodson, Danielle Michaan, David Kreigel, Cynthia Flynt, Karen Palmer, Jill Pearlman, Robert Boyd, Eli Fountain, Martin Guttman, Marina Budhos, Amy Kaufman, Susan Bell, and Cheryl Washington. I'd like to thank those who aided on the home front, namely Charles Nemetz and Peggy and Ben Miklas. And finally, there was my soul mate, Eli Gottlieb, who practically lived in the fabric of the experience, offered firm but gentle critique of the book, comforted me even though he was agonizing over his novel, ate more than the legal limit of spoonbread, and gave honest commentary on every recipe that crossed his lips. Thanking him on paper seems somewhat shallow, since he already understands the depth of my gratitude, but—thanks.

Contents

Preface

In the Old South it was said that rich folks ate for the body, poor folks ate for the soul. That certainly held true for the African slaves, a people who had to supplement their world with inmost pleasures in attempt to counteract their "peculiar" surroundings. During that period, soul satisfaction had more to do with eating than anything else, simply because there wasn't much else. Life for the slave began at dusk, after the fields had been tended and high domestic order had been achieved at the Big House. Music, dance, and religion formed the core of community for those miserably affected by colonial plantation life. And there was food. A steaming bowl of peppery collard greens; a tender hoecake, chock-full of freshly ground corn; sticky-sweet yams roasting over a pyramid of hot coals—all provided solace to the slave. This tradition of gentle consolation gave birth to one of the most original branches of American cuisine—that mixed marriage of kitchen cultures known as "down-home."

Introduction

When I first announced my intent to produce a "nutritionally correct" down-home cookbook, the initial responses of my friends ranged from mild incredulity to out-and-out skepticism. To most people, low-calorie down-home cooking seemed an oxymoron, however intriguing. Traditionalists suspected that tampering with the key flavor base of down-home cookery (read fat) would render it tasteless, dimming its unique charm. I'll admit, I had a moment of hesitation—after all, I was proposing to reconstruct America's very first comfort food, a surgery that could have resulted in an irreversible "cuisinectomy." But I eventually decided to carry on with my original idea: to shake up the ingredients in this wonderful, underappreciated cuisine for the sake of health. I had the future in mind too. Things that don't change end up extinct or in museums. And the truth is, down-home cooking has long outlived its status as a survival food.

In fact, last time I checked, it was killing us.

Many of the illnesses afflicting the American people, including the African-American community, are linked to nutrition: high blood pressure, diabetes, heart disease, obesity. What perplexes me is why no one, as of yet, has stepped forward with an alternative down-home diet.

Consider it done.

What I've managed to do is temper the unhealthier aspects of down-home cooking. Reinventing it has meant moderating its "terrible toos"—too much salt, too much fat, and too much sugar—and relying extensively on freshly ground spices and whole herbs. Traditional flavor bases—fatback, ham hocks, salt pork—have been eliminated and replaced with heart-friendly alternatives, such as smoked turkey or dried fish. Vegetarians have the option of using a fresh herb or sizzling pepper base.

Many people make the mistake of equating fat with richer flavor. The "magic" of cooking with fat simply lies in the way that it rapidly deepens the flavor of seasonings in foods. I prefer to let my flavors develop through time. Yes, I'm telling you to slow down. That's right, take off your seat belts, for I am not the Minute Chef. This doesn't mean that you cook your food to mush—it just means allowing the flavors to integrate on their own, sometimes off the stove.

About flavors: A few of my recipes remain true to tradition, but many have received some rather startling makeovers. For example, that old standby, candied yams, takes on a new dimension with the addition of grated gingerroot, citrus peel, and an intense Far Eastern spice, cardamom. Into a fluffy omelet (made only of egg whites!) I've folded a tart mixture of collard greens and shallots. For my Cowpea Chow Chow, cilantro, red-hot chili peppers, and lime juice are the splash of freshness that redefine the meaning of "jumping beans." A lot of the recipes were re-created with a sense of adventure in mind. And why not? I come from a culture of improvisers: artistic, athletic, and scientific. My people changed the course of American music because we found it difficult to cakewalk to Mozart. Who says I can't add a few changes myself?

When I began my research for this book, I discovered to my chagrin that there had been virtually no research into the African presence in Southern cooking, nor were there any works dedicated exclusively to slave cookery. The African influence is also conspicuously absent in a lot of Southern, ethnic, and "world" cookbooks. This void has allowed the notion to form that the spirit presiding over Early American cookery was none other than Betty Crocker.

Pure fiction.

This cookbook spotlights a simple fact: the African culinary contribution to American cooking was essential. The Yoruba tribe is an excellent place to begin.

The Yoruba were a progressive, highly sophisticated people, the flower of West Africa's Nigerian culture. If you're looking for a high-toned example of one of their gifts to America, here it is in a word: *jazz.* From the early 1600s until the middle of the nineteenth century, the Yoruba were brought over to the United States to be sold as cooks and agriculturists. Not only were they highly skilled in the arts of the kitchen, they were also accompanied by a garden's worth of herbs and plants that were virtually unknown in America. Among the foods that followed them here were okra, yams, cowpeas, peanuts, and sesame (benne) seeds, to name a few. Taking a cue from the Native Americans, the Yoruba made good use of corn (maize), which is indigenous to the United States. They tamed the bitter green. And with the help of rice crops brought over from the Ivory Coast, African rice farmers turned Charleston into one of the wealthiest cities in the land.

It's certainly not hard today to trace the similarities between West African and what we know as Southern cooking. An African corn cake is quite close to what's called a hushpuppy down South. Stewing and frying, the most popular cooking methods in the South, are traditional West African standbys. Gumbo, a thick Creole dish, is an African word meaning okra, which happens to be the star ingredient in this hearty stew. And Hoppin' John, a zesty rice and black-eyed pea dish still popular in the South, was daily fare aboard the slave ships taking the Middle Passage. Other one-pot dishes containing meat, vegetables, and miscellaneous spices, such as perleau (pilau) are analogous to Africa's jollof rice. Where West Africa and the American South differed was when it came to the matter of pork.

The consumption of pork was a relatively foreign experience for the newly arrived slave. Some Africans ate pork back home, but many—especially Muslims—abstained. They would soon acquire a taste for it, as it would become one of the main staples of their food ration. A large slab of salt pork, or fatback, was their essential protein source and flavor enhancer. But the slaves also made use of the undesired parts of the pig: feet, snout, tail, and the pigs' intestines, which were called chitterlings or "chitlins" (derived from the Middle English word *chiterling,* meaning viscera). And, depending on the personal relationship between slaveholder and slave, slaves were given limited license to fish or hunt, which afforded them access to game, fowl, and sometimes their own hog.

When it comes to cookware, the lineage is clear: the pots that were used in the Old South were borrowed almost directly from traditional African versions of the same. Large three-legged cast-iron kettles called spiders were used to cook up a mess of greens. Iron skillets were employed to fry up chicken. And the big wooden spoon clasped lyrically between Mammy's hands was the standard African utensil for "stirrin' de pots," as it's described in Gullah dialect.

Mammy's cooking technique was that of the senses: a pinch of this, a dash of that, tasting as she went along. But despite her apparent reign in the Big Kitchen, her recipes were never documented. Fortunately, they were passed through the generations. In my case, I've sifted out regional favorites and served them up with my own family's ancestral cooking—relying on hearsay and scattered bits, mustering up flavors and reminiscences long forgotten— and have arrived with an eclectic mix of tastes.

For nearly a century, cooks have run in my family. The most influential were my mother, grandfather, and great-grandmother. Each one's cooking represented something significant to me: a holiday, a day of the week, a season, or just a moment vividly captured.

Take Mom and Christmas. They are linked in my mind like Louis Armstrong and Ella Fitzgerald. Mom enjoyed Christmas even more than us kids, and for obvious reasons: It was her chance, starting a few weeks prior to the event, to search for the *best of everything.* Piling us into the car, she would roar off to the local maze of open-air markets, where right before our eyes she metamorphosed into the Shrewd Shopper, feared and admired by all the local merchants. (This was funny to me, because Mom is basically a timid, very proper soul, who cringed whenever we acted up in public.) And yet suddenly there she was, bellowing, "Drain those chitlins before you weigh them!" as we shrugged to the butcher apologetically. "Do you have a better turkey in the back?" she'd sweetly inquire of the poulterer. "Insects have been gnawing something fierce on the collards," she'd say to the greengrocer, with a judgmental nod. When Christmas Day finally arrived, it was always accompanied by the same scenes: a fortress of toys and gifts risen around the tree; Mom tottering, limp and bleary-eyed from her all-night stint in the kitchen; smells of the Motherland wafting before our noses, conjuring up the treasures that awaited us. All year long we looked forward to the butter-soft texture of the greens; the chewy, burnt-sugar crust that crackled atop the candied yams; the autumn-colored glaze of our roasted turkey, packed to the gills with savory cornbread stuffing; and much, much more. When, hours later, it was time for our satiated guests to leave, Mom would bid them good-bye by handing each one a sweet potato pie or a duplicate platter of the meal to go. To this day she upholds this tradition of generous hospitality.

Then there were Sundays, my favorite day of the week, thanks to Grand-pop Cothran. Grandpop was a Sunday cook, a self-taught amateur chef whose meals ranged from oxtail stew to coq au vin. Sundays would officially begin around 6:30 A.M., when Grandpop lulled us out of bed with stirring melodies of gospel music that played on the radio throughout the day. The air was thick with the smell of biscuits baking and coffee (off-limits to us, of course) brewing in the pot. By seven we were all at the table eating portions of baked shad with crisp sweet onions and eggs sunny-side-up.

In the afternoon Grandpop would begin preparing Sunday dinner. I loved watching him work. The kitchen was very large, and yet Grandpop seemed to tower over everything. He wore a white paneled apron with a small cloth tucked under the sash, which he frequently used to wipe off his work table, the stove, and the sides of pots whenever anything boiled over. On the Formica counter were the usual props: a chopping block, Ginsu knives, and a small jelly jar half-filled with iced Canadian whiskey. (Grandpop, now a very active churchgoer, has since become a solid teetotaler.) Grandpop was a slow, methodical cook who abhorred new-fangled gadgets like the Veg-o-matic, preferring instead the therapeutic concentration that comes from dicing and grating by hand.

I trusted Grandpop's judgment in food; he was the only person who could get me to eat macaroni and cheese, but that was because he deviated from the usual milk and cheese sludge I'd never acquired a taste for. He'd toss the macaroni in a little butter, with mushrooms, herbs, and a cheese I now recognize as Parmesan. Then he'd carefully craft a top layer with sliced tomatoes, crown it with a congenial mixture of shallots, celery, and bread crumbs, and broil it for five minutes. Scrumptious! Another one of my favorites was his corn pudding: freshly hulled corn, minced green bell peppers, and red chili peppers suspended in an airy custard base.

Grandpop wasn't much of a dessert maker, but he topped off each meal by washing all the dishes. And while Grandmom Cothran wasn't much for cooking, she always came through with after-dinner treats like fresh-picked grapes or banana pudding (remember the kind with vanilla wafers along the sides?). Grandmom is no longer with us, but memories abound of her great skills as a painter, milliner, and weaver.

Of all of my relatives, the most colorful was my great-grandmother Nana. Though long gone, she's left me with intense memories of the summers I spent at her place as a child, in a house filled with the scents of ripe bananas and Yuban coffee. She used to tell tales of all her siblings: two sisters named Charity and Missouri and two brothers named Dempsey and Joe-Floyd. Her mother was called Big-Six, because she was just that tall and "didn't take mess off of nobody." Big-Six's mother had been a slave cook who'd managed to pass down a lot of her recipes to Nana, recipes Nana used when she was a domestic for the Vanderveres on Long Island. But Nana wasn't necessarily domesticated. Not at all! Nana, in fact, fancied herself a glamour type, having been married four times. She loved an audience—as did her dog, a German shepherd named Liz (Taylor). I spent as much time as I could around Nana, who was as spunky and mischievous as one of the kids. She used to let me try on her fur coats and festive veiled hats, she fixed my hair in pretty adult styles, and granted me permission to wear lipstick around the house.

When it came to food, she managed to create quick, delicious meals with a minimum amount of effort. She was meticulous about what she ate and would eat ground meat only if she had ground it herself. Nana was a bit finicky—she didn't eat chitlins or pig's feet (neither did Grandmom, for that matter), she boiled her bacon before crisping it, and would spend an hour cleaning the fat off one chicken.

On Wednesday nights Nana would host Pokeno® parties in the cellar with the local ladies while Pop-Pop stayed upstairs watching TV. She'd prepare three or four types of dainty finger sandwiches and would serve them along with iced mint tea or strawberry limeade. Today I practice the ritual of afternoon tea in memory of Nana and her parties.

As a fourth-generation cook, I bring a flash of history, a brief family portrait, my most treasured recipes, and, most importantly, a means of self-empowerment through proper diet and nutrition.

The most valuable suggestion I can offer you is to trust your preferences and instincts while trying a recipe. Take into account the differences in stoves, altitudes, and other occurrences that could provide ten different results for one recipe. Cook with your soul and, most importantly, with your heart.

Welcome to my kitchen!

Danella Carter
New York, 1995

~1~

The Kitchen Basics

If home is where the "hearth" is, then it's easy to understand where down-home cooking begins its journey: in the kitchen. The kitchen is the womb of the house, the place where we best remember being nurtured. Some of us are fortunate to have large kitchens, filled with windows and sunshine pouring in from every angle, while others can make miracles happen in a tiny Pullman. Large or small, I like being in a cheerful, inviting place where people just naturally pull up a chair and chat while the food is cooking, nibbling things and offering their suggestions.

My kitchen doubles as my office, and because of that I have made it as functional as the inside of a boat, with everything within easy reach. On one side is the library, a collection of shelves and file cabinets stocked with articles, reviews, and recipes, and cookbooks from all over the world. On the other side is the storage area, racks for hanging pots and pans, drawers and cabinets for other cooking and eating utensils. There are deep shelves for appliances, and smaller shelves for spices. A small pantry stores dried and preserved foods. A nearby closet holds "atmospheric" items: table linens, napkins, candles and holders, salt and pepper shakers, vases, and special serving dishes. Please understand that a lot of these items are simply accumulated *frills* and are not at all necessary to produce a wholesome menu.

In fact, a down-home kitchen needn't be elaborate. It's much better to establish an intimate relationship with a few good pots and pans than to have a showcase of culinary gadgetry. Spend time with your cookware, get to know the rhythms of its heat distribution, and you'll be amply rewarded for your investment.

I appreciate the more traditional utensils, such as a good set of chopping knives over a food processor, simply because chopping by hand affords a better sense of participation in the meal and allows me to fine-tune the coarseness of the cut. It is an ideal way to work, and I often find it therapeutic. On the other hand, a processor is more suitable if you're making pastes and purees, to take just two examples out of many, so it may be a good idea to keep one around. Most people who love to cook, myself included, derive more satisfaction from doing in the kitchen than from having the kitchen do for them. But we know our limitations. The majority of us can't hand press apples into juice, nor can we craft the intricate shape of a waffle by hand. Therefore we are all happily at the mercy of certain electronic aids. But you don't actually need a machine to make bread or to steam rice—get what I'm saying?

Here is the basic equipment for a functional down-home kitchen:

Cast-Iron Cookware: Cast iron should be exposed to as little water as possible. After washing, dry thoroughly, and with a dry cloth dabbed with a little oil, coat the pan with the oil.

13-inch large skillet	Flat round or rectangular griddle
8-inch small skillet	Dutch oven with a lid

Stainless Steel and Nonstick Cookware: A nonstick coating allows you to cook with very little oil. The technology has come a long way since the days of Teflon. Excaliber® coating is a popular surface that works well with no oil.

1-quart saucepan with lid	3-quart saucepan with lid
2-quart saucepan with lid	5-quart stockpot with steaming basket

12-inch nonstick omelet pan
13-inch nonstick sauté pan

Roasting pan with rack

Cooking Implements

3 long-handled wooden spoons
4-sided grater
Wooden chopping board
Vegetable peeler (Oxo makes
    an excellent one)
Citrus zester
Garlic mandolin
Spatula
Mortar and pestle
Salt mill

Pepper mill
Kitchen shears
Balloon whisk
Pastry brush
Cherry pitter
Sifter
Rolling pin
Food mill
Meat tenderizing mallet
Stainless-steel mixing bowls

Knives

Serrated bread knife
Paring knife

Cleaver
10-inch chopping knife

Electric Appliances

Juice extractor
Waffle iron
Food processor

Coffee/spice grinder
Blender

FOOD BASICS

Behind every good cook is a stash of "kitchen magic," an entourage of flavor enhancers that are the true meal makers. My pantry of basic herbs, spices, and flavorings is flamboyant compared to Nana's sparse but resourceful cupboard, which consisted of only four items: salt, pepper, flour, and a copper-and-tin canister labeled tea, in which she kept strained chicken fat. Let's begin with the most basic of all the basics.

Salt

If you haven't done so before, do try the kind of coarse sea salt that has to be ground through a mill. There is pleasure in the handwork of grinding, but more important is the flavor bonus: sea salt is sharper, more intense than the additive-laden iodized salt you buy at the market. Therefore, less coarse salt can be used to achieve the same effect as the same quantity of table salt. Another way to reduce your salt intake is to make and use a salt blend, which may include a few dried herbs and spices.

～ Seasoned Salt ～

¼ cup sea salt
½ teaspoon garlic powder
½ teaspoon onion powder
2 tablespoons dried parsley
   flakes
Pinch of cayenne

½ teaspoon celery seed
¼ teaspoon paprika
1 tablespoon white peppercorns
¼ teaspoon ground thyme
½ teaspoon ground sage

Place all ingredients in a mortar and crush until fine, or process in a mini food processor or grinder. Store in a cool dry place for up to 3 months. *Makes ⅔ cup.*

Pepper

Peppercorns, to be exact. Red, white, black, pink, green—they store well, and you can keep a little of each mixed together in a clear glass tube, where the pretty little berries look like a painting. Grind small amounts as needed in a mill, or in a mortar for a coarser grind. Nothing in the world compares to freshly ground pepper; it's nature's wake-up call to sleepy flavors. If you haven't been grinding your own pepper, try it. I guarantee your shaker will take a long vacation in the back of the closet. Here are a couple of blends.

∽ Lemon Pepper ∽

I use lemon pepper in many of my dishes because of its subtle intensity. Few seasonings are as versatile as this indispensable blend. If you do not have a grinder or mini food processor, grate the lemon zest instead of cutting it into strips.

Zest of 1 lemon, cut into strips, avoiding bitter white pith

1 tablespoon black peppercorns

Grind the lemon zest and peppercorns in a mini food processor or grinder, until the desired texture has been reached. If you do not have a grinder, remove the zest from the lemon with a grater. Grind the peppercorns and mix with the grated zest. Store in a cool dry place for up to a week. *Makes 4 teaspoons.*

∽ Lemon Cayenne ∽

Zest of 2 lemons, avoiding bitter white pith

1 tablespoon Szechuan peppercorns

Grind the lemon zest and peppercorns in a mini food processor or grinder, until the desired texture has been reached. If you do not have a grinder, remove the zest from the lemon with a grater. Grind the peppercorns and mix with the grated zest. Store in a cool dry place for up to a week. *Makes 5 teaspoons.*

Herbs

Many of my recipes call for fresh herbs, but this is not an absolute necessity. If you prefer dried herbs to fresh ones, by all means use them. However, a lot of people are beginning to discover the contrast between the fragile fla-

vors on their spice rack and the rainbow of accents that are fresh herbs—
somewhat like the difference between recorded music and a live perfor-
mance. Unfortunately, many fresh herbs bought in a passion often end up as
bags of browned, unidentifiable foliage wasting away in the refrigerator. A
quick and easy method for preserving herbs with their taste intact is given
below. But if you have a sunny patch of earth or windowsill, there is another
alternative: a home herb garden. In my own case, I hesitated good and long
before beginning my own herb garden, because I'd developed a reputation
over the years as the "human herbicide," a smiling assassin of leafy things.
However, after weighing the flavor and cost differential between fresh-cut
herbs and seedlings, I realized I'd be ahead of the game even if they did
shrivel up and pass on to the big salad bowl in the sky. Well, they're still with
me. With a minimum of effort and just a few hours of sunlight a day, you can
have a windowsill full of herbs such as bay leaves, parsley, cilantro, thyme,
marjoram, savory, sage, sorrel, peppermint, spearmint, oregano, rosemary,
sweet basil, and French tarragon—lush leaves of flavor that are as functional
as they are beautiful. As an added bonus, they perfume the room with a
clean, expansive aroma that all the potpourri in the world can't duplicate.
Water them twice a week and make sure that they don't get too much sun.
The leaves flourish so quickly that you'll often have more herbs than you
need. In that case, you can blanch the leaves in boiling water for 5 seconds
and then plunge them into a bowl of ice water. Mix a cup of fresh herbs with
a teaspoon of olive oil and pulse a few times in a food processor. Place a tablespoon at a time of the mixture into small patches of plastic food wrap and
seal and freeze for future use.

You can also make care packages of various herbs to give to friends and
visitors on their way back home. My favorite herb bundle is the traditional
bouquet garni, the holy trinity of thyme, parsley, and a bay leaf that has been
my soup and stew saver for as long as I can remember.

～ Bouquet Garni ～

2 sprigs of thyme
5 sprigs of parsley
1 bay leaf

1 (6–inch) piece of sturdy string
   or a small cheesecloth bag

Tie herbs together with string or place in a small cheesecloth bag. *Makes enough for one soup or stew.*

Seasoning Blends

Of course it's easier to buy your seasonings pre-blended, but the sacrifice of flavor—not to mention value—is immense. Spice shops are sprouting up like chives these days, in ethnic marketplaces, in gourmet shops, in health food stores—and they often provide spice drawers from which you take only as much as you need for a few weeks. If you don't want to stockpile spices, carry the recipe and a set of measuring spoons with you, and buy only the amount you require. Or use dried herbs and spices to make new blends that beat anything premixed at the market.

～ Barbecue Shrimp Seasoning ～

1 teaspoon cayenne
1 teaspoon freshly ground white
   pepper
½ teaspoon salt

½ teaspoon crushed red pepper
½ teaspoon ground thyme
½ teaspoon dried rosemary
½ teaspoon dried oregano

Place all ingredients in a small jar with a tight-fitting lid and shake. Store in a cool dry place. *Makes enough seasoning for 2 pounds of shrimp.*

∽ Creole Spice Mix ∽

This will turn the most pallid gumbo into a Big Easy–style feast.

1 tablespoon cayenne
1 teaspoon celery salt
½ teaspoon garlic powder

½ teaspoon onion powder
1 teaspoon green peppercorns
½ teaspoon dried thyme

Place all ingredients in a mortar and crush until fine, or process in a mini food processor or grinder. Transfer to a small jar with a tight-fitting lid. Store in a cool dry place for up to a month.   *Makes 9 teaspoons.*

∽ Dried Herbs Mix ∽

1 teaspoon dried sage (not
   ground)
1 teaspoon dried basil
1 teaspoon dried parsley flakes

½ teaspoon dried tarragon
½ teaspoon dried chervil
¼ teaspoon ground thyme
¼ teaspoon fennel seed

Mix all ingredients together in a small jar with a tight-fitting lid and store in a cool dry place.   *Makes 4½ teaspoons.*

∽ Shellfish Boil ∽

This savory standby of Southern cooking is usually seen hard at work season-ing crabs, crayfish, and shrimp. Keep the cold beer close at hand!

1 teaspoon dried parsley flakes
1 teaspoon dried thyme
1 teaspoon celery salt
1 teaspoon paprika

1 teaspoon freshly ground black
   pepper
1 teaspoon grated lemon zest
1 teaspoon cayenne

¼ teaspoon dry mustard

¼ teaspoon ground ginger

¼ teaspoon mace

⅛ teaspoon ground cardamom

¼ teaspoon cinnamon

⅛ teaspoon ground cloves

Mix all ingredients together in a jar with a tight-fitting lid and shake before using. Can be stored up to a month. *Makes enough to season 3 dozen crabs, or up to 3 pounds of shrimp or crayfish.*

~ Seafood Seasoning ~

This is the blend I season catfish with, although it works with just about any fish or shellfish.

¼ cup sea salt

3 tablespoons white peppercorns

1½ teaspoons Szechuan peppercorns or 1 teaspoon cayenne

1 teaspoon dry mustard

1 teaspoon paprika

1 teaspoon ground sage

½ teaspoon nutmeg

Place all ingredients in a mortar and crush until fine, or process in a mini food processor or grinder. Transfer to a small jar with a tight-fitting lid. Shake before each use. Store in a cool dry place for up to a month.

~ Pie Spice ~

½ teaspoon cinnamon

¼ teaspoon nutmeg

½ teaspoon allspice

¼ teaspoon ground cloves

¼ teaspoon ground ginger

⅛ teaspoon ground cardamom

⅛ teaspoon freshly ground white pepper

Mix all ingredients together in a jar with a tight-fitting lid and store in a cool dry place. Shake before using. *Makes 2 teaspoons.*

Chili Peppers

The taste and fiery sizzle of chili peppers in certain dishes is essential, but gratuitous usage can be a masquerade for lack of flavor. When all you've got to say for a dish is *"Boy, is that hot,"* that dish is in serious trouble. I've got quite a few startling hot dishes in my repertoire, but they have more going for them than scoville units (scoville is the measure of heat in chilies). The most mouth-scorching, face-reddening, tear-inducing pepper is the notorious Scotch bonnet, a deceptively small sweet chili pepper that comes in about four Day-Glo shades. These are hotter even than the lantern-shaped habanero pepper, which rings in at 200,000 scoville units (to give you some perspective, the jalapeño has only 75,000). Know your limit before you plunge a whole pepper into the pot. Most of a pepper's heat is found in the seeds and membrane, so if you are inclined toward a milder palate, remove either or both. Use thin rubber gloves when touching peppers and keep your fingers away from your eyes. Most of my recipes call for fresh chilies, but in a pinch dried may be substituted.

Garlic

Fresh garlic, like fresh herbs, was pretty much nonexistent in our household when I was growing up. Mom used to enhance her flavors with Accent and garlic powder, which got no protests out of us. As obscure as it was to us, we understood one thing about garlic: when you ate it, you got bad breath, and people scattered from you as they did from Pepe le Pew, the amorous skunk of Saturday morning cartoon fame. The truth is, garlic is so tame when it's cooked that you can eat loads of it without the adverse effects (well, almost). As with fresh bay leaves, garlic can practically flavor a soup on its own. Use it in mashed potatoes, salad dressing, marinades; make butter with it; stuff a whole head into the cavity of a roasting chicken; in other words, become addicted to it, for garlic is one of nature's best antibiotics. If you are fortunate enough to live near a good nursery, try to find fresh young garlic, a bud whose tender flavor is so good when crushed that you can use it raw to make salad dressing. Fresh garlic heads, or bulbs, are also good roasted. The aroma of any garlic roasting in the oven is intoxicating, an appetite enhancer in itself, but fresh roasted garlic has an inimitable flavor and texture—just squeeze the garlic from its pulp and immediately find something to spread it onto.

∼ Roasted Garlic ∼

4 heads garlic
Olive oil

4 small sprigs of rosemary

Preheat oven to 400 degrees F. Slice each garlic head in half crosswise. Rub a small amount of oil over each half and put the halves together with a sprig of rosemary between them. Wrap each garlic head in aluminum foil. Place the heads on a baking sheet and bake for 25 minutes, or until garlic is soft. Serve immediately.

∼ Garlic Chips ∼

For ultra-thin slivers of garlic, I use an inexpensive garlic mandoline. You can obtain this invaluable gadget from most any kitchenware store, or see resources guide, page 268.

1 head garlic

2 tablespoons olive oil

Separate the cloves from the head and peel them. Slice each clove into very thin slivers. Heat the oil in a large skillet, preferably cast iron, over medium heat. Add the garlic and, working fast, toss until garlic is lightly browned. Remove garlic and drain on paper towels. Store in a jar with a tight-fitting lid. Use within three days.

Onions

Despite their having social consequences similar to garlic, onions can be used in an incredibly wide array of dishes. There are four types of onions in addition to the usual white and yellow: *red onions,* for slicing raw into thin rings for salads; *green onions,* or *scallions,* which impart a tart, almost lemony flavor to dishes; *shallots* (a bit confusing, since the Cajun version of a shallot is a scallion) for more delicate dishes; and *pearl onions,* marble-size gems that work well within a richly flavored stew. *Vidalia,* a big, sweet, and versatile yellow onion from Georgia, is used in quite a few down-home dishes. With their deep, rich flavor, Vidalia onions browned often compensate for the lack of pork in greens dishes and in dishes that would usually call for hocks or fatback as a flavor enhancer. Keep a jar of "brown onions" on hand and you'll have an instant flavor boost whenever you need it.

∽ Brown Onions ∽

2 tablespoons olive oil   **6 large onions**

Heat the oil in a large skillet, preferably cast iron, over medium-high heat. Cut the onions lengthwise and then crosswise into very thin half-rings. Add onions to the pan and let them cook for 5 minutes, until they begin to turn brown on the edges. Lower heat to medium, and continue cooking for 25 more minutes, turning occasionally with a spatula to cook evenly, until onions have turned reddish brown in color. Drain on paper towel. Store in a jar with a tight-fitting lid. Use within three days.   *Makes 2 cups.*

Oils

The first time I tasted olive oil was at Grandmom Cothran's house. I was making a grilled cheese sandwich, and there was no Mazola in sight. I spied something in an oil bottle that looked like oil, except for one thing: it was green—like limes or Granny Smith apples. I had no choice but to use it, since

I had already bonded the cheese to the bread. Gingerly, I poured a few drops in the pan and set my sandwich down on it. I wish I could tell you I liked it. I didn't. The oil ruined my lunch.

Many years later I met olive oil again, and a love affair was consummated on the spot. The oil was lighter this time: cold-pressed, extra-virgin, and delicious! Moral of the story: Put your money where your mouth is. Invest in a good-quality, extra-virgin oil, especially if you're a big salad eater.

~ Lemon Oil ~

Zest of 2 lemons, avoiding bitter white pith   **2 cups olive oil**

Cut the zest into strips and place them in a large jar with a tight-fitting lid. Add the oil and close the jar tightly. Store in a sunny place for at least 2 weeks. Strain, discarding lemon zest, and decant into a glass bottle. Seal and store in a cool, dark place.   *Makes 1 pint.*

~ Red Pepper Oil ~

3 long red-hot chili peppers (see page 10 for handling instructions)   **2 cups olive oil**

Slit the sides of the peppers and place them in a large jar with a tight-fitting lid. Add the oil and close the jar tightly. Store in a sunny place for 2 weeks. Strain, discarding chili peppers, and decant into a glass bottle. Seal and store in a cool, dark place.   *Makes 1 pint.*

~ Six-Pepper Oil ~

I've included allspice in this blend because it is technically a pepper berry. It is the fruit borne on the Jamaican pimento tree. I don't usually strain this blend, as I use it in salad dressings, but you may do so if you wish.

1 teaspoon black peppercorns	1 teaspoon Jamaican allspice
1 teaspoon pink peppercorns	berries
1 teaspoon white peppercorns	½ teaspoon Szechuan peppercorns
1 teaspoon green peppercorns	2 cups olive oil

Place all ingredients except oil in a mortar and crush until coarse, or process in a mini food processor or grinder. Funnel into a pint bottle with a tight-fitting lid. Add the oil and close the bottle tightly. Store in a sunny place for at least a week. Strain if desired and decant. Store in a cool dry place. *Makes 1 pint.*

Vinegar

I have fallen in love over and over again with good vinegars, pungent grace notes in salads and versatile flavor enhancers in a host of dishes. If salt is a health problem, vinegar can often provide an alternative that is easy on the blood pressure. There are also a variety of homeopathic treatment regimens that use cider vinegar as a toner and purifier of the blood. Drink up! Cider and balsamic vinegars are excellent for greens, but may be too overbearing for pickling, so keep some white distilled vinegar handy. I use white vinegar as a base for flavored vinegars.

~ Raspberry Vinegar ~

This is my favorite vinegar for deglazing a pan. It's expensive in the gourmet markets, and not as tasty as homemade, so I make my own. Buy raspberries in late July or September, when they are in season—you'll pay a lot less.

3 cups fresh raspberries   **2 tablespoons sugar**
2 cups white vinegar

Rinse 1 cup of raspberries and drain thoroughly. Place them in a large lid-ded jar and add the vinegar. Let the mixture sit for 24 hours in a cool, dark place.

Strain the vinegar into another jar, holding the second cup of raspberries, and let it sit for an additional 24 hours.

Repeat the process with the third cup of raspberries.

On the fourth day, strain the vinegar into a 2-quart saucepan, discarding berries; add sugar and simmer for 5 minutes.

Pour into two heavy bottles with tight-fitting lids and seal tightly while still hot. Store in a cool, dark place.   *Makes 1 quart.*

～ Peppered Vinegar ～

2 dozen small chili peppers   **2 cups white vinegar**
    (see page 10 for handling
    instructions)

Rinse the peppers and place them in a jar with a tight-fitting lid. Pour enough vinegar into the jar to cover the peppers. Cover tightly. Store in a sunny place for at least a week before using. Strain, discarding peppers, and decant into a glass bottle. Store in a cool, dry place.   *Makes 1 pint.*

Bread Crumbs

Bread crumbs had a primary function in our household—they stretched the meatloaf. Mom didn't use them for much else, but Grandpop loved crowning his baked dishes with tasty crumb concoctions. In today's era of soybean extenders and guar gum fillers, the humble bread crumb remains a wholesome, economical way to pump up the volume and impart flavor and texture to certain kinds of meals. I use them quite a bit, and have created a few variations in their honor.

∼ Bread Crumbs ∾

If you don't have any stale bread around, simply toast the available bread in the oven at a low temperature (250 degrees F.) for 30 minutes.

3 slices stale bread	¼ teaspoon paprika
¼ teaspoon onion powder	¼ teaspoon sage
¼ teaspoon garlic powder	⅛ teaspoon allspice
1 teaspoon dried parsley flakes	

Place the bread in a food processor and pulse until fine. Mix together the onion and garlic powders, parsley, paprika, sage, and allspice. Add to crumbs and pulse two or three more times. Sift the crumbs through a sieve and discard the large pieces. Transfer to a jar with a tight-fitting lid. Store in a cool dry place. Shake to mix before each use.   *Makes 1 cup crumbs.*

∼ French Bread Crumbs ∾

1 loaf of stale French bread, broken into small chunks	1 tablespoon dried parsley flakes
1 tablespoon Creole Spice Mix (page 8)	

Make sure bread is dry. Place the bread chunks in a food processor and pulse until fine. Add the spice mix and parsley to the crumbs and pulse once more. Sift the crumbs through a sieve and discard the large pieces. Transfer to a jar with a tight-fitting lid. Store in a cool dry place. Shake to mix before each use.   *Makes 2 cups.*

～ Cornbread Crumbs ～

1 cup crumbled stale cornbread	¼ teaspoon salt
¼ teaspoon cayenne	½ teaspoon freshly ground
½ teaspoon ground sage	white pepper
1 teaspoon dried parsley flakes	¼ teaspoon onion powder

Place all ingredients in a food processor and pulse until fine. Sift the crumbs through a sieve and discard the large pieces. Transfer to a jar with a tight-fitting lid. Store in a cool dry place. Shake to mix before each use. *Makes 1 cup.*

Sweeteners

Sugar has fallen out of favor with most health-oriented individuals, but I persist with my philosophy: moderation, moderation, moderation. I just can't fake it with artificial sweeteners. I'd rather have a sugarless dish before I impose that tinny aftertaste on any of my recipes. Sugar is a flavor enhancer, just like salt. Its sin is that it offers a lot of empty calories in the process. Honey and maple syrup are also guilty of being highly caloric and offering no more than a trace of nutrients, but the compensation is that they are less refined, and therefore more wholesome. Brown sugar and molasses are two sweeteners that carry a substantial nutrient value—potassium—but their unrefined taste and texture are too dominant for most dishes. The kind of sugar I use most is turbinado, a blond, granular, semi-raw type that takes a little longer to dissolve, but works well in recipes nevertheless. Keep a couple of sugar blends around for variety.

～ Vanilla Sugar ～

Nana used this in her Graham Cracker Crust (page 236).

2 cups sugar   **2 vanilla beans**

Pour the sugar into a jar with a tight-fitting lid. Split the beans lengthwise and flatten them out. Bury the beans in the sugar and cover tightly. Let the mixture sit for 2 weeks in a cool, dry place. Scrape the insides of the vanilla beans onto the sugar and mix well. Discard the beans. Store the sugar in a dry place.   *Makes 2 cups.*

～ Lemon Sugar ～

1 cup sugar
Zest of 2 lemons, cut in strips, avoiding bitter white pith

Pour the sugar into a jar with a tight-fitting lid. Insert the zest strips into the sugar and cover tightly. Shake jar and set aside for 2 weeks in a cool, dry place. Discard the zest. Store the sugar in a dry place.   *Makes 1 cup.*

2

Sunday Breakfast

Somewhere between the phrases Breakfast of Champions and Power Breakfast lies my preferred coinage: Sunday Breakfast. It's a natural phenomenon, like Old Faithful or the Northern Lights. Every Sunday I like to slow down, sit up straight, and take breakfast as something other than another morning meal in a chain of same. Sundays mornings are for resting, for relaxing, for eating long and good and slow.

Now, my daily breakfast involves nothing out of the ordinary. But my Sunday breakfast can put a few dinners in the shade. My sense of Sunday breakfast was, in part, inspired by Grandpop. His Sunday breakfast differed from mine in that it was earlier in the morning and much less elaborate, but his sensibility is forever etched in my heart: offer guests a variety of good selections, with something for everyone, make it wholesome, and encourage people to take their time eating. The operative word here is *people*. Like Grandpop, I love an audience for Sunday breakfast.

Nearly every weekend we have overnight guests who give us the pleasure of spoiling them for a couple of days. My partner, Eli, is the fire starter, the master of the grill, fireplace, and other flammable matters. He picks the flowers for the guest rooms, the fruits or vegetables and herbs for the meals, and makes a great tomato salsa. But unless we're having *huevos rancheros,* breakfast is my domain. Maybe it's because I tend to be more inventive and energetic in the morning. Sunday is a celebration of sorts; everyone is relaxed; gospel, jazz, or opera is playing. In the summertime goldfinches tumble about in the air over the daylilies and the breeze smells of mint and thyme. Wintertime brings the scent of maplewood burning in the hearth from the early morning fires, frosted windows, and mugs of steamy hot chocolate. Sunday is mine; I wouldn't trade it for any other day in the week.

I wake up early on Sunday morning, give thanks for a new day, and hit the kitchen—hard. Sunday breakfast may consist of freshly brewed teas and coffees, assorted breads, homemade lemon curd, poached plums, home fries, corn cakes, egg-white omelets, and waffles with warm maple syrup. Like most cooking for guests, the secret lies in the sequence and the pacing of the preparation. After all, I never know just who will be coming into the kitchen, and when. So I begin with the baking. Not only is it probably the most intricate of Sunday morning tasks, it also works fine as an alarm clock, rousting those sleepyheads from bed with the irresistible scent of homemade bread. Once the bread is in the oven, fresh fruits are sliced—an ambrosia of whatever's near at hand: peaches, plums, grapes, and pears—set to steep in each other's juice. Waffle or pancake batter is prepared and stored in the fridge until the guests are at the table. If sauces are to be served with the food, they are warmed in the double boiler until the time is right. By this time, the sun is up, the music's on, and the guests are at the table. Ripe oranges and grapefruits are squeezed, and sweet apples are pressed into juice and invigorated with a squirt of lemon. A fresh pot of coffee and a pot of tea are always on hand; for "anticaffeinators," a tisane or herbal infusion. And for those really special guests, I give the gift of chocolate.

~ Hot Cocoa ~

Nothing is as sure to float a smile onto a morning face as hand-whipped hot cocoa—especially in winter. Nana made it something like this, using the exquisite vanilla sugar she always kept around. She'd also whip up a little canned evaporated milk and put a dollop on top of each serving.

2 tablespoons unsweetened cocoa
2 tablespoons Vanilla Sugar
   (page 18)
Pinch of salt

½ cup boiling water
3 cups 1 percent fat milk
   Nonfat Whipped Cream
   (below)

In a medium saucepan, mix together the cocoa, sugar, and salt. While stirring with a wooden spoon, pour the water over the cocoa. Continue stirring until the mixture becomes dark and velvety. Slowly pour in the milk. Cook over medium heat, stirring often until the mixture comes to a near-boil. Place the hot cocoa in a large bowl and whisk for a minute, until frothy. Top each serving with nonfat whipped cream.   *Makes 4 servings.*

Per serving: 105 calories / 2 gm fat / 16 gm carbohydrate / 94 mg sodium

~ Nonfat Whipped Cream ~

½ cup evaporated skim milk
½ cup skim milk
¼ cup superfine sugar

½ teaspoon allspice
½ teaspoon vanilla extract

Place beater and a large whipping bowl in the freezer for 15 minutes. Pour both milks into the cold bowl and beat on high speed; add sugar while beating. Add allspice and vanilla, and continue to beat until stiff.   *Makes 2 cups of whipped cream.*

Per serving (2 tablespoons): 23 calories / 0 gm fat / 49 gm carbohydrate / 18 mg sodium

～ Watermelon Mimosa ～

Sometimes guests insist on having "the hair of the dog," a hangover remedy that involves more of the same pooch that bit you the night before. I serve breakfast rather early—too early for a Bloody Mary—so I offer this as a kinder, gentler animal.

3 cups watermelon chunks, seeded and chilled

1 bottle (750-ml) champagne, chilled

Put the watermelon in a blender and liquefy. Strain the juice into a container. Pour the watermelon juice into 8 tulip glasses, filling halfway. Fill to the top with champagne.　*Makes 8 drinks.*

Per serving: 112 calories / 0 gm fat / 6 gm carbohydrate / 1 mg sodium

～ Baked Apple Rings ～

A warming winter treat to have along with a Flat White Omelet (page 25) and Home Fries with Rosemary and Garlic (page 34).

2 Golden Delicious apples, peeled and cored
1 tablespoon butter, melted
2 tablespoons dark brown sugar

¼ teaspoon cinnamon
⅛ teaspoon allspice
⅛ teaspoon nutmeg

Preheat the oven to 400 degrees F. Slice the apples into ¼-inch rings. Pour the melted butter into a 9 × 12-inch glass baking dish. Using a pastry brush, distribute the butter evenly around the dish. Place the apples on the bottom of the dish. In a small cup, combine the sugar, cinnamon, allspice, and nutmeg, and sprinkle over the apples. Bake for 25 minutes, or until apples are bubbling brown sugar.　*Makes 4 servings.*

Per serving: 46 calories / 1 gm fat / 9 gm carbohydrate / 12 mg sodium

~ Poached Plums ~

The scent that wafts from this breakfast treat is heavenly. I'd like to bottle it and use it as kitchen potpourri!

12 medium to large plums, any variety	1 vanilla bean, split
1 cup water	1 cinnamon stick
¼ cup sugar	¼ cup evaporated skim milk

Cut the plums in half, remove the pits and set aside. Combine the water and sugar in a large pot over high heat and bring to a boil. Add the vanilla bean and cinnamon stick and reduce the heat to low. Add the plums to the pot and simmer, covered, for 15 minutes, until the plums are tender. Remove them with a slotted spoon and increase the heat to medium-high. Cook the syrup for 10 minutes, until it thickens slightly, and remove from the heat. When the syrup has cooled to room temperature, add the plums and milk and refrigerate for 1 hour, until thoroughly chilled.   *Makes 6 servings.*

Per serving: 145 calories / 1 gm fat / 35 gm carbohydrate / 6 mg sodium

~ Broiled Grapefruit ~

The trick to making this breakfast classic is to get the broiler very hot before-hand, and to sprinkle on the sugar right before you plunge the grapefruit into the broiler. The sugar caramelizes fast and gives you a delicious citrus sweet-and-sour taste.

3 grapefruit, split in half	6 teaspoons sugar

Preheat the broiler for about 10 minutes before putting in the grapefruit. Place the grapefruit halves in a shallow pan lined with crushed ice. Sprinkle

1 teaspoon sugar over each half and broil for about 2 minutes, until lightly browned.   *Makes 6 servings.*

Per serving: 52 calories / 0 gm fat / 13 gm carbohydrate / 0 mg sodium

∽ Broiled Figs ∾

Figs are the apples of the South, maybe a bit underappreciated in the North. I like to showcase their delicate flavor by cooking them with the least possible frills. Broiling takes them to yet another dimension. Great alongside a mound of thinly sliced smoked salmon.

12 fresh figs   **1 teaspoon butter, melted**

Preheat the broiler. Slice each fig lengthwise and brush lightly with butter. Place figs, cut side up, in a broiler pan, and broil for 1 minute, until figs are slightly browned.   *Makes 4 servings.*

Per serving: 119 calories / 1 gm fat / 28 gm carbohydrate / 13 mg sodium

Eggs

And now, a word about eggs. I love those versatile little ovals, and always have, but as everybody knows, they don't return the favor—at least when it concerns the heart. Egg yolks are notorious artery cloggers, and yet I really enjoy the taste of them. What to do? Well, since I don't believe in total abstinence when it comes to giving up the things I adore, I compromise by using only the whites. Yes, it's a bit wasteful, but I'd rather have the yolk in the garbage than inside of me adding to my cholesterol count. Besides, with the right seasoning you'll forget eggs were ever yellow. If you can't quite go cold turkey, then add one yolk to two whites and you've eliminated half the problem.

My brother Robert has been an egg lover from day one, begging for sunny-side-up eggs at breakfast, requesting egg salad sandwiches at lunch, and pleading for scrambled eggs for dinner. Mom, of course, didn't let him live on eggs the way he wished, and it was probably this deprivation that gave Robert a talent for making some of the lightest, fluffiest, most flavorful omelets I've ever tasted. He fills them with inspired ingredients and folds them so they actually appear to be smiling on the plate. The wonderful thing about omelets is that they are fast and practical, yet so sublime. And you can fill them with almost anything. I've been inspired by Robert to come up with a few good omelets.

If you are an "egger" like Robert, it would be wise to invest in a nonstick omelet pan. A nonstick pan keeps you from having to use a lot of oil, and thus allows the omelet a dignified exit from pan to plate. If you prefer not to use a nonstick pan, you can get similar results by seasoning a 12–inch sauté pan. To season the pan, pour a cup of oil into it and heat over very low heat for about 1 hour. Remove from the heat and let the oil cool down. Pour the oil into a container for future use and wipe off the excess oil from the pan. The pan is ready to receive your eggs. It's not necessary to do this every time you make an omelet; a little spray of oil and a preheated pan will do just fine.

～ Flat White Omelet ～

When making a plain omelet, I see no reason to fold. The only reason for the fold is to keep all the goodies inside well insulated and intact. I like a plain omelet flat, resting upon my plate like a cloud.

1 teaspoon butter	**¼ teaspoon freshly ground**
3 egg whites	**white pepper**
⅛ teaspoon salt	

In a 12-inch nonstick omelet or sauté pan, heat the butter over medium heat. In a medium bowl, combine the egg whites with the salt and pepper. With a whisk or fork, beat until frothy, about 1 minute. Increase the heat to medium-high and pour the egg mixture into the hot pan. Cook for 1 to

2 minutes, until the top begins to set and the bottom begins to brown. Turn the omelet over and cook a minute more, until it is springy to the touch.   *Makes 1 omelet.*

Per serving: 85 calories / 3 gm fat / 1 gm carbohydrate / 203 mg sodium

~ Brown Onion Omelet ~

My friend Kinnu makes the best brown onions: ultra-thin slices of sweet, dark crispness. The first time I tasted them I remember wondering what this would taste like on an omelet.

1 teaspoon butter	¼ teaspoon freshly ground
3 egg whites	white pepper
⅛ teaspoon salt	¼ cup Brown Onions *(page 12)*

Prepare the omelet according to the instructions for Flat White Omelet (see page 25). Add the onion mixture to one side of the omelet and gently fold.   *Makes 1 omelet.*

Per serving: 92 calories / 3 gm fat / 3 gm carbohydrate / 203 mg sodium

~ Collard Greens Omelet ~

This is the perfect answer to what to do with those leftover greens.

1 teaspoon butter	1 teaspoon Raspberry Vinegar
1 teaspoon minced shallots	*(page 14)* or balsamic vinegar
2 tablespoons cooked collard greens, minced	1 tablespoon chopped red bell pepper, seeded

¼ teaspoon freshly ground   ⅛ teaspoon salt
    black pepper   1 tablespoon orange juice
3 egg whites

In a small nonstick skillet, heat ½ teaspoon butter over medium heat. Add the shallots and sauté for 5 minutes, until they are translucent. Add the greens and cook for 8 to 10 minutes, until tender. Pour in the vinegar and cook for 2 to 3 minutes more. Mix in the red bell pepper and remove from the heat. Sprinkle in the black pepper and set aside.

In a medium bowl, combine the egg whites, salt, and orange juice. Whip until frothy. Heat the remaining butter in a 12-inch nonstick omelet pan and pour in the egg mixture. Cook for 2 minutes, until the top begins to set and the bottom begins to brown. Turn the omelet over and cook for 1 minute, until it is springy to the touch. Add the collard greens mixture to one side of the omelet and gently fold.   *Makes 1 omelet.*

Per serving: 99 calories / 4 gm fat / 5 gm carbohydrate / 208 mg sodium

Waffles

Maybe it's the complexity of the shape, or the delicate texture. Perhaps it's the contradiction between the lightness and the crunch that makes a waffle so satisfying. Waffles get a rise out of every one of my guests in a way that pancakes never do. Don't misunderstand, I love a hot stack of pancakes every now and again, ample syrup dripping down each tier, but the odds of getting a pancake with all the interesting elements of a waffle are slim. Even with the most precise pancake recipe, you can often wind up with one that is too thin, too thick, too cakey, or too doughy. A good waffle iron ensures a properly cooked product, leaving you the mere responsibility of providing the proper batter. Although I love seasoned waffles and plain waffles with seasoned syrups, I will never tire of the old-fashioned buttermilk waffles Nana used to make.

∼ Buttermilk Waffles ∽

2 cups all-purpose unbleached flour	1 egg
2 teaspoons baking powder	1 cup 1 percent fat buttermilk
½ teaspoon baking soda	1½ cups evaporated skim milk
1 tablespoon sugar	1 teaspoon butter, melted
½ teaspoon salt	2 egg whites

Preheat waffle iron. Sift together all the dry ingredients. Beat the whole egg and milks together and slowly mix into the dry ingredients, while adding the butter. Whip the egg whites until stiff and gently fold them into the batter. Lightly grease the waffle iron and pour the batter into the center of the iron and cook according to manufacturer's instructions. *Makes 6 waffles.*

Per serving: 238 calories / 2 gm fat / 45 gm carbohydrate / 289 mg sodium

∼ Gingerbread Waffles ∽

Instead of using maple syrup, try spreading a tablespoon of Lemon Curd (page 207) on top of these spicy waffles.

2 cups all-purpose unbleached flour	1 egg
2 teaspoons baking powder	2 cups evaporated skim milk
½ teaspoon baking soda	2 tablespoons finely minced crystallized ginger
1 tablespoon sugar	2 tablespoons grated gingerroot
½ teaspoon salt	1 teaspoon butter, melted
1 teaspoon Pie Spice *(page 9)*	2 egg whites
1 teaspoon ground ginger	

Preheat waffle iron. Sift together all the dry ingredients. Beat the egg and milk together and slowly pour the mixture into the dry ingredients. Add the crystallized ginger, gingerroot, and melted butter. Whip the egg whites until stiff and gently fold them into the batter. Lightly grease the waffle iron and pour the batter into the center of the iron and cook according to manufacturer's instructions.   *Makes 6 waffles.*

Per serving: 220 calories / 4 gm fat / 39 gm carbohydrate / 240 mg sodium

⌒ Country Chicken with Cornmeal Waffles ⌒

This was one of Nana's special meals, although her version had a lot less of the herbal frills. Liz, Nana's dog, used to beg for scraps whenever Nana wasn't watching. Normally we'd offer a tidbit or two, but this dish was too delicious to part with.

1 **pound skinless, boneless chicken breasts**	1 **tablespoon chopped chives**
2 **tablespoons dry sherry**	1 **teaspoon chopped dill**
1 **tablespoon butter**	1 **teaspoon grated lemon zest**
1 **tablespoon chopped shallots**	½ **teaspoon freshly ground white pepper**
1½ **tablespoons flour**	
2 **cups evaporated skim milk**	**Cornmeal Waffles (recipe follows)**
½ **teaspoon salt**	

Pound the chicken breasts flat with a heavy mallet. Heat a 13-inch nonstick sauté pan over medium-high heat and sear the breasts for about 3 minutes on each side. Add the sherry, scraping up the browned bits with a wooden spoon. Remove the breasts from pan, and let them cool. Mince. In the same skillet, melt the butter and sauté the shallots for about 1 minute. Add the flour and stir until the butter is absorbed into the flour. Add the milk slowly, stirring until the mixture thickens. (The mixture should be the consistency of a light soup.) Add more milk if a thinner sauce is desired. Add the chicken cubes to the sauce, followed by the salt, chives, dill, and zest, and simmer for about 5 minutes. Remove from the heat and add the pepper. Serve over Cornmeal Waffles (below).   *Makes 6 servings.*

Per serving: 327 calories / 6 gm fat / 62 gm carbohydrate / 546 mg sodium

Cornmeal Waffles

1 cup all-purpose unbleached
    flour
1 cup cornmeal
2 teaspoons baking powder
½ teaspoon baking soda
2 tablespoons sugar

½ teaspoon salt
1 egg
2 cups evaporated skim milk
1 teaspoon olive oil
2 egg whites

Preheat the waffle iron. Sift together all the dry ingredients. Beat the egg and milk together and slowly pour the mixture into the dry ingredients. Stir in the oil. Whip the egg whites until stiff and gently fold them into the batter. Lightly grease the waffle iron and drop the batter into the center of the iron. Cook according to manufacturer's instructions.   *Makes 6 waffles.*

∾ Rice and Shrimp Waffles ∾

The things I sacrifice for the luxury of shrimp in the morning! When I know shrimp is on the way for breakfast, even sleep seems a waste of time! Serve this with Red Pepper Gravy (page 203).

1 cup all-purpose unbleached
    flour
½ teaspoon baking soda
2 teaspoons baking powder
½ teaspoon salt
1 teaspoon freshly ground
    white pepper

1 egg
2 cups evaporated skim milk
1 teaspoon olive oil
1 cup cooked rice
1 cup minced cooked shrimp
2 egg whites

Preheat the waffle iron. Sift together all the dry ingredients. Beat the egg and milk together and slowly pour the mixture into the dry ingredients. Add the oil and beat until smooth. Fold in the rice and shrimp and set aside for 10 minutes. Meanwhile whip the egg whites until stiff and gently fold into the batter. Lightly grease the waffle iron and drop the batter into the center of the iron. Cook according to manufacturer's instructions. *Makes 6 waffles.*

Per serving: 204 calories / 3 gm fat / 32 gm carbohydrate / 205 mg sodium

∽ Corn Cakes ∽

On Sundays, Mom stacked plenty of steaming-hot corn cakes on our plates. Those heavenly discs tasted as if they were each stuffed with a fresh ear of corn. Warm maple syrup was the only dressing worthy to accompany them.

½ **cup cornmeal**	**1 egg**
1 cup all-purpose unbleached flour	**½ cup 1 percent fat buttermilk**
½ **teaspoon salt**	**1 cup evaporated skim milk**
½ **teaspoon baking soda**	**1 teaspoon olive oil**
2 tablespoons sugar	**2 ears of corn, cooked and kernels scraped from the cob**
¼ **teaspoon nutmeg**	**1 tablespoon snipped chives**

In a large bowl, combine the cornmeal, flour, salt, baking soda, sugar, and nutmeg. In another bowl, beat the egg and milks together and pour the mixture into the dry ingredients. Add the oil and beat until smooth. Stir in the corn and chives. Drop the batter onto a hot lightly greased griddle and cook for 2 minutes, until browned on each side. *Makes 8 cakes.*

Per serving: 268 calories / 4 gm fat / 53 gm carbohydrate / 158 mg sodium

~ Raspberry Pancakes ~

Sweet, juicy raspberries are plentiful in the summertime, and since they grow on the brambles right in our yard these pancakes are a regular treat around the house. Despite the many times I serve them this remains one of the favorites of the guests. I keep a piping-hot stack on the table, accompanied by a pitcher of maple syrup.

1½ cups all-purpose unbleached flour
2 teaspoons baking powder
2 tablespoons sugar
¼ teaspoon salt
1½ cups evaporated skim milk
1 egg
1 tablespoon butter, melted
1 cup fresh raspberries

In a large bowl, sift together the flour, baking powder, sugar, and salt. Add the milk and egg, and beat until smooth. Blend in the melted butter and the raspberries and stir lightly. Ladle the batter onto a hot griddle and cook for 1 minute, until bubbles form over the surface. Turn the pancakes over and cook for another minute, until browned.   *Makes 8 pancakes.*

Per serving: 99 calories / 2 gm fat / 16 gm carbohydrate / 136 mg sodium

∽ Oyster-Corn Griddle Cakes ∽

Try this one when fresh oysters "R" in season (that is, any month with an R in the name!). The sweetness of the corn highlights the briny taste of the shellfish, providing a little surf and turf where it's least expected—at the breakfast table. Serve with Brown Sherry Gravy (page 203) and Raspberry Applesauce (page 36).

12 oysters, drained, reserving oyster liquor *(see page 186 for preparation)*
½ cup all-purpose unbleached flour
½ cup cornmeal
1 tablespoon baking powder
½ teaspoon salt

1 tablespoon sugar
1 egg
1 cup evaporated skim milk
2 ears of corn, cooked and kernels scraped from the cob
1 tablespoon olive oil

In a large nonstick skillet, cook the oysters for 1 to 2 minutes, until the edges begin to ruffle. Remove them from the pan to cool; chop finely and set aside. In a large bowl, combine the flour, cornmeal, baking powder, salt, and sugar. Beat the egg and milk together and slowly add to the dry ingredients. Add the oysters, reserving their liquor, and corn and beat until well mixed, drizzling the oil in as you beat. Drop the batter by the tablespoon onto a hot griddle and cook for 1 minute, until bubbles form over the surface. Turn the cakes over and cook for another minute, until browned.   *Makes 6 cakes.*

Per serving: 283 calories / 5 gm fat / 53 gm carbohydrate / 347 mg sodium

∼ Potato Cakes ∼

This was an infrequent treat at our house, since we rarely had leftover mashed potatoes. But on occasions such as Thanksgiving or Christmas we'd hurry to put the potatoes away before they were gobbled up and the next morning we'd persuade Mom to make potato cakes for breakfast. They were perfectly suited to scrambled eggs, which made my brother Robert doubly happy.

2 cups cold Mashed Potatoes   **2 teaspoons olive oil**
    (page 151)
¼ cup all-purpose unbleached
    flour

Shape the potatoes into six patties. Dredge both sides of each patty in flour and refrigerate for at least 1 hour. In a nonstick skillet, heat 1 teaspoon oil over medium heat. Put three of the patties into the skillet and cook for 2 to 3 minutes, until golden brown and crisp. Turn the patties over and cook until golden brown on the other side. Drain on paper towels. Add the remaining oil to the pan and repeat cooking with remaining three patties. *Makes 6 cakes.*

Per serving: 106 calories / 4 gm fat / 17 gm carbohydrate / 242 mg sodium

∼ Home Fries with Rosemary and Garlic ∼

What is breakfast without home fries? This classic side dish is enhanced by the addition of lemon, rosemary, and garlic. The Swiss roesti *technique of flipping the potatoes ensures that everyone gets some of the crunchy crust. I generally do not peel the potatoes, since a lot of nutrients are on the surface, but feel free to do so, if you're so inclined.*

4 **large potatoes, scrubbed**
1 **tablespoon lemon juice**
2 **cloves garlic, minced**
1 **tablespoon minced**
   rosemary leaves

1 **tablespoon plus 1 teaspoon**
   olive oil
½ **teaspoon salt**
½ **teaspoon freshly ground**
   black pepper

Boil the potatoes in their skins until tender, about 25 minutes. Remove them from the water and when they have cooled, grate them, sprinkle with lemon juice, and set aside. In a 13-inch nonstick omelet pan over medium heat, sauté the garlic and the rosemary in 1 tablespoon of the oil for 30 seconds, until the garlic is lightly browned. Remove the garlic mixture from the pan and increase the heat to medium-high. Spread half of the potatoes in the hot pan, smoothing them out with a spatula. Sprinkle the garlic mixture on top. Spread the remaining half of the potatoes on top of the garlic, so that you have a perfect cake. Cook for 4 to 6 minutes, until potatoes turn a golden brown on the bottom. With a plastic spatula, gently slide the potatoes onto a plate, cooked side down. Cover the potatoes with another plate and flip the plates over. Add the remaining teaspoon of oil to the pan, and heat for a minute or so. Slide the potatoes back into the pan, cooked side up, and cook for another 4 to 6 minutes, until desired crispness has been achieved. Remove the potatoes to a platter and sprinkle with salt and pepper. *Makes 4 servings.*

Per serving: 123 calories / 4 gm fat / 21 gm carbohydrate / 247 mg sodium

～ Tart Apple Butter ～

Slather this on a piece of freshly baked Sweet Bread (page 61) and consummate a happy marriage of contrasting flavors.

4 Granny Smith apples, peeled and cored	1 teaspoon cinnamon
⅔ cup apple cider	1 teaspoon grated lemon zest
¼ cup firmly packed dark brown sugar	

Chop the apples coarsely. Pour the apple cider into a large pot and add the apples. Simmer, uncovered, for about 1 hour, or until apples are soft, adding additional cider if the liquid begins to evaporate. Remove the apples and puree in a food processor for about 30 seconds. Return the puree to the liquid in the pot and add the sugar, cinnamon, and lemon zest. Simmer, uncovered, for 30 minutes. The apple butter should be dark brown and thick. While hot, pour into 1 small sterilized jar (see page 207). Cover tightly and store in the refrigerator for up to 10 days.   *Makes ½ pint.*

Per serving: 67 calories / 0 gm fat / 18 gm carbohydrate / 5 mg sodium

～ Raspberry Applesauce ～

In late July our first crop of raspberries appears. In early October the raspberries appear again, along with a harvest of apples from the tree in our front yard. Energetic early risers often go out with small baskets and bring back both kinds of fruit. It was their efforts that inspired this side dish.

1 teaspoon sweet butter	1 pint fresh raspberries
3 large Golden Delicious apples, peeled and cored	½ teaspoon allspice
¼ cup sugar	¼ teaspoon thyme leaves, minced

Melt the butter in a 2-quart saucepan over medium heat. Chop the apples coarsely and add to the pan, along with half the sugar. Cook for 20 minutes, breaking up the apples as they soften. Add the raspberries and the remaining sugar, and continue cooking, stirring gently, for another 2 minutes. Add the allspice and thyme and remove from the heat. Serve cold or at room temperature.   *Makes 6 servings.*

Per serving: 59 calories / 1 gm fat / 14 gm carbohydrate / 2 mg sodium

~ Turkey Sausage Patties with Sage ~

I don't serve many meats at breakfast, because they're often a heavy, overpowering presence. But on occasion I'll get a craving for a piece of sausage with my waffle, and that's when I turn to ground turkey to lighten the load. It is wise to grind your own turkey breast, if possible. Crushed ice keeps the patties intact and gives them added juiciness.

1 **pound ground turkey**
1 **cup crushed ice**
1 **teaspoon salt**
1 **tablespoon finely minced sage**
1 **teaspoon ground sage**

½ **teaspoon freshly ground white pepper**
1 **teaspoon fennel seed**
¼ **teaspoon cayenne**
2 **teaspoons olive oil**

Put the turkey and crushed ice into a food processor and pulse until well blended. Add salt, fresh and ground sage, pepper, fennel seed, and cayenne, and pulse for a few more seconds. Shape the mixture into eight patties and refrigerate for at least 1 hour. In a nonstick skillet, over medium heat, heat 1 teaspoon oil. Put four of the patties in the pan and cook for about 3 minutes on each side, until browned. Drain on paper towels. Add the remaining oil to the pan and repeat cooking with the other four patties.   *Makes 8 patties.*

Per serving: 96 calories / 5 gm fat / 0 gm carbohydrate / 188 mg sodium

∼ Turkey Sausage Gravy ∼

There's nothing like sausage gravy over a plate of steaming-hot grits. I like them over biscuits as well.

4 **Turkey Sausage Patties with**	½ **cup water**
Sage *(page 36)*, **cooked**	1 **teaspoon grated lemon zest**
1 **tablespoon olive oil**	½ **teaspoon salt**
2 **tablespoons flour**	1 **teaspoon freshly ground**
½ **cup Chicken Stock** *(page 81)*	**white pepper**
1½ **cups evaporated skim milk**	

Crumble the sausage patties into a bowl and set aside. In a large cast-iron skillet, heat the oil over medium heat. Add the flour and stir for 2 minutes, or until lightly browned. Slowly add the chicken stock, then the milk, and finally the water, stirring and smoothing over any lumps with a wooden spoon. (Add more water for a thinner gravy; mix 1 teaspoon arrowroot with 1 table-spoon water for a thicker gravy.) Add the crumbled sausage and lemon zest, and stir to blend. Add the salt and pepper.   *Makes 6 servings.*

Per serving: 58 calories / 3.2 gm fat / 3 gm carbohydrate / 213 mg sodium

— 3 —

Down-Home Vegetables

As in most households in the 1960s, our family's daily diet revolved around meat as the main body of nourishment. We turned "high on the hog" into a family anthem, and weekends in particular were given over to breaking world records for cholesterol consumption. The culprits? Ribs, charred sticky-black beneath a spicy barbecue glaze; moist, tender pork loin, wading in its juices; Cornish hen, packed with rice and mushroom stuffing. Mom fussed over each production, and we ate without questioning. Back then, nutritional guidelines were as cloudy as smoke, and besides, it was communicated to us that meat was "serious eating," as in the kind of thing an adult was supposed to do. Vegetables? I adored them on instinct—the way they looked; the displays of the stems and stalks, the colors, the bulbs, and the aromas. But to the rest of my family, vegetables were side dishes—giddy little accessories to meat, the gustatory equivalent of toys.

Produce came in the local "rolling farm," a large turquoise truck that came up our street every day, driven by Miss Sally. We lived in the middle of the block and afternoons at four we could clearly hear her shrill, enthusiastic pitch of "Corn! Get your fresh corn here!" The truck would stop with a screech of brakes and we'd run from the house to look at the "day's catch"—

sweet peas, yams, collards, carrots, and onions, most of it picked fresh. Miss Sally was a short, round woman, with wavy hair hanging nearly to her waist. We thought she was special because she had a thin mustache, which darkened every time she smiled. She wore a big straw hat, which she'd let us children try on while she weighed and priced, often adding an extra ear of corn or a yam to our package.

For as long as I can remember, vegetables have been my truest love and dearest dietary ally, so that's why I'm featuring them early in the book. And in paying homage to the many African agriculturists who made profound botanical changes in this country, I'm placing the focus on the vegetables that either originated in Africa or were introduced to the New World by the Africans. I'll warn you right now, there are hot peppers in a lot of the recipes, so if you're not inclined to palate-tweaking hot, omit them—you'll still have plenty of taste to go around.

The art of vegetable shopping requires the same qualities as shopping for cars or clothes: astuteness, product knowledge, and awareness of seasonal value. Increasingly popular these days are food co-ops, communal buying organizations that you join for a fee. They provide you with regular access to fresh vegetables all year-round at prices that are generally lower than in supermarkets. Check around in your area, and if you like what you see, sign up—it's usually worth it.

From the point of view of health, nothing compares to organic vegetables. They taste better, too. Why? For one, organic vegetables are usually picked ripe, rather than picked green and expected to ripen on a truck or shelf. For another, they're not waxed, or sprayed with pesticides and herbicides. The average apple in a supermarket chain has had more wax applied to it than a showroom car. However, there is a catch to getting all that healthy, hand-grown goodness. It rhymes with honey, if you need a hint. The fact is, organic vegetables are often priced out of sight. Personally, I would prefer an expensive vegetable in my stomach to an expensive hat on my head, but the call is yours. Whether you choose organic or not, try at least to choose crisp, firm, well-colored vegetables that are free of blemishes. If your supermarket doesn't have a particular vegetable in stock and you know it's in season, order it directly from the produce manager. Most markets have one. The store will usually receive delivery within 48 hours.

Taste aside, one of the major reasons we eat vegetables is for wellness. Vegetables (and fruits) are nature's crowning nutritional achievements—healthy little soldiers outfitted for the battle against disease with trace elements, vitamins, minerals, and loads of fiber. Vegetables must be treated carefully, however, to maximize their health-giving properties. Try not to peel them before cooking, as the greatest concentration of vitamins and minerals lies near the surface. Also, remember that exposure to air not only detracts from appearance through discoloration, but oxidation decreases the nutritive value as well. Use as little water as possible to cook vegetables or consider steaming them when appropriate.

Collard Greens

I'm not sure why this is, but a down-home cook's worth is measured mostly by how well he or she prepares collard greens. Collards receive the most intense scrutiny of all the items in a down-home menu. I, too, am a picky greens eater, rating them by texture, size (which should vary with the dish), and, of course, flavor. I also take into consideration nutritional value, which, in the case of collards, is surprisingly high. A cup of collard greens contains as much calcium as a glass of milk. And collards are very low in fat and calories.

Arriving Africans, pleased to find an abundance of greens on American soil, introduced them into the colonial diet—a diet that until then was based exclusively on meat and carbohydrates. Until the slaves made them taste good, green vegetables were more or less reserved for the livestock. How's that for a fundamental contribution to American health?

When selecting collards, look for bunches that are tightly bound and have firm, dark green leaves. And remember, collards are a dirt-loving vegetable, so make sure all the dirt is removed before cooking.

To clean collards, fill a large basin or bowl with salted water and soak the greens for 10 minutes. The salt causes the dirt to fall to the bottom. Drain and, using unsalted water, repeat the process three more times. Remove the stem from each leaf, and chop leaves according to recipe instructions.

∼ Sautéed Mixed Greens ∼

Nana used to fix her greens this way, except she didn't use crushed pepper as liberally as I do. She also put a great deal more water in her pot, which produced an abundance of pot "likker," which she loved to drink. She made use of stale cornbread by crumbling large chunks on top of her greens and eating it only after it was saturated with the flavorful "likker."

2 pounds collard greens *(see page 41 for preparation)*, finely chopped

2 pounds mustard greens, finely chopped

1 bunch of watercress or sorrel, chopped

1 tablespoon olive oil

1 large onion, thinly sliced

5 cloves garlic, minced

1 small chili pepper, seeded and minced *(see page 10 for handling instructions)*

1 red or green bell pepper, seeded and diced

1 teaspoon salt

1 tablespoon sugar

2 tablespoons Raspberry Vinegar *(page 14)* or cider vinegar

1 cup dry white wine

½ teaspoon allspice

1 teaspoon freshly ground black pepper

Put the finely chopped collard and mustard greens in a large bowl, add watercress, and refrigerate. Heat the oil in a large, heavy skillet over medium heat for 1 minute or less. Add the onions and sauté for 20 minutes, until browned. Add the garlic and cook until lightly browned. Add the chili and bell peppers and cook for 1 minute. Add the greens and cook for 25 minutes. Mix together the salt, sugar, vinegar, wine, and allspice and pour over the greens. Cook for an additional 20 minutes, tossing the greens to mix. Add pepper and let sit, covered, off the stove for 15 minutes.   *Serves 8.*

Per serving: 72 calories / 2 gm fat / 11 gm carbohydrate / 389 mg sodium

~ Baked Collards with Smoked Hen ~

This zesty greens dish is very similar to one that is made often in Nigeria. Baking seems to concentrate its flavor. The Scotch bonnet pepper is quite hot, many times hotter than a jalapeño, so, as Nana would've said, "be particular." A lot of butchers sell smoked hens and will cut them up as you request. Smoked fish is an exquisite alternative to the hen.

1 tablespoon olive oil
1 large onion, chopped
2 cloves garlic, minced
2 pounds collard greens *(see page 41 for preparation),* coarsely chopped
1 fresh Scotch bonnet pepper, seeded and chopped *(see page 10 for handling instructions)*

1 red bell pepper, seeded and diced
1 large smoked Cornish hen, cut up into 6 pieces
1 cup Chicken Stock *(page 81)*

Preheat oven to 375 degrees F. Heat the oil in a medium skillet over medium-high heat. Add the onion and garlic and sauté for 5 minutes, until the onion is soft. Remove from heat. In a large mixing bowl, combine the sautéed onion and garlic with the collards and both peppers and set aside. Place hen parts in a large Dutch oven and smother with the collards mixture. Pour the stock over and bake, covered, for 1 hour.   *Makes 6 servings.*

Per serving: 123 calories / 4 gm fat / 14 gm carbohydrate / 152 mg sodium

~ Stewed Greens with Cornmeal Dumplings ~

These are the kinds of greens I imagine they ate back in the day: good and spicy, with plenty of pot "likker" to dunk your cornbread in. In this particular recipe, however, the cornbread is pre-dunked—that is to say, it is in the form of a dumpling. Mom's greens are similar, right down to the okra she tosses in for body. Mom's a traditionalist, but very open to new tastes, so she doesn't find the addition of crabmeat entirely radical. Codfish substitutes very well for the crabmeat, incidentally. This dish is best eaten out of a bowl.

3 **cloves garlic, minced**	1 **teaspoon salt**
1 **tablespoon olive oil**	2 **quarts Fish Stock** *(page 82)*
½ **cup chopped shallots**	¼ **cup Raspberry Vinegar**
½ **cup sliced trimmed okra**	**(page 14)**
(trimmed of tops and tails	2 **tablespoons dark brown sugar**
and sliced crosswise into	1 **recipe Cornmeal Dumplings**
¼-inch rings)	**(recipe follows)**
1 **chili pepper, seeded and**	½ **pound lump crabmeat or**
chopped *(see page 10 for*	**steamed codfish**
handling instructions)	
4 **pounds collard greens, finely**	
chopped *(see page 41 for*	
preparation)	

In a 5-quart Dutch oven, sauté the garlic in oil over medium heat for a minute or so until lightly browned. Add the shallots, okra, and chili pepper, and cook for 5 minutes more. Add the greens and salt and toss until well blended with the okra mixture. Add the stock, vinegar, and sugar. Reduce the heat and simmer, covered, for 45 minutes, while preparing the dumpling batter. Drop a tablespoonful of dumplings into the hot greens and cook for 5 minutes, until dumpling expands to twice the original size. Pick over the crabmeat to remove any cartilage. Ladle the greens into serving bowls and flake the crabmeat (or codfish) on top.   *Makes 6 servings.*

Per serving: 232 calories / 4 gm fat / 39 gm carbohydrate / 380 mg sodium

Cornmeal Dumplings

1 cup yellow cornmeal	1 tablespoon sugar
½ cup all-purpose flour, unbleached	1 egg
	¼ cup 1 percent fat milk
1 teaspoon baking powder	1 teaspoon melted butter
1 teaspoon salt	

Sift cornmeal, flour, baking powder, salt, and sugar into a large mixing bowl. Add egg, milk, and butter and mix until smooth. Let sit, covered, for 5 minutes. Drop dumplings by teaspoonfuls into the hot broth and cook over medium heat for 5 minutes.

Cowpeas (Black-Eyed Peas)

I'm a true lover of beans—any bean. But my favorite is the cowpea, also known as the black-eyed pea. Our New Year's Eve ritual, like that of many Southern and African-American families, involves eating a spoonful of them for luck. I remember once asking for another spoonful of the smoky-tasting little marvels, but Mom declined, saying two would be too much of a good thing. Mom is superstitious that way. She also feels it is good luck that the first person to enter the house after the stroke of midnight be a man.

Black-eyed peas were yet another gift the Africans gave to the South. Back home this "poor man's meat" was mixed with yams or corn to make a hearty stew. In some parts of the South, people have the luxury of eating black-eyed peas freshly picked and shelled. Up North they're mostly eaten dried.

African cooks also ground black-eyed peas into a paste to make a dough that could be fried, steamed, or made into bread. Of course, most people from the Deep South all the way to the sunny West Indian Islands prefer that perfect marriage of rice and peas called Hoppin' John (page 110).

To prepare black-eyed peas, pick out any stones that have made their way into the bag. Soak the beans overnight in a cool place. As you probably know, beans cause flatulence, which can be somewhat alleviated by draining the peas and tossing out the soaking water. As long as you haven't boiled the water you will not lose any of the precious vitamins and minerals.

∽ Black-eyed Peas ∾

Brown onions turn this simple dish into a pot of gold. Serve over rice.

1 pound black-eyed peas	1 tablespoon fresh thyme leaves, chopped, or 1 teaspoon dried
1 cup Brown Onions *(page 12)*	
2 quarts water	1½ teaspoons salt
1 large onion	½ cup beer
4 whole cloves	2 tablespoons tomato paste
2 bay leaves	1 teaspoon nutmeg
	Pinch of cayenne

Soak the peas overnight and drain. Put the brown onions into a large, heavy kettle. Add the water and peas and bring to a boil. Lower the heat to medium-low and add the onion, cloves, bay leaves, thyme, and salt. Simmer, covered, for 1 hour. Add the beer, tomato paste, nutmeg, and cayenne. Continue to simmer for 30 minutes more, until beans are tender. Remove and discard bay leaves before serving.   *Makes 8 servings.*

Per serving: 211 calories / 1 gm fat / 37 gm carbohydrate / 347 mg sodium

∽ Cowpea Stew ∾

Rosemary and sage add a bit of elegance to this ambitious but light stew. Accompany it with a hearty ale and you've got yourself a great winter meal!

1 pound black-eyed peas	½ cup sliced trimmed okra (trimmed of top and tails and sliced crosswise into ¼-inch rings)
1 tablespoon olive oil	
5 cloves garlic, minced	
1 cup pearl onions, or 1 large onion, finely chopped	
1 cup finely chopped celery	1 quart water
1 cup baby carrots or 1 cup diced carrots	1 quart Chicken Stock *(page 81)*
	2 bay leaves

4 sage leaves
1 large sprig of rosemary
1 (4-inch) square of cheesecloth
1½ teaspoons salt

1 teaspoon freshly ground
    black pepper
½ cup tomato paste

Soak the peas overnight and drain. Heat the oil in a large, heavy kettle over medium heat. Add garlic, and when lightly browned add onion, celery, carrots, and okra, and sauté for 5 minutes. Add peas, water, and stock and increase heat to high, bringing the mixture to a boil. Tie the bay leaves, sage, and rosemary in cheesecloth and drop into the boiling liquid. Add salt. Decrease the heat to low, and simmer, covered, for 1½ hours, stirring occasionally. Remove herb bundle and add the pepper and tomato paste. Let flavors develop off the heat for 15 minutes.   *Makes 6 servings.*

Per serving: 288 calories / 4 gm fat / 44 gm carbohydrate / 437 mg sodium

~ Black-eyed Peas with Yams ~

This combination of smoky and sweet is heaven, especially when accompanied by a side dish of Sautéed Mixed Greens (page 42) and a wedge of Cracked Pepper Cornbread (page 76).

1 pound black-eyed peas
1 tablespoon olive oil
1 medium onion, finely chopped
6 cups water
1 bay leaf
1 teaspoon minced thyme
    leaves

3 sprigs of marjoram
1 teaspoon salt
3 large yams, peeled and cubed
½ teaspoon nutmeg
    Pinch of cayenne

Soak peas overnight and drain. Heat oil in a large, heavy pot; add onion and sauté over medium-high heat for 5 minutes, until golden. Add peas and water and bring to a boil. Add bay leaf, thyme, marjoram, and salt and simmer, uncovered, for 1 hour. Add yams and nutmeg, and simmer for 30 minutes more. Remove from the heat and add cayenne. Remove and discard bay leaf before serving.   *Makes 6 servings.*

Per serving: 277 calories / 2 gm fat / 50 gm carbohydrate / 349 mg sodium

Okra

As with many children, it took me a while to get over my first experience with okra. When those dusky green prehistoric "fingers" were first plunked down on my plate, I took one look at them and said, *"You're crazy if you think I'm going to eat that!"* (to myself, of course). After much coaxing, I finally took a timid bite, and when that gummy extract oozed onto my tongue—"Phftoo!" I spat it back onto my plate and ran upstairs to wash out my mouth.

I have since learned that the mucilaginous substance inside okra makes a divine thickener for soups and stews. Okra has become the adopted crop of the South, where it is dredged whole in flour and deep fried, then munched pretty much the same way French fries are eaten.

When shopping for okra, look for pods that are a medium green color and deeply ridged. Pods should be between 2 to 4 inches long and should snap easily when broken. To cook, use aluminum or stainless-steel pots, as copper, brass, or iron will discolor the okra.

To clean and trim okra, rinse okra thoroughly, then clip the tops and tails.

A health note: Okra is low in calories, but supplies only a modest amount of vitamins and minerals, so it is best to supplement it with a green, leafy vegetable.

～ Okra, Corn, and Tomatoes ～

This recipe is one of Mom's specialties. Fresh corn gives the dish the perfect texture and crunch.

2 cloves garlic, minced
1 tablespoon butter
½ pound okra, trimmed of tops and tails and sliced crosswise into ¼-inch rings
4 ears of sweet corn, kernels removed

2 large tomatoes, coarsely chopped, peeled, and seeded
1 teaspoon salt
1 teaspoon sugar
1 teaspoon freshly ground white pepper

In a large skillet, sauté garlic in butter over medium heat until lightly browned. Add okra and cook for 20 minutes. Add corn and cook for 10 minutes more, tossing with the okra. Stir in tomatoes, salt, and sugar, and cook for an additional 5 minutes. Remove from the heat and stir in the pepper. *Makes 6 servings.*

Per serving: 133 calories / 3 gm fat / 25 gm carbohydrate / 219 mg sodium

∼ Okra Curry ∾

Curry flavor often shows up in the most unlikely places. If you think this is a case of strange bedfellows, try it and you'll think again. This goes well with Chicken Hash (page 131) and Sweet Potato Biscuits (page 72).

2 large onions, coarsely chopped
4 cloves garlic, minced
1 tablespoon olive oil
¼ cup Madras curry powder or
    curry powder with
    ¼ teaspoon cayenne added
1 teaspoon ground coriander
½ teaspoon turmeric
1 pound okra, trimmed of tops
    and tails and sliced cross-
    wise into ¼-inch rings

1 cup water
2 large tomatoes, peeled,
    seeded, and chopped
1 teaspoon salt
2 cups Vegetable Stock
    (page 85) or Chicken
    Stock *(page 81)*

In a large skillet, over medium heat, sauté onions and garlic for 5 minutes, until onions are translucent. Sprinkle in the curry, coriander, and turmeric and stir briskly to blend in with the onions. Add okra and water. Simmer, covered, for 25 minutes, adding more water as necessary if okra begins to dry out. Add tomatoes, salt, and stock, and cook for an additional 15 minutes. *Makes 6 servings.*

Per serving: 119 calories / 4 gm fat / 14 gm carbohydrate / 418 mg sodium

∼ Okra in Cornmeal Crust ∾

This snack or side dish is generally deep fried. I find that 4 teaspoons of oil and a good nonstick pan give similar results. Just make sure the pan is very hot before you introduce the okra.

1 cup cornmeal
½ cup flour
½ teaspoon cayenne
1 egg, beaten
¾ cup evaporated skim milk

4 teaspoons olive oil
1 pound okra, trimmed of tops
    and tails
½ teaspoon salt

In a medium mixing bowl, combine the cornmeal, flour, cayenne, egg, and milk, and beat until smooth. (It should be the consistency of thick pancake batter.) In a large nonstick skillet, heat 2 teaspoons oil over medium-high heat. Place half the okra in the batter and, with a slotted spoon, retrieve the okra (shaking off the excess batter) and place in the hot oil. Cook for 3 minutes on one side, until brown and crisp. Turn on the other side and cook for 2 minutes more, until evenly browned on both sides. Drain on a paper towel. Sprinkle with salt. Repeat with the remaining oil and okra.   *Makes 4 servings.*

Per serving: 72 calories / 2 gm fat / 11 gm carbohydrate / 389 mg sodium

Yams (Sweet Potatoes)

Yams were one of the most universally cultivated crops in West Africa, particularly among the Yoruba, who deemed them a symbol of fertility and wealth. Many people assume that the orange-colored potatoes are yams, while the ones with the pale yellow flesh are sweet potatoes. I've got news for you—both are sweet potatoes! African yams are so similar to the sweet potato in taste and texture, however, that when the slaves arrived here, they immediately adopted the sweet potato as their yam. (The word *yam,* incidentally, is a West African word for "to eat.") Throughout this chapter you'll see yam recipes that call for sweet potatoes. Do not be alarmed—for reason of tradition, I have chosen to maintain the original titles of the dishes, be it sweet potato or yam.

As a child, I watched Nana prepare sweet potatoes by first scrubbing them with castile soap and then rubbing their skins with oil. She'd place them in a hot (500 degree F.) oven for 15 minutes, then lower the heat to 325 degrees, and let them roast until they perfumed the kitchen with their distinctive nutlike aroma. As she pierced their skins with a sharp knife I could practically hear the sweet potatoes sigh as they emitted a burst of steam. What a treat!

∼ Baked Yams ∼

In the old days, when recipe ingredients were rarely measured, layering was used to ensure the proper distribution of seasonings. Nana did this with her baked yams, as well as with her fruit pies. I've adopted her method here.

6 large yams

3 apples, peeled and cored

1 tablespoon Pie Spice *(page 9)*

1 teaspoon grated lemon zest

3 teaspoons finely chopped
gingerroot

3 teaspoons butter

⅔ cup packed dark brown sugar

1 tablespoon dark rum

½ cup orange juice

Preheat the oven to 375 degrees F. Bake yams for 45 minutes, or until soft when a fork is inserted. Remove from the oven, cool, and peel. Lower oven temperature to 350 degrees. Butter a 9 × 12-inch glass baking dish. Thinly slice the apples and yams and divide into three parts, each consisting of two yams and one apple. Combine the pie spice mixture with the lemon zest and divide into three parts as well. Layer the bottom of the baking dish with one part of the yam-apple mixture. Sprinkle one third of the spice mixture, 1 teaspoon ginger, and 1 teaspoon butter, cut into small pieces, on top. Repeat with the two other portions. Heat the sugar in a small nonstick pan over medium heat until it caramelizes, stirring frequently until the sugar is cooked evenly and turns a golden brown. Add the rum and the orange juice to the sugar and continue cooking until the caramel dissolves. Pour over the yams and bake for 30 minutes, until browned and crusty on top. *Makes 6 servings.*

Per serving: 347 calories / 2 gm fat / 80 gm carbohydrate / 44 mg sodium

~ Mashed Yams ~

This is so delectable, I often wonder whether I should have placed it in the dessert chapter.

6 **large yams**	¼ **teaspoon allspice**
1 **tablespoon butter**	¼ **teaspoon nutmeg**
¼ **cup evaporated skim milk**	¼ **teaspoon ground cloves**
⅛ **cup lime juice**	½ **teaspoon salt**
1 **tablespoon dark rum**	1 **tablespoon freshly ground**
1 **teaspoon coconut milk**	**white pepper**
1 **tablespoon maple syrup**	¼ **teaspoon cayenne**
½ **teaspoon cinnamon**	

In water to cover, boil the yams in their skins for 45 minutes, or until soft when a fork is inserted. Cool, peel, and cube yams. Add butter, milk, lime juice, rum, coconut milk, and syrup and mash. Add cinnamon, allspice, nutmeg, cloves, salt, pepper, and cayenne and whip until smooth.   *Makes 6 servings.*

Per serving: 222 calories / 2 gm fat / 46 gm carbohydrate / 217 mg sodium

~ Sweet-Hot Yams ~

This simple dish really complements Crab Cakes (page 120) or Shrimp Cakes (page 174), and Cucumbers with Peppered Vinegar (page 142).

1 **tablespoon olive oil**	½ **teaspoon salt**
4 **large yams, peeled and cubed**	1 **teaspoon cayenne**
2 **tablespoons granulated dark**	
brown sugar	

Preheat the oven to 450 degrees F. Coat a 9 × 12-inch glass baking dish with the oil and place it in the oven for 5 minutes. Place the yams in the dish and bake for 25 minutes, tossing occasionally, until well browned. Remove from the oven. Combine the sugar, salt, and cayenne and sprinkle over the yams. Toss and serve.   *Makes 6 servings.*

Per serving: 244 calories / 3 gm fat / 51 gm carbohydrate / 284 mg sodium

～ Sweet Potato Waffles ～

This is always a hit at my table. These waffles are so versatile, they can be eaten with either syrup or Red Pepper Gravy (page 203). I like mine with a small pat of Cinnamon-Orange Butter (page 206). They're a great side dish with Skinless Fried Chicken (page 127) and Sautéed Mixed Greens (page 42).

2 **medium-sized sweet potatoes**	½ **cup flour**
1 **egg**	2 **egg whites**
1 **tablespoon butter, melted**	¼ **cup sugar**
2 **cups evaporated skim milk**	

Boil the sweet potatoes in their skins for 45 minutes, or until soft when a fork is inserted. Peel and mash the potatoes (you should have 2 cups mashed potatoes) and put them aside to cool. Beat the egg and stir it into the potatoes. Pour in the melted butter and the milk, and continue to beat. Add flour a little at a time, until the batter becomes smooth. Beat the egg whites, adding sugar a little at a time, until stiff peaks form. Gently fold the whites into the batter and let it sit for a few minutes. Drop a few large spoonfuls of batter onto a hot, well-oiled waffle iron, and cook following the manufacturer's instructions. Be patient. These waffles take longer to cook than standard flour waffles—often up to 12 minutes each.   *Makes 8 waffles.*

Per serving: 179 calories / 3 gm fat / 30 gm carbohydrate / 86 mg sodium

~ Sweet Potato Pone ~

To this day, I eat this delicious dish with bittersweet memories. One summer day, while we were staying at Nana's, I convinced my sister Diana to help me smuggle a large pot, a couple of weenies, and a long fork into our bedroom. With a bunch of crumpled-up comic books for fuel, we started a successful fire, and proceeded to roast weenies. Before they'd even had a chance to brown, Nana was in our room with a paddle, which she commenced to apply long and hard to our tender bottoms. I lay in bed sobbing for several minutes, and then suddenly stopped. My nose twitched. Could that be the aroma of sweet potatoes wafting up the stairs? Nana was baking sweet potato pone, my favorite treat. She had forgiven us after all!

Incidentally, this dish goes with anything but roasted weenies.

3½ **pounds sweet potatoes**	1 **teaspoon cinnamon**
1 **egg, beaten**	½ **teaspoon ground cloves**
¼ **cup evaporated skim milk, scalded**	2 **tablespoons grated orange zest**
1 **teaspoon butter**	1 **teaspoon grated gingerroot**
½ **cup sorghum or blackstrap molasses**	1 **teaspoon vanilla extract**
	1 **tablespoon dark rum**
½ **teaspoon nutmeg**	¾ **cup flour**

Preheat the oven to 375 degrees F. Butter an 8-inch-square baking dish. Boil the potatoes for 45 minutes, or until soft when a fork is inserted. Peel and mash the potatoes and put in a large saucepan. Add the egg, milk, butter, sorghum, nutmeg, cinnamon, cloves, orange zest, gingerroot, vanilla, and rum. Cook for 5 minutes over low heat. Remove from the heat and add the flour, a little at a time, until well mixed. Pour mixture into the baking dish and bake for 25 minutes, until golden brown.   *Makes 8 servings.*

Per serving: 237 calories / 1 gm fat / 50 gm carbohydrate / 44 mg sodium

～ Down-Home Stew ～

This is a personal favorite. The taste is both piquant and friendly—just like down-home itself. Serve with steamed rice or couscous.

2 large yams, peeled and cubed
1 cup water
3 cloves garlic, minced
1 large onion, chopped
1 tablespoon olive oil
1 teaspoon crushed red pepper
2 pounds collard greens *(see page 41 for preparation)*, finely chopped
¼ pound okra, trimmed of tops and tails and sliced crosswise into ¼-inch rings
2 bay leaves

1 tablespoon fresh thyme leaves or 1 teaspoon dried
¼ cup shelled peanuts
1 large tomato, peeled, seeded, and chopped
⅓ cup tomato paste
2 tablespoons peanut butter
2 cups water mixed with the juice of 1 lime
1½ teaspoons salt
1 teaspoon freshly ground black pepper

Place the yams in a steamer basket and steam over the water for 15 minutes over low heat. Reserve the liquid. Meanwhile, in a large skillet over medium heat sauté the garlic and onion in the oil for 5 minutes, until translucent. Add crushed pepper, greens, okra, bay leaves, and thyme. Stir to blend. Cook, covered, over low heat for 25 minutes. Add the steamed yams and their liquid, the peanuts and tomato. Mix the tomato paste with the peanut butter and lime-water, pour into the vegetable mixture, and simmer for 15 minutes more. Add the salt and pepper and let the stew flavors develop off the heat for 20 minutes, covered. The liquid should be the texture of gravy. Thin out with additional water, if necessary.   *Makes 8 servings.*

Per serving: 144 calories / 4 gm fat / 25 gm carbohydrate / 391 mg sodium

～ 4 ～

Bread

"Eating burnt toast will make you pretty," Nana used to say. (Has anyone else out there heard that?) I must admit, it was a brilliant lie. Whenever Nana overcooked our toast, did we complain? Of course not!

Nana was a wonderful baker. She baked bread to go with most of her meals. You see, Nana didn't believe in store-bought bread. She'd begin baking early in the morning, no matter what the temperature was. Her morning-kitchen potpourri was an intoxicating blend of yeast and baking buns, tea cakes, and my favorite, sweet potato bread. She also had a wonderful repertoire of biscuits: sage, buttermilk, cornmeal, even strawberry. Every time we turned around, Nana was wrist-deep in some intricate working of dough. In the same way that some people believe talking to plants promotes their growth, Nana was certain it was her loving handling of the bread that caused it to flourish into a work of art. What puzzles me is that she never used a recipe. Yes, she measured: a few teacups of this, a thimbleful of that, a pinch, dash, handful—whatever was available. And yet, the bread always arrived on the table perfectly shaped and crusty, yet moist and firm inside. I loved Nana's bread crusts, and used to pull them off and save them for last. Honestly, I don't know how she managed to bake perfect bread every time, using the tools she had to work with, but, of course, making an art of necessity is one of the main sensibilities of African culture. And although I tend to rely on guidelines, I do maintain one of Nana's principles: I bake with love.

FUNDAMENTALS OF YEAST-RAISED BREADS

If this is your first attempt at making bread, prepare to be humbled. For bread making, as elemental as it appears, happens to be an extremely technical art. And while you have license to perform aggressive acts on the dough, such as manipulation, punching down, and using your knuckles to check for doneness, you must also address your gentler side and wait patiently for its development—that is, if you want your dough to rise to the occasion. Every aspect of the process of bread making must be given equal attention and be well understood.

Yeast Activation

Yeast is a living organism. It needs to be fed properly in order to function for you. It feeds on sugar and thrives in warm water, although water that's too warm can put it in a state of hyperactivity, which can result in shock or burnout, and ultimately the death of your yeast. The best way to activate yeast is to dissolve it in ¼ cup lukewarm water, to which has been added 1 teaspoon sugar or honey.

Mixing

If you are using milk, you may want to scald it beforehand and let it come to room temperature. Scalding was always necessary when milk was unpasteurized. Among other things, it kills the enzymes that combine with yeast to produce soggy, rubbery loaves. Since most milk sold commercially is already pasteurized, this is not totally necessary; but it's best not to take chances, so scald. The mixing process is simple: You'll add the butter and eggs to the cooled milk, and in most cases, you'll mix the yeast-water with that mixture, which will then be enriched with the addition of flour and salt. I use all-purpose unbleached flour, which is more accessible than bread flour. Regarding salt, use it sparingly, as too much can retard the rising process. Mix in the flour 1 cup at a time. Though a recipe may require 5 cups of flour, slow down when you get to the last cup. Add the flour in small amounts and if the dough is the right consistency with 4 or 4½ cups, halt. The dough has reached the right consistency when it becomes stiff and easily pulls away from the side of the bowl. (You'll probably end up using the rest of the flour during the kneading process.)

Kneading

Once you've mixed all the ingredients, you must knead. This is the most essential, yet the most gratifying (I think), phase of bread making. Kneading releases the gluten and elasticizes the dough. In the process, it distributes the carbon dioxide bubbles the yeast has released, causing the dough to rise. (On a fitness tip: Kneading keeps the pecs and upper arms in shape.)

Here's how to knead: Sprinkle a clean, dry, preferably wooden, board with flour (often the leftover flour from the dough mixing). Dust your hands with flour and turn the dough out onto the board. Shape the dough into a ball and press down slightly to flatten it out. With your hands cupped, bring the sides of the dough toward you. Without losing your grip, take the heels of your hands and push down into the dough. *Ahhhh!* Slightly rotate the dough and continue kneading for 4 or 5 minutes. Turn the dough over and repeat the process.

Rising

If you are an impatient cook, this stage will drive you mad. It is important to allow dough the proper rising time. Rising times may vary, from 35 minutes to 1½ hours. A lot of circumstances factor in: altitude, brand of yeast, brand of flour, temperature. Stay the course. I guarantee it will rise, if you've made all the right moves. To prepare for the rising, place the ball of kneaded dough in a greased bowl (a large bowl, as the dough will be doubling in size), and lightly oil the top of the dough to prevent a skin from forming. Cover the bowl with a plate or a tea towel and place it in a warm, draft-free spot. Let it rise until doubled in bulk. And how do you know it has doubled in bulk? You press two fingers (down to the first knuckle) in the center of the dough. If the holes remain, the dough has doubled. With your fist and a little force, punch down right over the finger indentations to allow the gases to escape, and turn the dough back onto the board for 3 minutes of kneading. At this time, you may shape the dough into loaves or place it back in the bowl for a second rising, if the recipe calls for it. If that is the case repeat the kneading process once more.

Baking

Most breads bake for about ½ hour at 400–425 degrees F. The bread should bake until it is brown on top. To test for doneness, remove the bread from the oven and briskly knock on the base with your knuckle. If it sounds hollow, it is done.

∼ Nana's White Bread ∽

One of our summertime treats at Nana's was eating fresh-baked bread on a daily basis. This was her standard loaf of white bread: fluffy yet firm.

2 **packages active dry yeast**	1¼ **cups 1 percent fat milk,**
1 **tablespoon honey**	**scalded and brought to**
¼ **cup warm water**	**room temperature**
5½ **cups all-purpose unbleached**	2 **tablespoons butter, melted**
flour	1 **egg, beaten**
1 **teaspoon salt**	

Butter two 9 × 5 × 3-inch loaf pans. Dissolve the yeast and the honey in the water and let sit for 10 minutes. Into a large bowl, sift together the flour and salt. Put the cooled milk in another large mixing bowl and blend in the melted butter, egg, and yeast-water. Add the flour mixture, 1 cup at a time, until dough stiffens and pulls away from the bowl. Turn onto a floured board and knead for 10 minutes, or until dough is soft and flexible.

Put the dough into a large buttered bowl. Lightly oil the top of the dough, cover with a plate, and set aside in a warm, draft-free spot until the dough has doubled in size, about 1 hour.

Punch down the dough with your fist, and knead for 2 minutes. Return the dough to the buttered bowl, lightly oil top, and cover. Let rise for 45 minutes, until dough has doubled in size.

Divide the dough in half and shape it into the two loaf pans. Cover with a plate or tea towel and let rise for 45 minutes. Preheat the oven to 425 degrees F. Bake for 30 minutes, or until the tops have browned.   *Makes 2 loaves.*

Per serving (1 slice): 106 calories / 1 gm fat / 22 gm carbohydrate / 105 mg sodium

～ Sweet Bread ～

This is a sweeter version of Nana's white bread. In the morning she'd toast it and spread it with cinnamon butter all the way to the crust, then cut it into four triangles for me. To this day I cut my cinnamon toast into little triangles. Try this with Cinnamon-Orange Butter (page 206).

2 **packages active dry yeast**	1 **teaspoon salt**
1 **teaspoon honey**	1½ **cups 1 percent fat milk,**
¼ **cup warm water**	**scalded and brought to**
5½ **cups all-purpose unbleached**	**room temperature**
flour	2 **tablespoons butter, melted**
¼ **cup Vanilla Sugar (page 18)**	1 **egg, beaten**

Butter two 9 × 5 × 3-inch loaf pans. Dissolve the yeast and the honey in the water and let sit for 10 minutes. Sift together the flour, sugar, and salt. In a large mixing bowl, combine the milk, melted butter, egg, and yeast-water. Add the flour mixture, 1 cup at a time, mixing well until the dough stiffens and pulls away from the bowl. Turn onto a floured board and knead for 10 minutes, or until dough is soft and flexible. Put the dough into a large buttered bowl. Lightly oil the top of the dough, cover with a plate, and set aside in a warm, draft-free spot until the dough has doubled in size, about 1 hour.

Punch down the dough with your fist, and knead for 2 minutes. Return the dough to the buttered bowl and let rise, covered, for 45 minutes.

Divide the dough in half and shape it into the two loaf pans. Cover and let rise for 45 more minutes. Preheat the oven to 425 degrees F. Oil the tops. Bake for 30 minutes, or until the tops have browned.   *Makes 2 loaves.*

Per serving (1 slice): 116 calories / 1 gm fat / 25 gm carbohydrate / 103 mg sodium

∼ Sweet Potato Bread ∼

This bread has a rich orange color that deepens when buttered. This sweet bread goes wonderfully with spicy foods like Sautéed Mixed Greens (page 42) or Barbecued Shrimp (page 158).

2 packages active dry yeast	1 teaspoon cinnamon
⅓ cup plus 2 tablespoons honey	¼ teaspoon nutmeg
1½ cups warm water	¼ teaspoon ground ginger
5½ cups all-purpose unbleached flour	2 tablespoons butter, melted
1½ teaspoons salt	1⅓ cups mashed sweet potatoes, cooled
½ teaspoon allspice	

Butter two 9 × 5 × 3-inch loaf pans. Dissolve the yeast and 2 tablespoons honey in the water and let sit for 10 minutes. In a large mixing bowl, sift together the flour, salt, allspice, cinnamon, nutmeg, and ginger. Add the yeast-water, melted butter, remaining honey, and the sweet potatoes, mixing well into the flour until the dough stiffens and pulls away from the bowl. Turn onto a floured board and knead for 12 minutes, or until dough is soft and flexible. Put the dough into a large buttered bowl. Lightly oil the top of the dough, cover with a plate, and set aside in a warm, draft-free spot until the dough has doubled in size, about 1 hour.

Punch down the dough with your fist, and knead for 2 minutes. Return the dough to the buttered bowl and let rise for 45 minutes.

Divide the dough in half and shape it into the two loaf pans. Cover and let rise for 45 minutes. Preheat the oven to 425 degrees F. Oil the tops. Bake for 30 minutes, or until the tops have browned.   *Makes 2 loaves.*

Per serving (1 slice): 126 calories / 1 gm fat / 28 gm carbohydrate / 152 mg sodium

～ Lemon-Poppy Tea Bread ～

Nana used to serve this tart, sweet bread at her weekly Pokeno® party. I often helped her prepare for the party, which entitled me to as much of the tea bread as I wanted. I bake this bread at least four times a year, and still haven't the foggiest idea how to play Pokeno®.

1 tablespoon active dry yeast
1 teaspoon honey
¼ cup warm water
3 cups all-purpose unbleached
   flour
½ teaspoon salt
3 tablespoons sugar
½ teaspoon mace
4 tablespoons poppy seeds

2 tablespoons plus 1 teaspoon
   grated lemon zest
¾ cup 1 percent fat milk,
   scalded and brought to
   room temperature
1 egg, beaten
1 cup confectioners' sugar
3 tablespoons lemon juice

Butter a 9 × 5 × 3-inch loaf pan. Dissolve the yeast and honey in the water and let sit for 15 minutes. In a large mixing bowl, sift together the flour, salt, sugar, and mace. Stir in 2 tablespoons of the poppy seeds and 1 tablespoon of the lemon zest. Add the yeast-water, milk, and egg, blending well. Turn onto a floured board and knead for 2 minutes, or until dough is soft and flexible. Put the dough into a large buttered bowl. Lightly oil the top of the dough, cover with a plate, and set aside until the dough has doubled in size, about 1 hour.

Punch down the dough with your fist, and knead for 3 minutes. Shape it into the loaf pans. Cover and let rise for 1 hour. Preheat the oven to 400 degrees F. Oil the top. Bake for 30 minutes, or until the top has browned. Remove the loaf from the oven and cool thoroughly on a rack.

Combine the confectioners' sugar, lemon juice, and remaining zest to make a thin paste. Brush on the top of the loaf and sprinkle with the rest of the poppy seeds.   *Makes 1 loaf.*

Per serving (1 slice): 164 calories / 2 gm fat / 34 gm carbohydrate / 104 mg sodium

⁓ Black Currant Sugar Buns ⁓

These delicious buns are connected in my mind with—of all things—Grand-mom Cothran's dog. When we were kids, she had a Chihuahua named Penny, a delicate little thing who trembled all the time. One day Mr. Miller, Grand-mom's next-door neighbor, knocked on my door toting a half-dozen mouth-watering sugar buns and told me this funny story: His wife had baked these buns and had left a couple out on the porch while she ran in the house to get a glass of iced tea. Penny had jumped up on the rocker and begun licking the sugar off the top of one of the buns. Mr. Miller, coming home from work, had caught Penny red-handed. Penny—a veteran food-lifter—instantly rolled over and played dead. For years afterward, whenever Mr. Miller would see me, he'd cry, "Roll over, Penny," and split his sides laughing. Here's my interpreta-tion of those crunchy-sweet buns.

1 **package active dry yeast**	1 **cup 1 percent fat milk,**
2 **tablespoons honey**	**scalded and brought to**
¼ **cup warm water**	**room temperature**
2 **teaspoons butter, softened**	4 **cups all-purpose unbleached**
¼ **cup plus 2 tablespoons**	**flour**
Vanilla Sugar (*page 18*)	½ **teaspoon salt**
1 **cup black currants**	1 **teaspoon butter, melted**

Grease 2 baking sheets and set aside. Dissolve the yeast and honey in the water, and let sit for 10 minutes. Cream the butter with ¼ cup sugar and add currants. Pour in the milk. Add the yeast mixture and blend. Sift the flour with the salt, and add to the liquid, 1 cup at a time, until the dough begins to stiffen and pulls away from the bowl. Turn onto a floured board and knead for 10 minutes, or until dough is soft and flexible. Place the dough in a large buttered bowl, cover with a plate, and let rise in a warm, draft-free place for about 1 hour, or until dough has doubled in size. Punch down the dough with your fist and knead for 2 minutes. Divide the dough into eighteen pieces; roll them up to about 3 inches in diameter, and line up each piece side by side (1 inch apart) on the baking sheets. Let them rise until doubled in size, about 45 minutes. Preheat the oven to 425 degrees F. Brush tops with melted butter and sprinkle with remaining sugar on each bun. Bake for 15 minutes, until tops are browned.   *Makes 18 buns.*

Per serving: 181 calories / 1 gm fat / 40 gm carbohydrate / 111 mg sodium

∼ Yeast Rolls ∼

Mom's fame as a baker of exquisite yeast rolls quickly spread. Whenever we paid someone a dinner visit, Mom would always ask if there was something she could bring. The answer was always the same: "Please bring over some of those yeast rolls, Freda."

1 **package active dry yeast**	4 **tablespoons sugar**
1 **tablespoon honey**	¼ **teaspoon salt**
¼ **cup warm water**	5 **cups all-purpose unbleached**
2 **cups 1 percent fat milk**	**flour**
2 **tablespoons butter**	

Dissolve the yeast and honey in the warm water and set aside for 10 minutes. Scald the milk in a small saucepan. Add the butter, sugar, and salt, and let the mixture come to room temperature in a large mixing bowl. Add the yeast mixture. Add flour, a little at a time, until a soft dough is formed. Turn the dough onto a lightly floured board and knead until smooth, about 12 minutes. Shape the dough into a ball and place in a large buttered mixing bowl. Lightly oil the top of the dough, cover with a plate, and let stand in a warm, draft-free place for 1 hour, or until dough is doubled in bulk. Butter two muffin pans.

Punch down the dough with your fist, and knead for 3 minutes. Pinch off twenty-four pieces about 2 inches in diameter. Place each piece into a muffin cup. Cover and let sit for 45 minutes, or until rolls have doubled in size. Preheat the oven to 425 degrees F. Oil the top of each roll. Bake for 15 minutes, or until tops are golden brown.   *Makes 24 rolls.*

Per serving: 111 calories / 1 gm fat / 23 gm carbohydrate / 65 mg sodium

∼ Sweet Potato Buns ∼

Thanksgiving was the perfect holiday for us as kids: no one paid much attention to our mischief, and we could eat as much as our stomachs could contain. I always reserved space for Aunt Charity's sweet potato buns—a combination of two star carbohydrates in a single tasty handful.

1 package active dry yeast	3 tablespoons sugar
1 tablespoon honey	1 teaspoon butter
¼ cup warm water	1 cup 1 percent fat milk
1 large sweet potato	4 cups sifted all-purpose
½ teaspoon salt	unbleached flour

Butter two muffin pans and set aside. Dissolve the yeast and honey in the warm water. Boil the potato in its skin for 45 minutes. Peel, mash, and put in a large mixing bowl. Add salt, sugar, and butter, and beat vigorously. Heat milk; remove just before the boiling point and pour into the potato mixture. When cooled to room temperature, add the yeast mixture. Mix in the flour, 1 cup at a time, until the dough begins to thicken. Turn out onto a floured board and knead for 10 minutes, or until dough is soft and flexible. Put the dough into a buttered bowl. Lightly oil the top of the dough, cover with a plate, and let rise in a warm, draft-free place until the dough has doubled in bulk, about 45 minutes. Punch down with your fist.

Pull off twenty-four pieces about 2 inches in diameter, and shape into balls. Put each ball into a muffin cup. Cover and let rise again for 45 minutes, or until buns have doubled in size. Preheat the oven to 475 degrees F. Bake for 20 minutes, or until golden brown on top.   *Makes 24 buns.*

Per serving: 87 calories / 1 gm fat / 19 gm carbohydrate / 53 mg sodium

～ Orange Spice Buns ～

These buns are so scrumptious that I burn the roof of my mouth every time I eat them; that is to say, I can't wait for them to cool before I pop one into my mouth.

1 tablespoon active dry yeast	2 teaspoons Pie Spice (*page 9*)
½ cup 1 percent fat milk, scalded and cooled to room temperature	or pumpkin pie spice
	1 egg, beaten
	1 tablespoon butter, melted
½ teaspoon honey	2 tablespoons evaporated skim milk
1¾ cups all-purpose unbleached flour	
	2 teaspoons grated orange zest
½ teaspoon salt	2 tablespoons orange juice
2 tablespoons sugar	¼ cup confectioners' sugar

In a small bowl, combine the yeast, milk, honey, and ¼ cup of the flour, and let sit for 15 minutes. Into a large mixing bowl, sift together the remaining flour, salt, sugar, and pie spice. In a third bowl, mix the beaten egg, butter, evaporated milk, and 1 teaspoon zest, and combine it with the yeast mixture. Add the liquid mixture to the flour, and mix until a soft dough is formed. Turn onto a lightly floured surface and knead for 8 minutes, or until the dough is soft and pliable. Put the dough into a buttered bowl. Lightly oil the top of the dough, cover with a plate, and set aside in a warm, draft-free place until the dough has doubled in size, about 1 hour.

Butter a 9 × 11-inch baking pan. Punch down dough with your fist.

Knead the dough again for 3 minutes and divide into twelve pieces; roll each piece into a ball and place 1 inch apart in the baking pan. Cover and let rise again for about 45 minutes, or until rolls have doubled in size. Lightly oil the tops.

Preheat the oven to 375 degrees F. Bake for 25 minutes, or until golden brown. Cool on a wire rack. In a small bowl, mix together the orange juice, confectioners' sugar, and the remaining zest. Brush on top of the rolls.   *Makes 12 rolls.*

Per serving: 103 calories / 1 gm fat / 20 gm carbohydrate / 113 mg sodium

～ Sally Lunn ～

This cake has its origins in Britain, and was adopted in the Old South by way of the Virginians. We ate it regularly in our family, but I never knew it was called Sally Lunn. I just assumed it was Aunt Missouri's bread, because she was the one who made it. Aunt Missouri was Nana's sister, my great-great aunt, who used to baby-sit us from time to time. Freckle-faced Aunt Missouri was strict and stern, the kind of person around whom we yes-ma'amed and no-ma'amed in careful voices. In retrospect, I realize she was quite an elegant lady, and oh, what lovely doilies she made!

1 tablespoon butter	3 cups sifted all-purpose
1 cup 1 percent fat milk	unbleached flour
1 tablespoon active dry yeast	1 teaspoon salt
1 teaspoon sugar	2 tablespoons caraway seeds
2 eggs, well beaten	3 sugar cubes, crushed

Butter 2 9-inch cake pans. Melt the butter in the milk, but do not boil. When the milk has cooled to lukewarm, stir in the yeast and the sugar, and let sit for 10 minutes. Beat the eggs into the yeast mixture. Into a large mixing bowl, sift the flour with the salt and caraway seeds and add the yeast mixture. Beat for about 10 minutes, until dough is soft and shiny, but not gooey.

Pour into a large buttered bowl, cover with a plate, and set aside in a warm, draft-free place until the dough has doubled in size, about 1½ hours. Preheat the oven to 450 degrees F. Punch down dough and place equal portions of the dough into the cake pans. Sprinkle crushed sugar on top of the dough and bake for 35 minutes, until browned. Cut into 6 wedges each and serve hot.   *Makes 12 wedges.*

Per serving: 73 calories / 2 gm fat / 10 gm carbohydrate / 120 mg sodium

Biscuits

Nana was also an excellent biscuit maker, and as always, it was all done by "vibration." Her biscuits had the flakiest melt-in-your mouth texture, and when it came to the making itself, well, I've never seen anyone work fat into flour with such rapidity. Her fingers moved like hummingbird wings. One of her secrets? The liberal use of evaporated milk, which accounted for the rich taste of the biscuit. I'd like to tell you that I've inherited her intuitive method of cooking biscuits, but I'm afraid I must adhere to the guidelines if I expect to make a decent biscuit. And briefly, these guidelines are:

Preheat the oven properly. Often we can get away with baking in a cold or semiheated oven, but this definitely can't be done with biscuit dough. If you want to get a good rise out of your biscuit, preheat the oven at least 20 minutes prior to baking.

Be exact with the measurements. If the recipe calls for sifted flour, sift before you measure. And then sift all the dry ingredients together.

Chill the fat. You're working against time when cutting fat into flour. If you start off with warm fat, the heat of your fast-moving fingers will most likely melt the fat into the flour, and you'll be left with a greasy biscuit. *Tip:* If you aren't quick with your fingers, invest in a pastry cutter.

Cut the fat into the flour thoroughly. With your fingertips, briskly rub the fat into the flour until it is evenly distributed and resembles coarse grain. If the flour is not thoroughly incorporated into the fat, the gluten in the flour will overactivate upon mixing with a liquid. Unlike a yeast bread, which needs a high-gluten flour, biscuit dough that has too much gluten produces a heavy or doughy biscuit. You can alleviate part of this problem by using a low-gluten or pastry flour (see page 268 for mailing address, if you can't get these in your neighborhood).

Don't overknead. Unlike yeast bread, biscuit dough can't withstand heavy kneading. Knead gently, about eight or ten times.

Cutting. Nana used a jelly glass to cut her biscuits, and she got away with it. You may not. It's best to invest in a biscuit cutter that has sharp jagged edges to allow air to escape while cutting. Don't twist your cutter while cutting or you may end up with uneven biscuits. Dip the cutter in the flour, and bring it up clean.

∼ Old-Fashioned Biscuits ∼

Surprisingly, when it came to plain biscuits, Grandmom Cothran had both Mom and Nana beat. Grandmom wasn't much for cooking, but when you opened one of her hot biscuits, you'd recognize genius in the way she incorporated big taste into such a delicate object.

2 cups all-purpose unbleached flour	2 tablespoons sweet butter, chilled
1 tablespoon baking powder	2 tablespoons vegetable shortening, chilled
2 teaspoons sugar	1 cup evaporated skim milk
1 teaspoon salt	

Preheat the oven to 425 degrees F. In a large mixing bowl, sift together the flour, baking powder, sugar, and salt. Cut the butter and shortening into the flour mixture. Stir in the milk and turn out onto a lightly floured board to lightly knead ten times. Roll dough out to ¼-inch thickness and with a biscuit cutter cut into 2-inch rounds. Bake on an ungreased baking sheet for 20 minutes, until golden brown.   *Makes 12 biscuits.*

Per serving: 122 calories / 4 gm fat / 19 gm carbohydrate / 205 mg sodium

~ Cornmeal Biscuits ~

I know of only one way to eat these biscuits: pulled apart and placed face up on a saucer, with a puddle of sorghum in the middle of each half. Feel free to come up with some others!

1 cup cornmeal
1 cup all-purpose unbleached
   flour
1 tablespoon baking powder
2 tablespoons sugar

1 teaspoon salt
2 tablespoons sweet butter, chilled
2 tablespoons vegetable
   shortening, chilled
1 cup 1 percent fat milk

Preheat the oven to 425 degrees F. In a large mixing bowl, sift together the cornmeal, flour, baking powder, sugar, and salt. Cut the butter and shortening into the flour mixture until it resembles coarse meal. Stir in the milk until mixture holds together in a ball, and turn out onto a lightly floured board to lightly knead ten times. Roll dough out to ½-inch thickness and with a biscuit cutter cut into 2-inch rounds. Bake on a lightly greased baking sheet for 20 minutes, until golden brown.   *Makes 12 biscuits.*

Per serving: 135 calories / 4 gm fat / 21 gm carbohydrate / 205 mg sodium

~ Lemon Pepper Biscuits ~

This is a sassy biscuit. Split it open while it's still hot and pour a little Sawmill Gravy (page 204) over it for a quick breakfast treat.

2 cups all-purpose unbleached
   flour
1 tablespoon baking powder
1 teaspoon sugar
1 teaspoon salt
2 teaspoons Lemon Pepper
   (page 5)

2 tablespoons sweet butter, chilled
2 tablespoons vegetable
   shortening, chilled
1 cup 1 percent fat buttermilk

Preheat the oven to 425 degrees F. In a large mixing bowl, sift together the flour, baking powder, sugar, salt, and lemon pepper. Cut the butter and shortening into the flour mixture until it resembles coarse meal. Stir in the milk and turn out on a floured board to lightly knead ten times. Roll dough out to ½-inch thickness and with a biscuit cutter cut into 2-inch rounds. Bake on an ungreased baking sheet for 20 minutes, until golden brown.   *Makes 12 biscuits.*

Per serving: 113 calories / 4 gm fat / 17 gm carbohydrate / 191 mg sodium

～ Sweet Potato Biscuits ～

One of the many things Nana and I had in common was a love for sweet potatoes. She always kept a few on hand in a woven basket by the stove. She made plenty of foods with sweet potatoes, all of it inspired, she said, by the brilliant agriculturist George Washington Carver. Back then, study about great African innovators was limited to one week out of a year in school, so we were eager for any information obtained outside of "Negro History Week."

2 **large sweet potatoes**	2 **teaspoons sugar**
2 **cups flour**	2 **tablespoons sweet butter, chilled**
2 **teaspoons baking powder**	2 **tablespoons vegetable**
½ **teaspoon baking soda**	**shortening, chilled**
½ **teaspoon salt**	½ **cup 1 percent fat buttermilk**
¼ **teaspoon grated lemon zest**	

Preheat the oven to 450 degrees F. Boil the potatoes for 45 minutes, and drain. Peel and mash. In a large mixing bowl, sift together the flour, baking powder, baking soda, salt, zest and sugar. Blend the butter and shortening into the flour with your fingertips until it has the texture of coarse meal. Add the milk, a little at a time, until well blended. Add the potatoes and blend with a wooden spoon until a soft dough has been formed. Turn the dough out onto a lightly floured board and roll out to ½-inch thickness. Using a

2-inch round cutter, cut the dough into rounds. Lightly grease a baking sheet and place the biscuits ½ inch apart. Bake for 15 minutes, or until lightly browned on the top. *Makes 12 biscuits.*

Per serving: 158 calories / 4 gm fat / 26 gm carbohydrate / 219 mg sodium

～ Sage Biscuits ～

Nana loved to always keep a little sage somewhere about in the kitchen, as she felt it represented longevity. She often hung it upside down to dry. She generally used the dry mixture in her biscuits, crumbling it until superfine and lightly kneading it into the dough. I use fresh sage, moderately air-dried.

2 cups all-purpose unbleached flour
1 tablespoon baking powder
½ teaspoon baking soda
½ teaspoon salt
2 tablespoons sweet butter, chilled

2 tablespoons vegetable shortening, chilled
½ cup 1 percent fat buttermilk
1 egg, beaten
2 tablespoons chopped sage

Preheat the oven to 400 degrees F. In a large bowl, sift together flour, baking powder, baking soda, and salt. With your fingertips, rub the butter and the shortening into the flour mixture until it resembles coarse meal. Stir the buttermilk into the egg. Pour buttermilk mixture into the flour mixture and stir until it holds together in a ball. Turn out onto a lightly floured surface. Knead in sage (ten times). Roll out to ½-inch thickness. With a biscuit cutter, cut into 2-inch rounds. Place biscuits on a lightly greased baking sheet, at least 1 inch apart. Bake 15 minutes until well browned. *Makes 12 biscuits.*

Per serving: 121 calories / 4 gm fat / 17 gm carbohydrate / 212 mg sodium

∼ Strawberry Biscuits ∼

Pale yellow, flecked with pink, these biscuits add a touch of tea-and-sympathy elegance to an old standard.

2 cups all-purpose unbleached flour	½ teaspoon salt
1 tablespoon baking powder	4 tablespoons sweet butter, chilled
½ teaspoon allspice	¾ cup evaporated skim milk
2 tablespoons sugar	1 cup minced fresh strawberries

Preheat the oven to 425 degrees F. In a large mixing bowl, combine the flour, baking powder, allspice, sugar, and salt. Cut the butter into the flour mixture until it resembles coarse meal. Combine the milk with the strawberries and add to the flour mixture. Turn out onto a floured board and gently knead ten times. Roll out to ½-inch thickness and with a biscuit cutter cut into 2-inch rounds. Bake on a lightly greased baking sheet for 20 minutes, until well browned.   *Makes 12 biscuits.*

Per serving: 129 calories / 4 gm fat / 21 gm carbohydrate / 205 mg sodium

∼ Skillet Cornbread ∼

Nana wouldn't bake cornbread in anything other than a cast-iron skillet. She often cooked it over medium heat right on top of the stove. She'd cut it into wedges, slide a little butter in between, and that was all she wrote. It was all she ever needed to.

2 cups yellow cornmeal	½ teaspoon freshly ground white pepper
1 cup flour	
2 tablespoons sugar	1 egg
4 teaspoons baking soda	1¾ cups 1 percent fat milk
1 teaspoon salt	1 tablespoon butter, melted

Preheat the oven to 425 degrees F. Grease a 9-inch cast-iron skillet. In a large mixing bowl, sift together the cornmeal, flour, sugar, baking soda, salt, and pepper. Add the egg, milk, and butter and beat with a wooden spoon until smooth. Place the skillet in the oven for 10 minutes, prior to pouring in the batter. Bake for 25 minutes, until golden brown on top. Cut into wedges. *Makes 8 wedges.*

Per serving: 258 calories / 1 gm fat / 49 gm carbohydrate / 310 mg sodium

～ Buttermilk Cornbread ～

Buttermilk and cornbread have always had a harmonious relationship. In the old days, people used to crumble up day-old cornbread, pour buttermilk over it, and eat it with a spoon. Here, the marriage has been prearranged.

2 cups cornmeal	2 tablespoons sugar
1 cup all-purpose unbleached flour	1 egg
1 tablespoon baking powder	1½ cups 1 percent fat butter-milk
1 teaspoon baking soda	1 cup evaporated skim milk
1 teaspoon salt	1 tablespoon butter, melted

Preheat the oven to 425 degrees F. Butter an 8-inch-square baking dish. In a large bowl, combine the cornmeal, flour, baking powder, baking soda, salt, and sugar. In a large mixing bowl, beat together the egg, milks, and butter and pour liquid mixture into dry; stir until well blended. Pour into pan and bake for 30 minutes, until browned on top.   *Makes 9 squares.*

Per serving: 228 calories / 2 gm fat / 45 gm carbohydrate / 396 mg sodium

∾ Sweet Potato Cornbread ∾

You guessed it! Another one of Nana's masterpieces.

1 cup all-purpose unbleached
   flour
1 cup cornmeal
¼ cup sugar
1 tablespoon baking powder
½ teaspoon salt
½ teaspoon cinnamon
¼ teaspoon nutmeg

1¾ cups evaporated skim milk
2 tablespoons freshly grated
   coconut meat
1 large sweet potato, cooked
   and mashed
1 egg
1 tablespoon butter, melted

Preheat the oven to 475 degrees F. Grease an 8-inch-square baking dish. In a large mixing bowl, combine flour, cornmeal, sugar, baking powder, salt, cinnamon, and nutmeg. Add milk and stir until smooth. Mix in coconut, sweet potato, egg, and butter and beat until well blended. Pour batter into baking dish and bake for 25 minutes, or until top is golden brown.   *Makes 9 squares.*

Per serving: 267 calories / 2 gm fat / 52 gm carbohydrate / 312 mg sodium

∾ Cracked Pepper Cornbread ∾

This recipe works well with a blend of peppercorns. I often eat this as a side dish, alongside Mom's Chicken Bouillon (page 130) and String Beans with Potatoes (page 148).

2 cups yellow cornmeal
1 cup all-purpose unbleached
   flour
2 tablespoons sugar
2 teaspoons baking powder
1 teaspoon baking soda

½ teaspoon salt
1 egg
1¾ cups evaporated skim milk
1 teaspoon butter, melted
2 tablespoons mixed peppercorns, cracked in a mortar

Preheat the oven to 425 degrees F. Grease an 8-inch-square glass baking dish. In a large mixing bowl, sift together the cornmeal, flour, sugar, baking powder, baking soda, and salt. Add the egg, milk, and butter, and beat with a wooden spoon until smooth. Pour the batter into the baking dish and sprinkle cracked pepper on top. Bake 25 minutes, until golden brown on top. Cut into squares to serve. *Makes 9 squares.*

Per serving: 224 calories / 2 gm fat / 43 gm carbohydrate / 319 mg sodium

～ Red and Green Pepper Cornbread ～

My brother Robert, omelet maker extraordinaire, also makes a mean cornbread. He has thoroughly eclectic taste buds—sometimes, I have to admit, just a touch too strange for me. But his zany experiments with food occasionally yield a treasure such as this one.

2 cups yellow cornmeal
1 cup all-purpose unbleached
    flour
2 tablespoons sugar
2 teaspoons baking powder
1 teaspoon baking soda
1 teaspoon salt
½ teaspoon freshly ground
    white pepper

1 egg
1¾ cups evaporated skim milk
1 teaspoon butter, melted
2 ears fresh corn, kernels
    removed from the cob
1 red bell pepper, seeded and
    diced
1 green bell pepper, seeded and
    diced

Preheat the oven to 425 degrees F. Grease an 8-inch-square baking pan. In a large mixing bowl, sift together the cornmeal, flour, sugar, baking powder, baking soda, salt, and white pepper. Add the egg, milk, and butter, and beat with a wooden spoon until smooth. Add the corn and bell peppers. Pour the batter into the pan, and bake for 25 minutes, or until golden brown on top. *Makes 9 squares.*

Per serving: 247 calories / 2 gm fat / 49 gm carbohydrate / 355 mg sodium

～ Cornbread Muffins ～

I don't much go for those cakelike muffins that can put you into a sugar shock in the morning. Good muffins are pretty scarce these days, so I resort to making my own.

2 cups yellow cornmeal	1 teaspoon salt
1 cup all-purpose unbleached flour	2 tablespoons sugar
1 teaspoon baking powder	1 egg
1 teaspoon baking soda	1¾ cups evaporated skim milk

Preheat the oven to 350 degrees F. Butter a 12-cup muffin pan and set aside. In a large mixing bowl, combine cornmeal, flour, baking powder, baking soda, salt, and sugar. Add egg and milk and beat briskly until well blended. Spoon into muffin cups and bake for 15 minutes, until muffins are golden brown on top.   *Makes 12 muffins.*

Per serving: 144 calories / 1 gm fat / 28 gm carbohydrate / 295 mg sodium

～ Cranberry Corn Muffins ～

A mixture of fresh and dried cranberries turns this into a memorable muffin.

2 cups yellow cornmeal	1 tablespoon grated orange zest
1 cup all-purpose unbleached flour	⅓ cup plus 2 tablespoons sugar
1 teaspoon baking powder	1 egg
1 teaspoon baking soda	1¾ cups evaporated skim milk
1 teaspoon salt	¼ cup orange juice
1 teaspoon Pie Spice *(page 9)* or pumpkin pie spice	1 teaspoon butter, melted
	½ cup fresh cranberries
	½ cup dried cranberries

Preheat the oven to 350 degrees F. Butter a 12-cup muffin pan and set aside. In a large mixing bowl, combine cornmeal, flour, baking powder, baking soda, salt, pie spice, zest, and ⅓ cup sugar. Add egg, milk, orange juice, and butter, and beat briskly until well blended. Fold in cranberries, and spoon batter into muffin cups. Sprinkle the remaining sugar on the top of each muffin and bake for 15 minutes, until muffins are golden brown.   *Makes 12 muffins.*

Per serving: 178 calories / 2 gm fat / 36 gm carbohydrate / 322 mg sodium

~5~

Hot Pot:
Soups and Stews

Soup is a democrat, the culinary equivalent of a dream lover: stable, long-lasting, and low-maintenance on the one hand, but, with a little dressing up, a luminous star. It can arrive at the table as the main course or as a small accent in a larger design. Mix whatever you have handy into your soup, and if your base is robust and your ingredients friendly, you've got a match. Soup was a standby of the slave kitchens, an accommodating base for those early, wondrously resourceful cooks who stretched scraps from the Big House, adding a little okra, salt, and the rare bit of meat for flavor to a dish that gave the comfort of steaming warmth to those in need of it.

Soup means winter to me. It means friends arriving at our house, snow-capped and shivering, a sight which sends my nurture meter way over the legal limit. I lead them to a cushiony sofa by the fire, and immediately slip a hot mug of spice tea or buttered rum between their hands. Winter brings out my sociability at dinnertime because it's the only season that I can prepare a dish—and only one dish—and leave it to cook on its own while I sit and chat. This is when my Dutch oven works overtime to make some of the most robust meals of the year. And I'm not just talking about stews, I'm talking about soups as well, hearty enough to be headliners, with a wedge of tasty bread on the side. The hot pot is economy in motion, saving me time, energy, and most importantly, money.

Here's something else: the consumption of soup brings with it an instant feeling of community, of shared participation, unique to its steaming, nutritious self. I even like the sounds of soup eating—regular clink of spoon on bowl, the hiss and sigh of the happy palate which tells me I've done something right. Candles illuminate the steam-blanketed windows, the wind blows snow against the pane outside, we raise our gleaming tablespoons, and sup.

Stocks

It is really a pain to prepare both soup and broth in the same day, so having some on hand will eliminate that last minute temptation to run out and get canned broth, which is mostly laden with salt, or bouillon cubes, which are laced with the much-dreaded MSG. We won't even mention taste. Long before I prepare any of my soups, I prepare my base. Homemade stock rules all the way. Stocks keep for 2 to 3 days in the refrigerator, but can be frozen and used at a later time.

~ Chicken Stock ~

Of all the soup bases, chicken stock is the most elemental. When in doubt as to what kind of nonvegetarian soup base you should use, lean toward chicken stock. It's also the most versatile blend. Chicken backs are very inexpensive, and if you catch a butcher in a good mood, he'll often give them to you for free.

2 pounds chicken backs	**1 Bouquet Garni** (*page 7*)
2 quarts water	**1 tablespoon black peppercorns**
2 large carrots, coarsely chopped	**1 whole head garlic, slightly**
2 stalks celery	**crushed**
1 large onion, quartered	**1 cup dry white wine**
1 bay leaf	

Combine the chicken, water, carrots, celery, onion, bay leaf, bouquet garni, peppercorns, garlic, and white wine in a large 5-quart kettle. Bring to a vigorous boil over high heat. Reduce heat and simmer, uncovered, over low heat for at least 2 hours. Cool and strain. Place in refrigerator for at least 8 hours. Remove hardened layer of fat at the top. Freeze or use within a few days.   *Makes 2 quarts.*

Per cup: 85 calories / 2 gm fat / 3 gm carbohydrate / 121 mg sodium

~ Fish Stock ~

Fish heads and bones are another item you most likely can get for free or next to nothing. Try to stay away from the bones of oily fish, such as mackerel, trout, bluefish, or shad.

5 pounds fish bones and heads	6 sprigs of thyme
4 quarts water	1 bay leaf
1 teaspoon salt	1 bunch of parsley
1 cup dry vermouth	2 whole cloves
2 whole leeks	½ lemon

Coarsely chop the fish bones and heads and put into a large stockpot. Pour water over the heads, add salt, and bring to a rapid boil over high heat. With a slotted spoon, skim off the scum as it rises. Add wine, leeks, thyme, bay leaf, parsley, and cloves. Cover and simmer for 20 minutes. Add the lemon, cover, and let sit off the heat for 10 minutes. Strain. Use within 3 days or freeze for future use.   *Makes 4 quarts.*

Per cup: 38 calories / 0 gm fat / 4 gm carbohydrate / 142 mg sodium

∼ Herb Stock ∼

This is more like a fusion than a true stock—a brew of sorts. This anise-flavored stock mixes well with both chicken and fish broths, and infuses flavor to sluggish but receptive beans like navy or butter beans. Vegetarians will appreciate it.

¼ **cup chervil**	2 **stalks celery**
¼ **cup chopped parsley**	1 **medium onion**
¼ **cup tarragon**	6 **sprigs of thyme**
3 **slices gingerroot (1-inch slices)**	1 **bay leaf**
2 **quarts boiling water**	1 **teaspoon salt**
1 **large carrot**	¼ **teaspoon fennel seed**

Into a large bowl, put the chervil, parsley, tarragon, and ginger. Pour 1 quart of boiling water over the herbs and steep for 5 minutes. Strain liquid into a large stockpot and discard herbs. To the pot add the remaining water, carrot, celery, onion, thyme, and bay leaf. Bring to a boil over high heat and add salt and fennel seed. Cover and simmer for 20 minutes. Strain and use within 3 days or freeze.   *Makes 2 quarts.*

Per cup: 28 calories / 0 gm fat / 5 gm carbohydrate / 91 mg sodium

∼ Shrimp Stock ∼

Since I eat shrimp as often as once a week, I usually don't have to buy shrimp in order to make stock. I just keep a plastic container in the freezer filled with shells. By the time I get around to making stock I've usually an accumulation of shells from at least 10 pounds of shrimp. But if you're looking for something to do with the cooked shrimp left over from the following recipe, consult page 143 for a great shrimp salad. If you manage to collect the shells from 10 pounds of shrimp, you may eliminate the first step of steaming fresh shrimp and proceed to the part in the recipe where it calls for the shells.

2 **pounds shrimp**
4 **quarts water**
3 **sprigs of thyme**
3 **bay leaves**
5 **cloves garlic, crushed with**
    skins on

1 **teaspoon paprika**
1 **cup dry white wine**
¼ **teaspoon fennel seed**

Cook shrimp in water until pink, drain shrimp, and set aside the shrimp-water. Peel and devein shrimp, reserving shells. (Use shrimp for another dish, or chill and eat.) Place shrimp-water and shells into a 5-quart stockpot. Add thyme, bay leaves, garlic, paprika, wine, and fennel seed, and bring to a high boil. Lower heat and simmer, uncovered, for 20 minutes, occasionally skimming the top with a spoon. Strain and use within 3 days, or freeze for future use.   *Makes 4 quarts.*

Per cup: 74 calories / 1 gm fat / 1 gm carbohydrate / 85 mg sodium

～ Pepper Stock ～

This stock is not for the timid. Like the Herb Stock, this one works best when used in conjunction with a chicken, fish, or vegetable stock. Use it also to spice up gravies and sauces, but use it sparingly—the Scotch bonnet pepper is one of the hottest ever grown. You may substitute a milder pepper for it.

1½ **quarts water**
2 **carrots**
3 **stalks celery**
1 **head garlic**
5 **whole cloves**
½ **cup white vinegar**
½ **cup dry white wine**

1 **Scotch bonnet pepper,**
    seeded and chopped *(see page*
    10 for handling instructions)
1 **red chili pepper, seeded**
    and chopped *(see page 10 for*
    handling instructions)
1 **tablespoon black peppercorns**

Place all the ingredients in a 3-quart saucepan and bring to a boil over high heat. Reduce heat to low and let simmer for 20 minutes. Strain stock and freeze, or refrigerate and use within 3 days.   *Makes 1½ quarts.*

Per cup: 37 calories / 0 gm fat / 6 gm carbohydrate / 28 mg sodium

～ Vegetable Stock ～

2 quarts water	2 teaspoons whole peppercorns
2 large onions, coarsely chopped	1 Bouquet Garni *(page 7)*
1 pound carrots, coarsely chopped	5 allspice berries
	2 cups carrot juice
5 stalks celery, cut into chunks	1 cup dry white wine
1 head garlic, crushed	

Combine all the ingredients in a 5-quart stockpot and bring to a boil over high heat. Reduce the heat to low and simmer, covered, for 1 hour. Strain, mashing the vegetables with the back of a spoon to extract all the juices. Use within 3 days, or freeze for future use.   *Makes 2½ quarts.*

Per cup: 34 calories / 2 gm fat / 8 gm carbohydrate / 34 mg sodium

～ Cabbage Soup ～

I take pleasure in eating something tasty that is also good for me. Cabbage belongs to the group of vegetables we know to be anticarcinogens, and it also has anti-cancer properties. The juice of cabbage contains vitamin K, apparently good for peptic ulcers. Cabbage is also loaded with vitamin A, a great source of beta-carotene, which is known to strengthen the eyes. (And you thought chicken soup was the greatest tonic.) In this particular soup, I cook the cabbage over a high flame to caramelize it along with the onion, giving it a sweet-sour taste. This seemingly rich soup has only 4 grams of fat per serving. Serve with a wedge of Red and Green Pepper Cornbread (page 77).

1 large onion, diced
1 tablespoon butter
1 head cabbage, finely chopped
1 teaspoon salt
1 teaspoon fennel seed
1 bay leaf
6 cups Vegetable Stock *(page 85)*
   or Chicken Stock *(page 81)*
1 large carrot, shredded

1 large apple, peeled, cored, and
   shredded
1 cup dry white wine
¼ teaspoon nutmeg
   Pinch of cayenne
2 cups evaporated skim milk,
   heated
1 teaspoon freshly ground
   white pepper

In a 5-quart Dutch oven, sauté onion in butter over medium heat, stirring occasionally until well browned, about 20 minutes. Add cabbage, salt, fennel seed, and bay leaf, and cook for 25 minutes, tossing occasionally with the onions until cabbage begins to caramelize. Lower heat, pour in stock, and let simmer, covered, for 20 minutes. Add carrot, apple, and wine, and cook, uncovered, for 10 minutes. Remove from heat and stir in nutmeg, cayenne, milk, and pepper.   *Serves 8.*

Per serving: 165 calories / 4 gm fat / 16 gm carbohydrate / 499 mg sodium

∼ Roasted Yam and Pepper Soup ∼

Bright red sweet peppers and sweet potatoes decorate my food basket year-round. Often I'll sit in my kitchen contemplating a marriage of vegetables, and the following is a result of my matchmaking. You might find the roasting of the peppers a little time-consuming, but what music these two roasted veggies make together when teamed up in this delightful soup. Serve with Corn-bread Muffins (page 78).

6 large sweet potatoes, peeled
   and cubed
3 red bell peppers
½ cup dry red wine

½ teaspoon allspice
½ cup chopped leeks, white
   parts only
1 tablespoon olive oil

1 **small chili pepper, seeded
  and chopped** *(see page 10
  for handling instructions)*
3½ **cups Vegetable Stock** *(page 85)*
  or Chicken Stock *(page 81)*
½ **cup dry vermouth**

1 **teaspoon salt**
1 **bay leaf**
⅛ **teaspoon marjoram leaves**
1 **teaspoon Lemon Pepper**
  (page 5)

Preheat the oven to 475 degrees F. Lightly oil a large glass baking dish and place in the oven for 5 minutes. Add the potatoes and bake for 25 minutes, until browned. Rub a small amount of oil on the peppers. Place the peppers on a long-handled fork and roast over an open flame, rotating to char evenly (try to get it as close to the heat as possible). Roast until evenly blackened, about 5 minutes. Remove the peppers and immerse in cold water. The charred skin should come off easily. Peel peppers and quarter. Puree the peppers with the wine and allspice in a food processor and set aside. In a large stockpot, sauté the chopped leeks in the oil for 5 minutes, until translucent, over medium heat. Add the chili pepper, stock, vermouth, and salt, and bring to a boil. Add potatoes, pepper puree, bay leaf, and marjoram and simmer, covered, for 30 minutes. Remove and discard the bay leaf. Add lemon pepper and serve.   *Serves 8.*

Per serving: 195 calories / 3 gm fat / 30 gm carbohydrate / 343 mg sodium

～ Buttermilk Soup with Cornbread Croutons ～

Buttermilk and cornbread have a successful down-home union from the start. The cornbread was generally broken into small chunks and placed in a bowl. Buttermilk was poured directly over it, and it was eaten with a spoon. Here I've made it easy for you.

1 cup Brown Onions *(page 12)*
4 cups Vegetable Stock *(page 85)*
 or Chicken Stock *(page 81)*
1 bay leaf
1 cup dry white wine
2 cups 1 percent fat buttermilk, warmed
2 teaspoons chopped fresh
 tarragon or 1 teaspoon dried

⅛ teaspoon nutmeg
 Pinch of cayenne
1 teaspoon salt
1 teaspoon freshly ground
 white pepper
 Cornbread Croutons
 (recipe follows)

Put onions and 1 cup stock into a blender or food processor and puree. Put pureed onions into a large stockpot and add bay leaf, remaining stock, and wine. Bring to a boil over high heat and then simmer over low heat, uncovered, for 15 minutes. Add buttermilk, tarragon, nutmeg, cayenne, salt, and pepper and simmer for 5 more minutes. Garnish each bowl with chopped parsley, a thin slice of lemon, and a cornbread crouton.   *Serves 8.*

Per serving: 181 calories / 3 gm fat / 26 gm carbohydrate / 552 mg sodium

Cornbread Croutons

These croutons also work well in a bowl of collard greens.

½ cup cornmeal
¾ cup all-purpose unbleached
 flour
½ teaspoon salt
2 teaspoons sugar

½ teaspoon baking powder
1 egg, beaten
1 cup evaporated skim milk
2 egg whites

Preheat the oven to 425 degrees F. Butter a large jelly-roll pan. In a large mixing bowl, combine cornmeal, flour, salt, sugar, and baking powder. In a small bowl, mix the egg together with the milk and add to the dry mixture, stirring well to blend. Whip egg whites until stiff and fold into batter. Spread into the baking pan and bake for 15 minutes, or until bread is golden brown on top. Remove from oven and reduce heat to 250 degrees F. When bread has cooled slightly, cut into 1-inch squares. Put the squares on a baking sheet and bake for 1 hour.   *Makes 4 cups croutons.*

Per cup: 202 calories / 2 gm fat / 37 gm carbohydrate / 387 mg sodium

∽ Pureed Turnip Soup ∽

I used to steer clear of the astringent taste of turnips. I'd always thought they had the taste and texture of something attempting to imitate a vegetable, but not quite succeeding. No matter how many ways she prepared them, Mom could never convince me I'd want to have turnips in my shopping basket when I grew up. And then I did grow up—and realized how tasty they were. This soup goes very well with Cracked Pepper Cornbread (page 76).

4 **pounds turnips**	1 **bay leaf**
4 **cups Vegetable Stock** *(page 85)*	½ **teaspoon salt**
or Chicken Stock *(page 81)*	¼ **teaspoon allspice**
2 **cloves garlic, minced**	1 **teaspoon freshly ground**
2 **teaspoons very finely minced**	**white pepper**
rosemary	2 **cups evaporated skim milk,**
½ **cup dry white wine**	**warmed**

Peel and cube turnips and place in a 3-quart saucepan. Add just enough water to cover and cook over medium-high heat for 25 minutes. Drain. Place turnips in a blender or food processor, along with a cup of stock, and puree. In a large stockpot quickly sauté the garlic and rosemary for 1 minute over medium-high heat, stirring often until browned. Add the remaining stock, wine, turnip puree, bay leaf, and salt, and bring to a boil. Reduce heat and simmer for 25 minutes. Remove from heat and add allspice and pepper. Strain into a large bowl and stir in the warmed milk.   *Serves 8.*

Per serving: 163 calories / 2 gm fat / 21 gm carbohydrate / 402 mg sodium

∾ Shrimp and Okra Stew ∾

This Low Country favorite is a big hit in the fall, when okra is at its peak. Accompanied by a basket of piping hot Lemon Pepper Biscuits (page 71), it proves to be a crowd pleaser every time.

1 pound shrimp, peeled and deveined
3 cloves garlic, minced
4 teaspoons olive oil
1 teaspoon Lemon Pepper *(page 5)*
1 teaspoon lemon juice
1 medium onion, finely chopped
1 pound okra, trimmed of tops and tails and sliced crosswise into ¼-inch rings
1 teaspoon salt

1 chili pepper, seeded and chopped *(see page 10 for handling instructions)*
4 cups Shrimp Stock *(page 83)* or Vegetable Stock *(page 85)*
1 cup water
1 cup beer
¼ cup tomato paste
1 bay leaf
4 sprigs of thyme
3 large tomatoes, peeled, seeded, and chopped
1 teaspoon freshly ground black pepper

Cut each shrimp into thirds and set aside. In a large stockpot, sauté garlic in 2 teaspoons oil for 1 minute over low heat, until browned. Add shrimp and lemon pepper and cook for 2–3 minutes, just until shrimp begins to turn pink. Add lemon juice and toss to mix. Remove the shrimp from the pan and set aside. To the same pan, add the remaining oil and onion and cook over low heat for about 5 minutes, until softened. Mix in the okra, ½ teaspoon salt, and the chili pepper, and simmer, covered, for 20 minutes, stirring occasionally to prevent the okra pieces from sticking to the pan. Add the stock, water, beer, tomato paste, bay leaf, thyme, and the remaining salt and simmer, covered, for 20 more minutes. Add tomatoes, shrimp, and pepper and remove from heat. Let develop for 15 minutes.   *Serves 6.*

Per serving: 203 calories / 4 gm fat / 13 gm carbohydrate / 599 mg sodium

～ Chicken and Peanut Stew ～

In Senegal, this stew is called mafe. *In Ghana, it's called* hkatenkwan. *In Zimbabwe, it's referred to as* dovi, *and in Uganda,* chickenat. *It's known generically as groundnut stew, a peanut-based chicken stew of African origin. This stew was, at one time, very popular among the early English settlers in colonial Williamsburg.*

1½ pounds skinless, bone-in
    chicken breasts
¼ cup finely chopped shallots
2 stalks celery, chopped
1 carrot, coarsely chopped
2 teaspoons olive oil
2 tablespoons curry powder
1 cup beer
4 cloves garlic, minced
2 bay leaves
3 large tomatoes, peeled,
    seeded, and chopped

1 chili pepper, seeded and chopped
    **(see page 10 for handling
    instructions)**
2 tablespoons chopped
    parsley
¼ cup peanut butter mixed
    with ½ cup hot water
1 tablespoon salt
4 cups Chicken Stock
    (page 81)
2 tablespoons chopped cilantro

In a large nonstick sauté pan, sear chicken breasts for 1 minute on each side over high heat, and set aside. In the same pan, sauté shallots, celery, and carrot in 1 teaspoon oil for about 5 minutes over a low flame, until softened. Sprinkle in the curry powder and toss to mix well. Slowly add the beer and continue stirring as curry begins to thicken. Remove from the heat. In a large stockpot, sauté garlic in the remaining oil over medium heat for a minute, until garlic begins to brown. Add chicken, bay leaves, and tomatoes, and simmer for 20 minutes, stirring occasionally. Add the curry mixture to the chicken and tomatoes, followed by the chili pepper, parsley, peanut butter, and salt. When all is well mixed add stock and simmer, covered, for 30 minutes. Remove and discard bay leaf. Sprinkle in cilantro and serve.   *Serves 8.*

Per serving: 199 calories / 7 gm fat / 11 gm carbohydrate / 381 mg sodium

~ Mom the Fisher Stew ~

Compared to other families' diets, ours was abundantly enriched with fish. At least twice a week we ate fish, and once a week it was freshly caught. Here I've compiled a stew of my three favorite fish. A fish stew should be nothing more than that: mostly fish, with not many vegetables to deter the flavors of the fish but lots of good herbs and spices to enhance. It's as a tribute to Mom, gifted fisher and the original frugal gourmet, that I present the following recipe. Have some hot, crusty Skillet Cornbread (page 74) on hand.

3 **cloves garlic, finely minced**	1 **sprig of thyme**
¼ **cup chopped shallots**	1 **bay leaf**
2 **teaspoons olive oil**	2 **cups dry white wine**
1 **pound catfish**	2 **cups water**
1 **pound shrimp, peeled and**	1 **cup Herb Stock** *(page 83)*
deveined	3 **tablespoons chopped**
1 **pound cod fillets**	**parsley**
1 **leek, both white and green**	½ **teaspoon salt**
parts, chopped	**Pinch of cayenne**
1 **carrot, finely chopped**	1 **teaspoon freshly ground**
¼ **teaspoon saffron threads**	**black pepper**

In a Dutch oven, sauté garlic and shallots in oil over medium heat for 5 minutes, until softened. Add catfish, shrimp, and cod to the pot and sauté for 3 minutes, until shrimp turns pink, tossing to mix. Add leek, carrot, saffron, thyme, and bay leaf. Pour in the wine, water, and stock, and simmer, covered, for 10 minutes. Add parsley, salt, cayenne, and pepper and let develop off the heat for 1 hour. Remove and discard bay leaf before serving.   *Makes 8 servings.*

Per serving: 196 calories / 3 gm fat / 4 gm carbohydrate / 269 mg sodium

～ Red Beans and Chicken with Wine ～

Grandpop used to order lots of cookbooks through the mail; each highlighted the cuisine of a different country. I enjoyed the French cookbooks most, and would encourage Grandpop to lean more toward French cookery. He never minded—he'd say, "I'll cook whatever you all want, just as long as you don't waste your food." We never let one crumb get by us. One of my favorite classics was coq au vin, tender chicken cooked in a broth infused with brandy, herbs, and red wine. In its own way, coq au vin is a down-home kind of stew—I've made it more so by adding red beans. Make sure you've got a basket of garlic-buttered Sage Biscuits (page 73) to accompany it.

1 **pound red beans**	2 **tablespoons brandy**
10 **cloves garlic, minced**	4 **cups Chicken Stock** *(page 81)*
2 **teaspoons olive oil**	1 **teaspoon salt**
4 **skinless bone-in chicken**	1 **Bouquet Garni** *(page 7)*
breast halves	2 **cups dry red wine**

Soak beans for at least 8 hours; drain and set aside. In a Dutch oven, sauté garlic in 1 teaspoon oil for 1 minute over medium heat, until browned. Remove garlic from the pot and set aside. Add remaining oil and brown chicken for 3 minutes on each side. Add brandy, toss chicken around, and remove chicken from the pot. Add stock and bring to a boil. Add beans, salt, and bouquet garni, and bring to a second boil. Reduce heat, cover, and simmer for 2 hours, stirring occasionally. Add chicken, browned garlic, and red wine, and cook for 1 hour more.   *Serves 8.*

Per serving: 325 calories / 3 gm fat / 38 gm carbohydrate / 321 mg sodium

～ White Beans and Shrimp ～

White beans are one of my favorites, just as long as I've got plenty of garlic and herbs to go with them. This dish is laden with garlic, both sautéed minced cloves and the paste from a whole head of roasted garlic. The shrimp, in this case, take a backseat to the beans, but are a divine addition nonetheless.

1 **pound white beans**	1 **quart Vegetable Stock**
1 **pound shrimp, peeled and**	**(page 85)**
deveined	1 **bay leaf**
2 **teaspoons Lemon Pepper**	2 **teaspoons chopped oregano**
(page 5)	½ **teaspoon chopped marjoram**
1 **large onion, chopped**	1 **cup dry white wine**
2 **teaspoons olive oil**	1 **head Roasted Garlic (page 11)**
3 **cloves garlic, minced**	¼ **cup chopped parsley**

Soak beans for 4 hours and drain. Put the shrimp in a bowl, sprinkle with lemon pepper, and set aside. In a Dutch oven, sauté onions in 1 teaspoon oil for 20 minutes over medium heat, until well browned. Add the garlic and cook for 2 minutes more, until garlic has browned. Pour in the stock and bring to a boil. Add the beans and bring to a second boil. Reduce heat, add bay leaf, and simmer, covered, for 1 hour. Add oregano, marjoram, and wine, and simmer, covered, for 30 minutes more, until beans are firm but tender. Meanwhile, sauté the shrimp and lemon pepper in a nonstick skillet over medium-high heat for 2 minutes, until shrimp begin to turn pink. Remove from heat and chop coarsely. Squeeze the softened garlic from the head and stir it into the beans. Add the shrimp and parsley to the beans, tossing to mix. Remove from heat and let flavor develop for 10 minutes. Remove and discard bay leaf before serving.   *Serves 8.*

Per serving: 311 calories / 3 gm fat / 40 gm carbohydrate / 228 mg sodium

~6~

Down-Home Grains

When I speak of down-home grains, I am usually referring to rice and corn—two cornerstones of good cooking and healthy diets. Interestingly, I've found that most people assume rice to be an indigenous American crop. Not so. Rice, in truth, is yet another African contribution to the culinary happiness of the New World. Experts in rice agriculture all along the Rice Coast of Africa were "selected" and brought to this country to be used as field slaves in order to duplicate their ingenious technique of cultivation. It worked—as did they, you can be sure—and as a result, Charleston, South Carolina, was for a time the wealthiest city in the land.

While rice is an adopted grain, corn *is* an indigenous American grain. More American than apple pie (an unfair comparison, since apple pie is of British origin), corn has been around in this country for thousands of years, discovered and cultivated by the Native Americans. Both grains represented at one point abundance and survival, and often, spirituality.

Corn

Corn played an important role in the early African-American slave diet. Cornmeal was one of three staple food rations that were given to slaves on a weekly basis—the other two being salt pork and molasses. Back home, Africans pounded beans and yams into a coarse meal with which they enriched their breads and porridges, so the adaptation of recipes to cornmeal was no major transition. During harvest season on the plantation, corn shucking was a major event and, oddly enough, one of the few activities where tasks were divided by gender. Generally the men shucked the corn, while the women—surprise, surprise—prepared a huge meal.

Corn is prepared today the way it was then—as simply as possible. The reason for this is that corn belongs to that very small group of foods we have no desire to adorn. We are happy to eat it directly from the cob, with a little salt or butter. We appreciate the way it shows subtlety, even when it's the principal player, in such preparations as corn pudding or corn chowder. We love its sunny color, its ambrosial flavor, its humility.

∽ Roasted Corn in the Husk ∽

This is the most primal way to eat corn—right out of the husk. Roasting adds a smoky complexity to the natural sweetness.

8 ears of corn, in their husks

Pull the husks back from the corn, taking care not to completely remove them; remove corn silk and wrap the husks back over the corn, securing with a piece of twine. Soak the corn in water for ½ hour. Roast over hot coals for 20 minutes, turning occasionally. Season with a sprinkling of salt.   *Serves 8.*

Per serving: 43 calories / 0 gm fat / 9 gm carbohydrate / 8 mg sodium

∾ Oven-Grilled Corn on the Cob ∾

Here's compensation for those of you who don't have access to a grill.

8 ears of corn	**4 teaspoons Garlic Butter** *(page 205)*
4 teaspoons Herb Butter *(page 205)*	

Preheat broiler. Strip the corn of its husk; remove silk and rinse. Spread ½ teaspoon each of herb and garlic butter on each ear and wrap with aluminum foil. "Grill" under the broiler for 15–20 minutes, turning occasionally. *Serves 8.*

Per serving: 77 calories / 4 gm fat / 9 gm carbohydrate / 47 mg sodium

∾ Succotash ∾

Although this dish has many names—Msakwitash, Misick-quotash, Sukqut-tash, etc.—it is one of the most universal Native American dishes. And one of the oldest. The original succotash was a stew made from corn and kidney beans, with a flavor base which included bear grease. Often other items were added to this stew, such as potatoes, meats, and herbs, and ultimately the kidney bean was replaced by the lima or butter bean. Today it is mostly prepared as a side dish, alongside meat or fish. Here, I've prepared it as a main course. I hope you don't mind that I've omitted bear grease from my recipe.

1 pound dried baby lima beans	**6 ears of sweet corn, kernels**
1 large onion, finely chopped	**scraped from the cob**
1 tablespoon olive oil	**¼ cup chopped parsley**
4 cups Vegetable Stock *(page 85)*	**1 cup dry white wine**
or Chicken Stock *(page 81)*	**½ teaspoon cayenne**
1 bay leaf	**½ teaspoon ground sage**
3 sprigs of thyme	**¼ teapoon nutmeg**
1 teaspoon salt	**1 tablespoon freshly ground**
4 cloves garlic	**white pepper**
1 tablespoon butter	**1 teaspoon lemon zest**

Soak beans for at least 8 hours; drain. In a Dutch oven sauté onion in oil over medium heat for 15 minutes, until slightly browned. Add beans and stock, and bring to a boil. Lower heat, add bay leaf, thyme, and salt, and simmer, covered, for 1½–2 hours, until beans are tender, adding water to the pan if the beans begin to dry out. Remove from heat and set aside. In a large skillet, sauté the garlic in butter for 1 minute, until browned; add corn kernels and cook over medium heat for 3 minutes. Remove pan from heat and toss in parsley. Pour corn mixture into the beans pot and add wine, cayenne, sage, and nutmeg. Simmer for 5 minutes and remove from heat. Add pepper and lemon zest and let develop off the heat for 30 minutes. Discard bay leaf. *Serves 8.*

Per serving: 392 calories / 6 gm fat / 61 gm carbohydrate / 438 mg sodium

Cornmeal

Cornmeal, a pedigree product of the American soil, has as many uses as there are days of the year, from breading catfish to making delicious dumplings. For its first harvesters, the Native Americans, corn was color-coded. Yellow corn was the prime corn for eating, while white corn was used for mush and bread. The Native Americans soaked the corn in a mixture of ashes and water, which made the corn swell and whiten. The Algonquin Indians named it Tackhummin, corn without skin, from which we derived the name hominy. Often it was then dried and ground into meal. African slaves used this meal to make a series of delicacies, many of which were adaptations of the Native American methods.

Most of today's hominy meal is sold in the supermarket, in little cardboard drums. This may suffice, but if you want to receive the full benefit of ground hominy, it's best to buy the stone-ground. If you can't find it in your neighborhood, don't despair: it is easy to find places that will ship. Cornmeal is the finer grind of hominy; it is used in baking breads and cooking porridges. There is an ongoing Dixie/Yankee argument about whether white meal is superior to the yellow. I see no real difference, and therefore will establish no hierarchy. Go with whatever color appeals to you. It's all delicious.

∼ Couche-Couche (Cornmeal Mush) ∼

This classic cornmeal recipe takes me way back. Grandmom Cothran used to cook this so that it was crunchy on the outside and creamy inside. She drizzled a little buttermilk over it and poured a teaspoon of thick syrup on top: Alaga syrup, which tasted an awful lot like molasses.

2 cups cornmeal	1 teaspoon sorghum or
½ cup boiling water	blackstrap molasses
1½ cups 1 percent fat milk	1 teaspoon salt
1 egg, beaten	1 tablespoon butter
1 teaspoon baking powder	

Put the cornmeal into a large mixing bowl. Stir in the water, then add the milk. Add the egg, baking powder, sorghum, and salt. In a large cast-iron skillet, melt the butter over medium-high heat. Pour the meal mixture into the pan and lower the heat. Cook without stirring, until a crust forms on the bottom. Scrape the browned crust into the rest of the mush and continue scraping until most of the mush is browned.   *Makes 4 servings.*

Per serving: 338 calories / 6 gm fat / 59 gm carbohydrate / 451 mg sodium

∼ Toasted Cornmeal Mush ∼

I enjoy preparing this porridge for breakfast. The smell of popcorn roasting is intoxicating enough, but when I smell the actual roasted kernels being ground, I lose my head. It won't do to take the quick method of partially air-popping the corn before grinding—only roasting will provide the fine grind that you're seeking.

1 cup popcorn kernels	¼ cup sweetened condensed milk
1 cup 1 percent fat milk	1 cup water

Preheat oven to 450 degrees F. Toast the popcorn in a shallow pan until one kernel actually pops. Immediately remove from oven before the rest begin to pop, and cool. Grind the kernels in a food processor or coffee grinder. Let sit for at least 8 hours or overnight. Heat the milk, condensed milk, and the water to near-boiling point. Pour the meal into a bowl, add milk mixture, and stir until well mixed. Cover with a plate and let sit for 5 minutes. Serve immediately. *Makes 2 servings.*

Per serving: 189 calories / 4 gm fat / 29 gm carbohydrate / 110 mg sodium

∿ Hoecake ∿

This is a basic down-home staple, to be eaten as you would eat bread. Originally, the batter was poured on a hoe and placed on a bed of hot coals to cook.

2 cups cornmeal	1 tablespoon sugar
1 teaspoon salt	1 cup scalded 1 percent fat milk

Into a mixing bowl, sift together the cornmeal with the salt and sugar. Moisten the cornmeal with just enough milk to give it the texture of thick pancake dough. If it is too runny, allow the batter to stand for 1 hour. Drop the batter on a hot, well-greased griddle. Spread it out to make a round cake about ½ inch thick. Cook over low heat for 15 minutes, until bottom is well browned. Turn over and cook the other side, for another 12 minutes.   *Serves 8.*

Per serving: 139 calories / 0 gm fat / 28 gm carbohydrate / 283 mg sodium

∿ Corn Dodgers ∿

Dodgers are cooked a few ways. This is the way Nana cooked them, and it's the way I like them. Serve hot with maple syrup.

1 cup cornmeal	½ teaspoon salt
2 cups evaporated skim milk	1 egg
½ cup all-purpose unbleached flour	1 teaspoon butter, melted
	1 teaspoon olive oil

In a large saucepan, combine the cornmeal with the milk and cook over low heat while stirring. Cook for 5–8 minutes, until slightly thickened. Remove from heat and add the flour, salt, egg, and butter. Heat oil in a large griddle until very hot. Drop spoonfuls of batter onto the hot griddle and brown for 2 minutes on both sides.   *Makes 6 dodgers.*

Per serving: 176 calories / 3 gm fat / 29 gm carbohydrate / 237 mg sodium

∾ Buttermilk Pone Bread ∾

This is a no-nonsense bread made the way a lot of Southerners make it. Unlike a lot of the cornmeal breads of the North, this one is free of sugar and eggs.

2 cups cornmeal	1 teaspoon baking soda
1 cup boiling water	½ teaspoon salt
1 cup 1 percent fat buttermilk	

Preheat the oven to 425 degrees F. Butter an 8-inch-square baking pan. In a large mixing bowl, combine the cornmeal with the boiling water. Mix the buttermilk with the baking soda and add to the cornmeal, along with the salt. Beat thoroughly and pour into the baking pan. Bake for 30 minutes, until browned on top. Cut into squares.   *Makes 9 squares.*

Per serving: 123 calories / 0 gm fat / 25 gm carbohydrate / 298 mg sodium

～ Spoonbread ～

Spoonbread is a souffléd version of cornbread—light and airy, with a light custardy base. The trick to making this dish is to coordinate the baking time so that the spoonbread arrives from the oven to the table just at the moment you are ready to serve. Eat it as you would stuffing or rice—or grits for that matter. Here I've made a sizzling addition of chili pepper.

3 cups evaporated skim milk
1 cup cornmeal
1 teaspoon salt
1 teaspoon butter, melted
1 egg

1 chili pepper, seeded and minced *(see page 10 for handling instructions)*
2 tablespoons sugar
2 teaspoons baking powder
½ teaspoon baking soda
2 egg whites

Preheat the oven to 375 degrees F. Butter a 2-quart baking dish. In a medium saucepan, combine 2 cups milk, cornmeal, and salt, and bring to a boil over high heat. Cook until thickened, about 10 minutes. Mix the remaining milk with the butter, egg, pepper, sugar, baking powder, and baking soda. Pour the milk mixture into the meal mixture, and beat well. Whip the egg whites until stiff and fold into the batter. Pour into dish and bake 30 minutes, until puffed and golden brown.   *Serves 8.*

Per serving: 156 calories / 1 gm fat / 26 gm carbohydrate / 397 mg sodium

～ Sweet Potato Spoonbread ～

A most satisfying side dish—but of course I'm biased. I could eat sweet potatoes twice a day.

3 cups 1 percent fat milk
2 cups cornmeal
½ teaspoon salt
2 cups mashed sweet potatoes

3 tablespoons dark brown sugar, packed
1 teaspoon butter, melted
1 egg

2 teaspoons baking powder   **2 egg whites**
½ teaspoon baking soda

Preheat the oven to 375 degrees F. Butter a 2-quart baking dish and set aside. Put 2 cups milk into saucepan, stir in meal and salt, and bring to a boil. Cook for 5 to 8 minutes, until thickened, and add sweet potatoes and sugar. Mix the remaining milk with the melted butter, egg, baking powder, and baking soda and combine with the sweet potato mixture. Whip the egg whites until stiff and fold into the batter. Pour into dish and bake 30 to 35 minutes. Center will be custard-like and should jiggle when fully cooked.   *Serves 8.*

Per serving: 270 calories / 1 gm fat / 48 gm carbohydrate / 483 mg sodium

∼ Boiled Grits ∼

Grits are the coarser grind of hominy, and when cooked they resemble porridge. I eat my grits at dinnertime, with a little butter and salt, usually beside a plate of fish. Others just eat them for breakfast. It's best to avoid the instant or quick grits unless, of course, you don't mind the lack of texture.

4 cups water   **1 cup grits**
½ teaspoon salt

In a 2-quart saucepan, bring water to a boil over high heat and add salt. Sprinkle grits in by the tablespoon, stirring continuously to avoid clotting. Reduce heat to low and simmer for 15 minutes, continuing to stir until grits become creamy and thick.   *Serves 8.*

Per serving: 72 calories / 0 gm fat / 15 gm carbohydrate / 133 mg sodium

~ Fiery Grits ~

Just add some chopped chili pepper and your gentle grits will turn scorching!

4 cups water	½ teaspoon chopped chili pepper
½ teaspoon salt	(see page 10 for handling
1 cup grits	instructions)
	1 tablespoon butter

In a 2-quart saucepan, bring water to a boil over high heat and add salt. Sprinkle grits in by the tablespoon, stirring continuously to avoid clotting. Reduce heat to low and simmer for 15 minutes, continuing to stir until grits become creamy and thick. Add pepper and butter and stir to mix.   *Serves 8.*

Per serving: 85 calories / 1 gm fat / 15 gm carbohydrate / 148 mg sodium

~ Fish and Grits ~

Whenever I've got a little leftover cod, I make this for breakfast, and eat it alongside a bowl of raspberries.

4 cups water	¼ cup evaporated skim milk, warmed
1 cup grits	1 teaspoon salt
1 cod fillet, steamed and flaked	1 teaspoon freshly ground
(see instructions in glossary	white pepper
for steaming fish)	½ teaspoon paprika

In a 2-quart saucepan, bring water to a boil over high heat. Sprinkle grits in by the tablespoon, stirring continuously to avoid clotting. Reduce heat to low and simmer for 15 minutes, continuing to stir until grits become creamy and thick. Pour grits into a warm, buttered bowl and add cod, milk, salt, and pepper, and toss to mix. Sprinkle paprika on top and serve.   *Serves 4.*

Per serving: 254 calories / 1 gm fat / 33 gm carbohydrate / 347 mg sodium

～ Lemon-Garlic Grits ～

This is more of a side dish for dinner, alongside a plate of shellfish, since a lot of people (excluding myself) cannot tolerate garlic in the morning.

4 cups water
1 teaspoon salt
1 cup grits
1 tablespoon minced Garlic Chips
   (page 11)

1 tablespoon grated lemon zest
Freshly ground white pepper

In a 2-quart saucepan, bring the water to a boil over high heat. Add salt, and sprinkle in the grits. Simmer, for 15 minutes, stirring as grits begin to thicken. Remove from heat and stir in garlic chips and lemon zest. Add pepper and serve.   *Serves 8.*

Per serving: 73 calories / 0 gm fat / 15 gm carbohydrate / 137 mg sodium

～ Green Onion and Cheese Grits ～

An excellent match!

1 tablespoon butter
4 cups water
½ teaspoon salt
1 cup grits

½ cup chopped scallions, green and
   white parts
¼ cup freshly grated Parmesan
   cheese

In a 2-quart saucepan, bring water to a boil over high heat. Sprinkle grits in by the tablespoon, stirring vigorously to avoid clotting. Reduce heat to low and simmer 15 minutes, continuing to stir until grits become creamy and thick. Remove from heat and immediately pour into a lightly buttered serving dish. Sprinkle scallions and cheese on top and serve.   *Serves 8.*

Per serving: 98 calories / 2 gm fat / 16 gm carbohydrate / 195 mg sodium

∽ Pumpkin Grits ∽

We'd always eat these around the winter holidays, when there was an abundance of sweet, enormous pumpkins around.

3 **cloves garlic, minced**
1 **teaspoon olive oil**
2 **cups chopped fresh pumpkin**
1 **teaspoon salt**
 1 **cup Chicken Stock** *(page 81)*

2 **cups cooked grits** *(page 103)*
1 **chili pepper, seeded and chopped**
   (see page 10 for handling
      instructions)

In a large skillet, sauté garlic in oil for 1 minute, until lightly browned, over low heat. Add pumpkin, salt, and stock, and cook for 20 minutes, mashing pumpkin as it softens. When the pumpkin is fully mashed, add grits and chili pepper and cook for 10 minutes.   *Serves 8.*

Per serving: 89 calories / 1 gm fat / 16 gm carbohydrate / 130 mg sodium

Rice

There are almost as many ways to prepare rice as there are cultures. The Japanese sprinkle vinegar and sesame seeds on it and call it seasoned rice; Indians soak it for hours, to produce the whitest, lightest basmati; Italians obsess over the creamiest risotto; and the Chinese like it sticky, so as to keep it intact for chopsticks. I like it prepared all ways.

I grew up on white rice; at our dinner table it was as commonplace as the salt and pepper shaker. But later on, when I began comparing the nutritional differences between white and brown rice, I jumped ship. It wasn't a hard choice to make, because, aside from the added fiber and minerals in brown rice, I began loving its nutty, unrefined flavor. But I had to face a painful truth: brown rice doesn't complement a lot of the down-home dishes in the way that white rice does. Although brown rice is too precious for me to give up for any extended period of time, I do give it up when I'm preparing certain down-home dishes. If you find it hard to give up brown rice even on a temporary basis you may substitute it in all my white rice recipes. Just remember to add an additional ½ cup water per cup of rice and cook 25 minutes extra.

～ Plain White Rice ～

4 cups water	1 teaspoon butter
½ teaspoon salt	2 cups uncooked long-grain rice

In a heavy pot, bring water to a boil over high heat. Add salt and butter, and sprinkle rice into pot. Bring to a second boil. Stir, reduce heat to low, and simmer, covered, for 18 minutes, until rice is dry and tender, but firm. Fluff up and serve.   *Serves 6.*

Per serving: 169 calories / 1 gm fat / 40 gm carbohydrate / 189 mg sodium

～ Herbed Rice ～

This goes well with spicy dishes, such as Shrimp Creole (page 163) and Barbe-cued Shrimp (page 158).

4 cups water	½ teaspoon dried sage
½ teaspoon salt	¼ teaspoon dried tarragon
2 cups uncooked long-grain rice	¼ teaspoon dried chervil
	2 teaspoons butter, melted

In a heavy pot, bring water to a boil. Add salt and sprinkle rice into pot. Bring to a second boil. Stir, reduce heat to low, and simmer, covered, for 18 minutes. Mix the herbs with the butter and pour over cooked rice. Fluff and serve. *Serves 6.*

Per serving: 169 calories / 1 gm fat / 40 gm carbohydrate / 189 mg sodium

~ Dirty Rice ~

This is an old Louisiana favorite—the giblets make the rice look "dirty."

3 cloves garlic, minced
2 teaspoons olive oil
¼ pound chicken livers
¼ pound chicken giblets
¼ cup chopped onions
½ cup chopped celery
¼ cup chopped green bell
   pepper, seeded

1 cup uncooked long-grain rice
2½ cups Chicken Stock *(page 81)*
1 teaspoon thyme leaves
1 teaspoon salt
½ teaspoon freshly ground
   black pepper
Pinch of cayenne

In a large skillet, sauté garlic in 1 teaspoon oil for 1 minute, until lightly browned. Add livers and giblets, and cook over medium heat for 5 to 8 minutes, until livers are nearly done, but still pink inside. Remove from heat, coarsely chop livers and edible giblets, and set aside.

To the same skillet add the remaining oil. Sauté onions, celery, and pepper for 5 minutes over low heat, until softened. Add rice and sauté 2 minutes more, stirring constantly. Add stock and thyme, and bring to a boil. Cover, and simmer for 20 minutes, until rice is just about done. Stir in salt, pepper, cayenne, livers, and giblets, and continue cooking for 5 minutes, until rice is dry and tender, but firm to the bite.   *Serves 6.*

Per serving: 265 calories / 6 gm fat / 29 gm carbohydrate / 299 mg sodium

~ Red Rice ~

I've added sun-dried tomatoes and lemon pepper to this Low Country favorite.

3 cloves garlic, minced
1 onion, finely chopped
1 red bell pepper, seeded and
   chopped
½ red chili pepper, seeded and
   chopped *(see page 10 for
   handling instructions)*
1 tablespoon olive oil
2 teaspoons chopped fresh
   thyme leaves or
   ½ teaspoon dried
1 tablespoon chopped fresh
   basil or 1 teaspoon dried

1 teaspoon chopped fresh
   marjoram or ½ teaspoon
   dried
1 teaspoon salt
¼ teaspoon cayenne
1 teaspoon Lemon Pepper *(page 5)*
½ cup finely chopped sun-dried
   tomatoes
2 tablespoons tomato paste
1 teaspoon Worcestershire sauce
2½ cups Chicken Stock *(page 81)*
   or Vegetable Stock *(page 85)*
1 cup uncooked long-grain rice

In a 2-quart saucepan, sauté garlic, onion, and peppers in oil for 2–3 minutes over low heat, until peppers are cooked, but not wilted. Add thyme, basil, marjoram, salt, cayenne, lemon pepper, tomatoes, tomato paste, Worcestershire sauce, and stock, and bring to a boil. Stir in rice and bring to a second boil. Cover and simmer for 18 minutes, until rice is tender but firm to the bite. Fluff with a fork and let develop off the heat for 5 minutes.   *Serves 6.*

Per serving: 160 calories / 3 gm fat / 28 gm carbohydrate / 420 mg sodium

∼ Greens and Rice ∼

The perfect companion to this dish is a large roasted sweet potato.

1 tablespoon olive oil
3 cloves garlic, crushed
1 large onion, chopped
2 teaspoons crushed red pepper
2 pounds collard greens, finely
    chopped *(see page 41 for*
    preparation)
2 tomatoes, peeled, seeded, and
    finely chopped

1½ quarts Chicken Stock *(page 81)*
    or Vegetable Stock *(page 85)*
1 teaspoon salt
1 teaspoon freshly ground
    pepper
1 cup uncooked long-grain rice

Pour the oil into a large heavy kettle and add garlic, onion, and crushed pepper. Cook over medium heat for 2–3 minutes, until onion is softened. Add greens and simmer for 20 minutes, tossing occasionally, until greens are cooked, but not wilted. Add tomatoes, stock, salt, and pepper and bring to a boil. Add rice and bring to a second boil. Reduce heat to low, cover, and simmer for 20 minutes, until rice is tender, but firm.   *Serves 6.*

Per serving: 248 calories / 5 gm fat / 37 gm carbohydrate / 428 mg sodium

∼ Hoppin' John ∼

There are many conflicting myths as to where the name originated. I truly don't care—it's as close to my heart as mashed potatoes. In the West Indies, they make the same dish with pigeon peas, a smaller version of the black-eyed pea. Try this with Escoveitched Catfish (page 119).

1 pound black-eyed peas
1 large onion, chopped
3 cloves garlic, minced
2 carrots, finely chopped

1 stalk celery, sliced ¼ inch thick
1 tablespoon olive oil
2½ quarts water
1½ teaspoons salt

| 1 bay leaf | 2 cups uncooked long-grain rice |
| 2 teaspoons chopped thyme | 2 tablespoons coconut milk |

Soak beans for at least 8 hours and drain. In a Dutch oven, sauté onions, garlic, carrots, and celery in oil for 5 minutes over low heat, until celery is cooked but firm. Add water, salt, and beans and bring to a boil over high heat. Add bay leaf and thyme and return heat to low. Simmer, covered, for 1½ hours, until beans are firm but tender. Add rice and coconut milk and simmer for 20 minutes more, until rice is tender.   *Serves 8.*

Per serving: 352 calories / 3 gm fat / 67 gm carbohydrate / 493 mg sodium

∼ Shrimp Pilau ∼

Practically every culture has a rice and meat dish such as this one, which accounts for the numerous ways this dish is spelled: pilaf, perleau, purlo, pilaw, pullao, just to name a few.

1 recipe Shrimp Marinade (page 115)	1 tablespoon Seafood Seasoning (page 9)
1 pound shrimp, peeled and deveined	2 teaspoons chopped thyme leaves
3 cloves garlic, minced	½ cup beer
1 red bell pepper	1 cup uncooked long-grain rice
½ cup chopped shallots	2 cups Shrimp Stock (page 83)
1 cup chopped celery	1 teaspoon salt
2 tablespoons freshly grated gingerroot	1 teaspoon Lemon Pepper (page 5)
1 tablespoon butter	¼ cup chopped parsley

Pour marinade over shrimp and let sit for at least 4 hours in the refrigerator. Preheat the oven to 350 degrees F. Butter a large baking dish with a lid. In a large skillet, sauté garlic, pepper, shallots, celery, and gingerroot in butter over medium heat for 5 minutes, until cooked but not wilted. Add shrimp, seafood seasoning, and thyme, and toss 2 minutes more, adding beer while stirring. Remove the mixture from heat just as the shrimp are beginning to turn pink, and spoon into the baking dish. Sprinkle the rice over the shrimp mixture and pour the stock over the rice. Add salt, lemon pepper, and parsley; cover and bake for 45 minutes, until rice is firm but tender.   *Serves 6.*

Per serving: 261 calories / 3 gm fat / 32 gm carbohydrate / 471 mg sodium

7

Fish

Back in the day when other moms were baking brownies or sewing clothes in their spare time, what was our mom up to? Well, she did a few of those things, sure. But there was something else, something a little stranger, something a little closer to Mom's heart than any of those "cheery" domestic crafts: Mom fished. Not casually, as background music to something else, but passionately and whole-hog. It relaxed her, put her back in touch with her roots. Every week she "put out to sea" (usually a local stream or lake— often a river), leaving home on a sunny Tuesday or Wednesday morning, equipped with hook, hat, line, sinker, and the highest hopes in the world. Eight hours later, if she'd had a good day, back Mom would come, carrying a bucket filled to the, er—gills with fish. Glistening trout, sole, flounder, and a delicate fish called weakfish lay thick in the water, and several hours later, in the pots and pans of our neighborhood, steaming and frying and perfuming the air with their special eau de pond. A good day for Mom meant fine eating all over our part of town, for Mom took as much pleasure in parceling out her fishy haul to friends as she did in catching it.

What she didn't catch, she bought. She'd travel far north to find the perfect geoducks for clam chowder, and far south to get the biggest Sallies for succulent, flaky crab cakes. Although she went on hiatus in the winter months, she'd compensate by going to the specialty fish market in town to bring back "weird" specialties like octopus, squid, and frogs' legs. Mom loved what was foreign and encouraged us to be more experimental. "How can you say you hate it if you haven't tried it?" she'd ask. "Don't worry—I *know*" was my smug reply. And at the time, I was right. But finally my curious taste buds began to get the best of me. To my amazement, frogs' legs, once cooked in a sauce, lost their greenness and even tasted like chicken. The same with the little baby octopi—though it remained hard for me to eat them because it always looked like they were holding hands on the plate.

Of course, exotic fish cost the exotic money that we didn't have, so most of the time we had to settle for the more mundane catches and purchases of the week. My favorite on the higher-priced side were shrimp, which Mom would steam in their shells with a ground hot pepper concoction. She'd put them into a large bowl in the center of the table within easy reach of itching fingers. On the low end, I loved codfish and the way Mom wed them with mashed potatoes to produce a pan-fried marriage of crispness, garlic, and essence of fish. But my all-time favorite was catfish. That ugly monster, when properly trimmed and dressed by Mom, turned into an ambassador of the deep. I've eaten a lot of fancy fish in my time, but Mom's humble fried "cat" could keep up with any of them.

And speaking of things fishy, how do you determine whether a fish is fresh? You look him dead in the eye. The eyes should be clear, bright and rounded, never dull or sunken. The fish should be firm to the touch and not leave an imprint when handled. I have a general rule that I follow whenever fish shopping: if the store reeks of fish odors, stay away. Fresh fish don't carry any obvious odors, so sniff your fish (even if it's been packaged) before you leave the store. Touch the scales to make sure they are intact, and not dropping with your every prod. Look at the belly and gills, which should be no darker than the rest of the fish.

~ Fish Marinade ~

This marinade ensures your fish a sense of identity whenever it's being added to other dishes.

Juice of 1 lemon
1 tablespoon olive oil
3 tablespoons chopped parsley
1 clove garlic, crushed

1 teaspoon Lemon Pepper
    (page 5)
½ teaspoon salt
2 tablespoons vermouth

Put all ingredients in a small jar with a tight-fitting lid and shake. Use as recipe requires.   *Enough for a pound of fish*

~ Shrimp Marinade ~

Recipes often call for the addition of shrimp at the last minute. The only problem is that the shrimp hardly get a chance to absorb the host flavors. This marinade allows the shrimp to contribute much more flavor to the pot.

Juice of 1 lemon
1 tablespoon olive oil
3 tablespoons chopped sweet
    basil
1 clove garlic, crushed

1 teaspoon grated lemon zest
½ teaspoon salt
1 tablespoon Raspberry Vinegar
    (page 14)

Put all ingredients in a small jar with a tight-fitting lid and shake. Use as recipe directs.   *Enough for 1 pound shrimp.*

～ Smothered Catfish ～

The first time I saw a catfish I nearly fainted. I was out playing Double Dutch with my friends, when I heard a shriek. I ran into the house to find my sister Diana poking at something with a fork. It resembled a miniature whale with whiskers. We sat silently inspecting it until Mom came into the kitchen. "Catfish? That—thing is what we're having for dinner?" Needless to say, one taste conquered my queasiness—forever. A lot of people are still leery of this whiskered piscine, mainly because of its reputation as a scavenger in the deep and muddy bottoms of the river. Today, most catfish are farmed and fed a proper diet of corn and similar vegetarian pleasures, which gives them a milder taste in the pan.

1½ **pounds catfish fillets**	1 **small onion, chopped**
1 **tablespoon Seasoned Salt** *(page 4)*	1 **small green bell pepper, seeded and diced**
1 **teaspoon olive oil**	1 **cup Fish Stock *(page 82)***
1 **tablespoon Roux *(page 201)***	½ **cup dry white wine**

Split catfish in half lengthwise. Sprinkle half the seasoned salt evenly over back and front of fillets. In a large nonstick skillet, heat 1 teaspoon oil over medium-high heat. Sauté fillets for 2 minutes on each side, until slightly browned, and reduce heat to low. Cover and cook for 8 minutes, until fish flakes when pulled apart. Remove fish from pan and increase heat to medium. Add roux, onion, and pepper and stir to mix, adding stock slowly to the mixture. Sprinkle the remaining salt in the pan and add wine, stirring to remove any lumps that have formed. Put catfish back in the pan and let sit off the heat for 5 minutes.   *Serves 4.*

Per serving: 130 calories / 4 gm fat / 4 gm carbohydrate / 377 mg sodium

~ Catfish with Cornmeal Crust ~

I have the same philosophy about frying catfish as I do with chicken: it doesn't need to be immersed in a vat of hot oil to qualify as tasty. Invest in a good nonstick skillet and the promise of good taste awaits you. And don't waste the drippings. Just add a tablespoon of Roux (page 201) to the pot, blend in a little Fish Stock (page 82) or Shrimp Stock (page 83), and you've got a great gravy for grits, the perfect side dish.

2 **large catfish fillets**
1 **teaspoon lemon juice**
½ **cup cornmeal**
¼ **cup flour**
½ **teaspoon Seafood Seasoning**
   (page 9)
1 **teaspoon ground sage**
½ **teaspoon cayenne**
2 **teaspoons olive oil**

Split the fish lengthwise, right down the middle. Put the fish in a shallow bowl and pour lemon juice over it. Toss to mix and let it sit in the refrigerator for 30 minutes. Combine the cornmeal, flour, seafood seasoning, sage, and cayenne and spread the mixture out on a plate. Dredge each fillet in the corn-meal mixture and set on a plate. Chill for 30 minutes. Heat the oil in a nonstick skillet over medium heat. Place the fillets in the pan (do not crowd) and cook for 3–5 minutes on each side, or until well browned. Place on a paper towel to drain and if necessary repeat with the remaining oil and fish.   *Serves 4.*

Per serving: 188 calories / 4 gm fat / 19 gm carbohydrate / 301 mg sodium

~ Catfish with Plantain ~

Here's a case of South meets West (Indies). This dish is somewhat stewlike; the plantain becomes soft and breaks down around the catfish, and it often looks a little discouraging. Don't lose hope! With the addition of red bell peppers and sweet peas, the dish reaches higher aesthetic ground, and attains a new dimension of taste.

3 large catfish fillets	1 ripe plantain, sliced ¼ inch thick
2 teaspoons olive oil	
1 large onion, finely chopped	1 teaspoon salt
2 tablespoons curry powder	2 cups Pepper Stock *(page 84)*
¼ teaspoon ground cardamom	½ cup dry white wine
½ teaspoon turmeric	1 red bell pepper, seeded and diced
¼ cup water mixed with 1 tablespoon lime juice	½ cup sweet peas

In a large nonstick skillet, brown the fillets in oil over medium-high heat for about 2 to 3 minutes on each side. Remove from pan, and set aside. Reduce the heat to medium and sauté the onions for 5 minutes, until softened. Combine the curry powder with the cardamom and turmeric and sprinkle over the onions. Pour in the lime juice mixture and stir until curry is well mixed with the onions. Reduce heat to low and add fish, plantain, salt, stock, and wine, and simmer, covered, for 25 minutes, until the liquid is the consistency of light gravy, stirring occasionally to break up the plantain. Add water if mixture begins to dry out. Add pepper and peas and simmer, uncovered, for 5 minutes more.

NOTE: 2 cups water and 1 diced chili pepper can be substituted for pepper stock.

Per serving: 183 calories / 3 gm fat / 67 gm carbohydrate / 493 mg sodium

～ Escoveitched Catfish ～

Another West Indian–inspired dish. This fiery dish is not for the timid. Scotch bonnet peppers are as hot as acetylene, a few scorching scoville units hotter than the habanero. Have plenty of water on hand and loads of cornbread muffins, or feel free to use a milder pepper.

3 medium onions	3 large catfish fillets
1 small Scotch bonnet pepper *(see page 10 for handling instructions)*	1 tablespoon Seasoned Salt *(page 4)*
2 teaspoons olive oil	½ cup white vinegar

Peel onions and cut each in half, lengthwise. Cut each half into ¼-inch slices and separate the half-rings. Put in a bowl and set aside. Seed the Scotch bonnet pepper, chop up, and place in the bowl with the onions. In a large cast-iron skillet, heat the oil over medium-high heat. Season the catfish with the salt and place in the pan to brown for 4 minutes on each side, until fish is firm to the touch. Remove fish from the pan, and increase the heat. Add onions and pepper to the pan and cook for 1 minute. Add vinegar and re-move from heat. Stir the mixture well and place the catfish back in the pan to absorb the vinegar mixture.   *Serves 6.*

Per serving: 110 calories / 3 gm fat / 5 gm carbohydrate / 72 mg sodium

～ Codfish Cakes ～

I can't remember better codfish cakes than those my Mom made. Somehow she always knew the exact ratio of codfish to mashed potato, and was able to quickly crisp the outer crust while keeping the patty perfectly tender. I recall wanting to slap buns on either side of it and make a cod burger of the tasty bundle on my plate—but that was forbidden. According to Mom, bread at the dinner table was meant to be eaten with butter or jam, and nothing more.

1 pound cod fillets, steamed
   (see Glossary for instructions)
1 teaspoon lemon juice
1 cup Mashed Potatoes
   (page 151)
2 cloves garlic, minced
1 tablespoon finely minced
   rosemary leaves

3 teaspoons olive oil
1 teaspoon salt
1 teaspoon Lemon Pepper
   (page 5)
½ teaspoon dry mustard
2 tablespoons bread crumbs
2 tablespoons flour

Put steamed fish into a large mixing bowl. Sprinkle on lemon juice and toss. Add potatoes and gently fold into the fish. In a small saucepan, sauté garlic and rosemary in 1 teaspoon oil over medium heat for 1 minute, until garlic is lightly browned. Add garlic mixture, salt, lemon pepper, and mustard to the fish mixture and knead with your hands to mix thoroughly. Shape into eight patties, and dredge in a combined mixture of bread crumbs and flour. Let chill in refrigerator for ½ hour. In a large nonstick skillet, heat 1 teaspoon oil over medium-high heat. When hot, add four patties and cook for 3 minutes on each side, until well browned. Remove and drain on paper towels. Repeat with the remaining oil and patties.   *Makes 8 patties.*

Per serving: 107 calories / 3 gm fat / 8 gm carbohydrate / 400 mg sodium

~ Crab Cakes ~

Because crabmeat is not only divinely delicate and flavorful, but quite expensive too (unless you spend the time picking it from the shell), I limit crab cakes to a couple of special occasions each year. And because it is such a rare treat, I handle the fish with loving care. I spend an hour picking it over to remove every bit of cartilage. I also take care not to overcook it, since the crabmeat is precooked. And I never pat down my crab cake to compress it—I like it light, with very little breading, so that it floats on the plate like a sea-cloud.

1 pound lump crabmeat, cartilage
   removed

1 egg, beaten
1 teaspoon cayenne

1 tablespoon snipped chives
2 tablespoons minced parsley
2 teaspoons grated lemon zest
1 tablespoon reduced-fat
  mayonnaise

½ tablespoon dry mustard
1 tablespoon lemon juice
2 tablespoons bread crumbs
2 teaspoons butter

Put the crabmeat in a large mixing bowl. In another bowl put the egg, cayenne, chives, parsley, lemon zest, mayonnaise, mustard, and lemon juice, and whisk until well blended. Add the mixture to the crabmeat and toss gently, so as not to break up the crabmeat. Sprinkle on the bread crumbs, and toss again. Shape into eight flattened patties and refrigerate for 1 hour. Heat 1 teaspoon butter in a large nonstick skillet over medium heat. Place four crab cakes in the skillet and cook for about 3–5 minutes on each side, until well browned. Do not pat the crab cakes down. Put another teaspoon of butter in the skillet and repeat with the remaining crab cakes.   *Makes 8 cakes.*

Per serving: 75 calories / 2 gm fat / 1 gm carbohydrate / 204 mg sodium

~ Salmon Croquettes ~

Whenever Grandmom Cothran made a rare appearance at the stove, the result was immensely satisfying. Some Fridays, when we arrived for one of our frequent visits, we'd be met by the aroma of these delicate pink cakes. Grandmom would always serve them with a little spaghetti on the side and Cucumbers in Peppered Vinegar (page 142).

3 cloves garlic, minced
3 teaspoons olive oil
1 pound salmon fillet
½ cup dry vermouth
2 teaspoons butter
1 tablespoon flour
½ cup evaporated skim milk
½ cup Mashed Potatoes *(page 151)*
1 teaspoon salt

2 teaspoons Lemon Pepper *(page 5)*
2 tablespoons chopped parsley
2 tablespoons chopped chives
1 tablespoon chopped dill
1 egg, beaten
2 teaspoons lemon juice
¼ cup flour
2 tablespoons bread crumbs

Sauté garlic in 1 teaspoon oil and set aside. Steam salmon in vermouth for 10 minutes, until firm, set aside to cool, and flake. In a large saucepan, melt butter. When butter begins to bubble, stir in the flour. Slowly add the milk, stirring while pouring, until mixture is smooth and thickened. Add salmon, garlic, potatoes, salt, lemon pepper, parsley, chives, dill, egg, and lemon juice. In a plate combine flour and bread crumbs. Run hands under cold water and shape salmon into eight patties and dredge in flour mixture. Chill for at least ½ hour.

In a nonstick skillet or cast-iron skillet, heat 1 teaspoon oil. Place four patties in the pan and cook 3 minutes on each side, until well browned. Drain on paper towels. Add remaining oil to the pan and cook the remaining four patties.   *Makes 8 croquettes.*

Per serving: 129 calories / 4 gm fat / 11 gm carbohydrate / 379 mg sodium

～ Red Snapper with Hot Pickled Lemons ～

The best results with this dish come from using the whole fish. Have the fish cleaned and gutted at the fish market and leave the head intact.

1 teaspoon olive oil	½ cup dry white wine
3 cloves garlic, chopped	2 tablespoons chopped parsley
1 large red snapper, cleaned, head intact (optional)	½ Hot Pickled Lemon, minced (page 215)

Preheat the oven to 350 degrees F. In a large cast-iron skillet, sauté garlic in oil for 1 minute, until lightly browned; add snapper and cook on each side for 4 minutes over medium-high heat, until it becomes firm. Remove fish from the pan and set aside. Add wine, parsley, and lemon to the pan and stir to mix. Put fish back into the pan and toss around to coat with wine sauce. Cover the pan with foil and bake for 20 minutes, until fish flakes with a fork. *Makes 2 servings.*

Per serving: 178 calories / 3 gm fat / 13 gm carbohydrate / 442 mg sodium

∾ Baked Redfish with Herbs ∾

Parchment paper seals in the flavors and produces a tender, flaky fish.

6 redfish fillets
1 teaspoon salt
2 teaspoons Lemon Pepper
   (page 5)
½ cup dry vermouth

6 12-inch squares of parchment
   paper or aluminum foil
2 teaspoons Dried Herbs Mix
   (page 8)

Preheat the oven to 325 degrees F. Sprinkle redfish with salt and lemon pepper, and place in a shallow dish. Pour the vermouth into the dish and let sit for 1 hour in the refrigerator. Place each fillet in the middle of a square of parchment paper and sprinkle with herbs. Seal the edges together to form an airtight wrap. Place wrapped fish on a large baking sheet and bake for 12 minutes. Remove from oven and let sit for 5 minutes before opening.   *Serves 6.*

Per serving: 188 calories / 2 gm fat / 2 gm carbohydrate / 460 mg sodium

∾ Steamed Crabs ∾

At least twice during the summer months, the whole family drove to Baltimore to get a barrel of live crabs. On the way back, we'd continually peek into the barrel to see if the crabs were still alive, and those feisty rascals were invariably alive and kicking. Mom would make an all-day event out of this, with friends and relatives pouring in the door, full of anticipation. The table was lined with newspapers, mallets, and nutcrackers. There was a trash barrel filled with ice-cold beer for the adults, and root beer and cream soda for the kids.

24 live blue crabs
3 cloves garlic
1 teaspoon olive oil
1 small chili pepper, seeded
   *(see page 10 for handling
   instructions)*

¼ cup white vinegar
2 cups beer
½ cup Shellfish Boil *(page 8)*
   or Old Bay Seasoning

Rinse crabs under cool water. With tongs, and a bit of patience, lift crabs one by one into a steamer basket and cover. In a large stockpot (large enough to accommodate the steamer basket), sauté garlic in oil for 1 minute, until lightly browned. Add pepper, vinegar, and beer and bring to a boil. Carefully lower the basket into the hot mix, and sprinkle seasoning on top of the crabs. Secure the lid. Steam for 10 minutes, until crabs are deep red in color. Let them come to room temperature before serving.   *Serves 6.*

Per serving: 144 calories / 2 gm fat / 9 gm carbohydrate / 428 mg sodium

∽ Steamed Shrimp ∽

I love simple, communal meals: a large bowl of shrimp and eager hands— plenty of beer, music, and good conversation.

2 **pounds fresh shrimp**	½ **cup vinegar**
1 **cup water**	¼ **cup Shellfish Boil** *(page 8)*
½ **cup beer**	**or Old Bay Seasoning**

Place the shrimp in a large steaming basket. In the steampot, combine water, beer, vinegar, and shellfish boil and bring to a vigorous boil. Lower shrimp basket into the pot and cover the pot, cooking over low heat for 3 to 5 minutes. You may need to toss the shrimp so that they cook evenly. Drain, remove shells and intestinal tract, and serve hot or chilled.   *Serves 6.*

Per serving: 277 calories / 4 gm fat / 8 gm carbohydrate / 215 mg sodium

～8～

Chicken:
The Preacher's Bird

Chicken has a long and tasty history in the early African community in the United States, dating back to the 1860s when this feathered fowl was sometimes known as the Preacher's Bird. The name commemorates the fact that in the South at that time, the church was the center of the newly freed African community and the preacher was often invited to Sunday dinner at the homes of his parishioners. The proud hosts would often kill and roast a precious chicken for the occasion. As the honored guest, the preacher had first claim on the meatiest part of the bird. I wonder if these men of the cloth had any idea that they were making a health-conscious choice, since the meatiest part of the bird—the breast—happens to be the most healthful. In fact, chicken, when cooked right, is remarkably low in saturated fat. In addition, it ranks near the top of all meats in practicality. Economical, versatile, equally at home dressed in fancy finery or humbly roasted, chicken, in reality, is a kind of supermeat. In fact, I've known more than one person who had contemplated the path of vegetarianism, and decided against it because they felt a chicken-free lifestyle was too great a sacrifice.

When it comes to buying chicken, I recommend patronizing a shop that specializes in poultry. Most butchers offer a higher grade of chicken than the standard supermarket. For obvious reasons, you should steer clear of any chicken that has been synthetically boosted with hormones. How will you know if this is the case? Usually you won't. Trust your instincts, use your judgment, and keep your eyes wide open for the fine print on labels. You'll have to find a brand that makes a specific claim. It's like the labeling of vegetables: if it doesn't indicate in black and white that it is organic—then it's probably not. Free range, or organic, chickens have a slightly more powerful flavor than store-bought birds, and have the additional bonus of being drug-free.

Although flavorful enough to be eaten simply with a little salt and pepper, chicken has a chameleon-like quality. It adapts with equal generosity to fruit-based dishes as to those built around hot chilies. It accommodates a white sauce as elegantly as a brown gravy. Nonpartisan when it comes to red or white wine, chicken provides the meatiness that certain people can't live without, and yet it does so mildly, without being overbearing in a dish. Thus your basic chicken—a blank slate awaiting the writing of culinary poetry.

～ Poultry Marinade ～

It's a good idea to marinade chicken before cooking whether the recipe calls for it or not. Marinading tenderizes the chicken and enhances the flavor in just an hour. I leave the marinade on overnight for extra flavor.

1 **tablespoon lemon juice**	½ **teaspoon dry mustard**
2 **teaspoons olive oil**	1 **teaspoon balsamic vinegar**
2 **teaspoons dry sherry**	3 **tablespoons chopped rosemary**
1 **clove garlic, crushed**	**leaves**

Mix all ingredients in jar with a tight-fitting lid and shake. Pour over chicken, cover, and refrigerate.   *Makes enough for 1 pound of chicken.*

~ Skinless Fried Chicken ~

A healthy change rung on the old standby. All that is needed for this mouth-watering classic is a well-seasoned coating, a great cast-iron pan, and a side of mashed potatoes and gravy, and you'll hear no complaints from anyone.

6 skinless, bone-in chicken
    breast halves
2 cups 1 percent fat buttermilk
½ teaspoon salt
1 teaspoon freshly ground
    pepper
1 tablespoon lemon juice
1 teaspoon Seasoned Salt
    (page 4)

2 teaspoons ground sage
2 teaspoons paprika
¼ cup finely ground cracker
    crumbs
1 teaspoon baking powder
¼ cup olive oil
1 cup flour

Split each halved chicken breast in half again. Soak each chicken piece in the buttermilk for 1 hour. Remove chicken from buttermilk mixture and pat dry. Discard milk. Place chicken on a plate and sprinkle with salt, pepper, and lemon juice. Toss to mix evenly. In a paper bag, combine the seasoned salt, sage, paprika, cracker crumbs, and baking powder; shake the bag to mix. In a large cast-iron or nonstick skillet, heat the oil over medium-high heat. Dredge chicken in flour and shake off the excess. When oil is very hot, lay the chicken pieces in the pan, fleshy side down, and immediately reduce heat to medium. Cook for 10–12 minutes and turn the chicken over to cook for another 8–10 minutes, until chicken is golden brown. Remove and drain on paper towels.   *Serves 6.*

Per serving: 308 calories / 7 gm fat / 25 gm carbohydrate / 487 mg sodium

~ Smothered Chicken with Mushrooms ~

When I was a child, I was perplexed by mushrooms: Were they meat? Vegetable? The rubbery texture made me nervous. Any meal that Mom made with mushrooms required my combing through the entire dish and piling the mushrooms on the side of the plate. It wasn't that I disliked them—I was indifferent because they had no taste! Grandpop proved me wrong one day, by giving me my first taste of a fresh mushroom. The conversion was instantaneous.

6 skinless bone-in chicken breast halves, boneless	1 teaspoon Lemon Pepper *(page 5)*
1 recipe Poultry Marinade *(page 126)*	1 tablespoon chopped parsley
2 onions, chopped	1 tablespoon chopped chives
3 teaspoons olive oil	1 bay leaf
1 pound mushrooms, sliced	1 cup Chicken Stock *(page 81)*
½ teaspoon Seasoned Salt *(page 4)*	½ cup dry white wine
	2 teaspoons arrowroot
	¼ cup water

Put the chicken in a large bowl and pour marinade on top. Toss well and set aside for 1 hour.

After chicken has been marinating for ½ hour, sauté onions in 1 teaspoon oil in a large skillet, over medium heat for 20 minutes, or until onions turn golden brown. Add mushrooms and cook for 7–10 minutes more, or until mushrooms have browned. Remove chicken from marinade and discard marinade. Lower heat and put the chicken pieces, fleshy side down, in the pan and add seasoned salt, lemon pepper, parsley, chives, and bay leaf. Cover and cook for 20 minutes on each side, until chicken is tender but firm. Remove chicken from the pan and discard bay leaf. Add stock and wine to the pan. Increase heat to medium-high and mix arrowroot with water; slowly add arrowroot mixture while stirring. When gravy is well mixed, put chicken pieces back in the pan and reduce heat to low. Cover and simmer for 10 minutes.   *Serves 6.*

Per serving: 197 calories / 4 gm fat / 7 gm carbohydrate / 334 mg sodium

~ Grilled Barbecued Chicken ~

I am always amused to see a person standing over a grill, brush in hand, diligently slathering barbecue sauce on a piece of chicken that's reached the last stages of cooking. The chicken is coated with sauce, and when the sauce dries, a second and often a third coating is added. Although the coating may be delicious, the chicken itself often seems to have no flavor whatsoever. I avoid this by marinating the chicken in the sauce the night before. You may not have time to marinate overnight, but give this sauce at least two hours with your grill-bound bird.

6 skinless chicken bone-in breast halves, boneless	½ teaspoon freshly ground pepper
½ teaspoon salt	1 cup Barbecue Sauce *(page 199)*

Put chicken in a shallow dish and sprinkle with salt and pepper. Pour on barbecue sauce, toss well, and let sit in refrigerator for at least 2 hours. Discard sauce or use as a baste for immediate use only.

Preheat grill for 15 minutes. Put chicken pieces, fleshy side down, on the hot grill and cook for 10 minutes, until chicken is slightly charred. Turn over and cook for 10 minutes more, basting occasionally.   *Serves 6.*

Per serving: 204 calories / 3 gm fat / 14 gm carbohydrate / 421 mg sodium

~ Baked Chicken with Benne Seeds ~

Benne seeds were introduced to the New World by the Africans. Most people recognize them by the name sesame seeds. They were thought to possess luck-giving powers. Nana used benne seeds a lot, mostly to make sweets, like benne seeds brittle or benne wafers. Occasionally, she'd use them to dress a chicken—and this was one of the best-dressed birds of them all.

6 skinless boneless chicken
   breast halves
1 teaspoon salt
1 tablespoon Lemon Pepper
   (page 5)
¼ cup grape or raspberry
   preserves

½ teaspoon ground sage
½ teaspoon dry mustard
1 tablespoon tomato paste
¼ teaspoon cayenne
1 tablespoon cider vinegar
¼ cup dry red wine
1 cup sesame seeds

Preheat the oven to 350 degrees F. Butter a long rectangular baking dish and set aside. Put chicken in a shallow dish, sprinkle salt and lemon pepper over it, and set aside. In a small bowl, combine preserves, sage, mustard, tomato paste, cayenne, vinegar, and wine. Beat well and pour on top of the chicken, tossing to coat each piece well. Spread sesame seeds out on a plate and dredge each piece of chicken with seeds. Place chicken in baking dish, and pour remaining sauce over chicken. Bake for 30 minutes, until chicken is tender but firm.   *Serves 6.*

Per serving: 272 calories / 4 gm fat / 26 gm carbohydrate / 449 mg sodium

～ Mom's Chicken Bouillon ～

Okay, so it's not chicken bouillon—but that's what Mom called it, and that's what I call it too. The only other name I have for it is delicious.

2 large onions, sliced into
   ¼-inch-thick rings
1 tablespoon butter
3 skinless bone-in whole
   chicken breasts
2 teaspoons Lemon Pepper
   (page 5)

¼ cup chopped parsley
¼ cup dry white wine
½ cup Chicken Stock *(page 81)*
½ cup nonfat sour cream
1 teaspoon salt

In a large skillet, sauté onion rings in butter over low heat for 10 minutes, until onions are translucent. Increase heat to medium-high and when quite hot, place chicken breasts, fleshy side down, into skillet. Cook for 2 minutes on each side, until browned. Add lemon pepper, parsley, wine, and stock and return the heat to low. Simmer, covered, for 25 minutes. Remove from heat and add sour cream and salt.   *Serves 6.*

Per serving: 175 calories / 3 gm fat / 4 gm carbohydrate / 474 mg sodium

~ Chicken Hash ~

I love hashes of all sorts—low-tech, high-flavor cooking at its best, with flavors combined brilliantly and haphazardly in a pan. The beauty of this dish, as in jazz music, lies in its improvisation.

3 cooked large skinless, boneless chicken breasts	1 tablespoon flour
2 large potatoes, boiled and grated	½ cup Chicken Stock *(page 81)*
1 tablespoon lemon juice	¾ cup evaporated skim milk
½ cup chopped celery	2 tablespoons chopped parsley
½ cup chopped carrots	1 tablespoon chopped tarragon
1 small onion, chopped	½ teaspoon salt
1 red bell pepper, seeded and chopped	1 teaspoon freshly ground white pepper
1 teaspoon butter	⅛ teaspoon mace
1 tablespoon Raspberry Vinegar *(page 14)* or balsamic vinegar	2 teaspoons olive oil

Shred chicken finely and put in a large bowl; add potatoes and lemon and toss to mix. In a large nonstick skillet, sauté celery, carrots, onion, and red bell pepper in butter over medium heat for 5 minutes, until softened. Pour in vinegar and toss to blend. Add flour to the pan and stir to mix. Stirring, slowly pour in stock until it thickens, and blend in the milk. Add the chicken-potato mixture and follow with parsley, tarragon salt, pepper, and mace. Toss and remove the mixture from the pan.

Heat the oil in a large nonstick pan over medium-high heat. When hot enough to sizzle a drop of water, add the chicken mixture. Cook for 15 minutes, until the edges turn a golden brown, and slide the chicken out of the pan onto a large plate. Cover the plate with another of the same size and flip over. Slide the mixture back into the pan, browned side up. Cook for another 10 minutes, until well browned, and remove from heat. Cut into wedges and serve.   *Serves 6.*

Per serving: 199 calories / 4 gm fat / 16 gm carbohydrate / 388 mg sodium

～ Chicken Pot Pie ～

This classic is a quintessential down-home dish. Unfortunately the traditional preparation makes it hard on the heart. I've managed to lighten the typically creamy filling and alter the crust dramatically. Phyllo dough is wonderfully light and crisp, yet so tasty.

4 **skinless, boneless chicken breast halves**	2 **cups Chicken Stock** (*page 81*)
2 **teaspoons olive oil**	¼ **cup dry sherry**
¼ **cup shallots, chopped**	10 **tarragon leaves, minced**
2 **stalks celery, chopped**	2 **teaspoons arrowroot mixed with ¼ cup water**
2 **carrots, sliced into ¼-inch rings**	½ **teaspoon salt**
1 **large sweet potato, peeled and cubed**	1 **teaspoon freshly ground white pepper**
1 **cup sweet green peas**	4 **sheets phyllo dough**
	1 **teaspoon butter, melted**

Preheat the oven to 375 degrees F. In a large nonstick skillet, cook the chicken pieces in 1 teaspoon oil over medium-high heat for 3 minutes, until browned on both sides. Remove from pan and set aside. Lower the heat to medium and add the remaining oil to the pan. Add shallots, celery, carrots, potato, and peas and sauté for 5 minutes, until cooked but firm. Add stock, sherry, tarragon, and arrowroot mixture, and stir until sauce begins to thicken. Add salt, pepper, and chicken, and remove the mixture from the heat. Lay the phyllo dough on a flat surface and brush each sheet with melted butter. Line the bottom of an 8-inch-square baking dish with two sheets of the dough. Spoon the chicken mixture into the dish and place the remaining phyllo sheets on top, tucking into the sides of the pan. Bake for 30 minutes, until phyllo is crisp and golden brown.   *Serves 6.*

Per serving: 235 calories / 5 gm fat / 24 gm carbohydrate / 333 mg sodium

～ Chicken Fricassee ～

I always knew when Nana was making fricassee; the kitchen was lit up with the aroma of sautéed onions and herbs. She cooked the chicken until the meat nearly fell off the bones, and when she made the gravy it all seemed so effortless. It took me sixteen tries to duplicate it, but with a few additions and substitutions, I have more or less re-created it the way Nana made it. The aroma stirs up memories so intense I feel as if Nana is in the kitchen with me.

6 **large skinless bone-in chicken breast halves**
1 **recipe Poultry Marinade** *(page 126)*
3 **teaspoons olive oil**
¼ **cup flour**
2 **small onions, chopped**
1 **cup Chicken Stock** *(page 81)*
1 **teaspoon Worcestershire sauce**
1 **bay leaf**
1 **teaspoon chopped thyme leaves**
1 **tablespoon chopped parsley**
¼ **teaspoon mace**
   Pinch cayenne
1 **teaspoon salt**
1 **teaspoon Lemon Pepper** *(page 5)*
1 **teaspoon arrowroot mixed with ¼ cup water**

Put the chicken pieces in a large bowl and pour marinade on top. Toss and set aside for an hour.

Heat 1 teaspoon oil in a large nonstick skillet over medium heat. Remove chicken from marinade and discard marinade. Dredge chicken pieces in flour, shaking off excess, and add as many pieces as you can to the pan without crowding to brown for 2–3 minutes on each sides. Remove them from the pan and repeat with another teaspoon oil and the remaining chicken until all the chicken has been browned. Set the browned chicken aside and add the remaining oil to the pan. Add the onions and cook for 15 minutes, until onions are well browned. Add stock, Worcestershire, bay leaf, thyme, parsley, mace, cayenne, salt, lemon pepper, and arrowroot mixture and stir until thickened. Reduce heat to low, put the chicken pieces back into the pan, and simmer for 40 minutes, until chicken is tender. Remove and discard bay leaf before serving.   *Serves 6.*

Per serving: 171 calories / 4 gm fat / 3 gm carbohydrate / 458 mg sodium

∽ Stewed Chicken with Dried Fruit ∽

This is a variation of a recipe I received from my friend Jill, who's living in Paris at the moment. She writes of the many open-air markets, stocked with produce and delicacies from almost every culture. (She can even find ingredients for a down-home meal.) This particular dish mingles the sweet with the hot in a particularly fluent—and satisfying—way.

6 **skinless bone-in chicken breast halves**
1 **teaspoon salt**
1 **teaspoon lemon juice**
1 **tablespoon olive oil**
1 **cinnamon stick**
5 **whole cloves**
5 **whole allspice berries**
2 **teaspoons ground ginger**
1 **teaspoon turmeric**
1 **small chili pepper, seeded and minced (*see page 10 for handling instructions*)**

2 **cups Chicken Stock (*page 81*)**
1 **cup red wine**
½ **cup dried cranberries**
¼ **cup dried cherries or apricots**
¼ **cup black currants or raisins**
1 **tablespoon grated lemon zest**
2 **tablespoons chopped parsley**
2 **tablespoons chopped cilantro**

Cut halved chicken breasts in half again. Put chicken pieces in a bowl. Sprinkle on ½ teaspoon of the salt and the lemon juice and toss. In a large skillet, heat the oil over medium-high heat. When oil is hot, add the cinnamon, cloves, and allspice. Put the chicken in the hot oil and cook for 2–3 minutes, until browned on each side. Remove chicken and set aside. Add ginger, turmeric, and chili pepper to the pan and stir. Immediately pour in the stock and wine. Bring to a boil and add the cranberries, cherries, and currants. Lower heat, add remaining salt and the cooked chicken, and simmer, covered, for 35 minutes, until tender. Sprinkle in zest and cook over medium heat for 10 more minutes. Add parsley and cilantro, remove from heat, and serve.   *Serves 6.*

Per serving: 247 calories / 5 gm fat / 14 gm carbohydrate / 478 mg sodium

～ Stewed Chicken with Mashed Potato Dumplings ～

I used to avoid dumplings at all cost, until I tried one that was made with mashed potatoes. They were much lighter than the traditional flour and cement balls I'd become so adept at avoiding.

2 cups cold Mashed Potatoes *(page 151)*	2 teaspoons olive oil
	2 onions, chopped
1 egg	5 cloves garlic, minced
¼ cup flour	3 cups Chicken Stock *(page 81)*
1 teaspoon baking powder	2 cups water
2 tablespoons 1 percent fat buttermilk	1 cup dry white wine
	1 Bouquet Garni *(page 7)*
1 large stewing chicken, cut up, skin removed	½ teaspoon salt

In a large mixing bowl, combine potatoes, egg, flour, powder, and buttermilk and refrigerate until needed.

In a Dutch oven, brown chicken in 1 teaspoon oil over medium heat for 3 minutes on each side, until lightly browned. Remove from pan and set aside. Add remaining oil and onions and cook for 15 minutes, stirring occasionally, until onions begin to turn brown on the edges. Add garlic, tossing around to mix. Add chicken stock, water, and wine and bring to a boil. Reduce heat to low. Drop in bouquet garni, add chicken and salt, and simmer, covered, for 45 minutes, until chicken is tender. Drop potato mixture by tablespoonfuls into the hot chicken base for 5 minutes, until puffed and doubled in size.   *Serves 6.*

Per serving: 271 calories / 8 gm fat / 26 gm carbohydrate / 670 mg sodium

~ Chicken with Brown Celery Sauce ~

Pop-Pop loved this dish. He'd mop the sauce up with a rolled piece of bread, a practice which was outlawed at the table. He always looked so sheepish whenever he was caught perpetrating this tableside "don't."

6 **skinless bone-in chicken breast halves**
½ **teaspoon ground sage**
1 **teaspoon paprika**
2 **teaspoons Lemon Pepper** *(page 5)*
2 **teaspoons olive oil**
1 **cup chopped shallots**
6 **celery stalks, sliced 1 inch thick**
2 **tablespoons dry vermouth**

2 **cups Chicken Stock** *(page 81)*
½ **teaspoon salt**
1 **teaspoon celery salt**
1 **teaspoon celery seed**
1 **Bouquet Garni** *(page* 7*)*
¼ **teaspoon cayenne**
½ **cup red wine**
2 **teaspoons arrowroot mixed with ¼ cup water**
1 **teaspoon Burnt Caramel** *(page 202)*

Season chicken with sage, paprika, and lemon pepper. Heat 1 teaspoon oil in a nonstick skillet over high heat, and sear chicken for 3 minutes on each side, until browned. Remove chicken from the pan and set aside. Add the remaining oil to the skillet and sauté shallots over medium heat for 5 minutes, tossing occasionally, until softened. Add celery and cook for 10 minutes more. Pour in vermouth and stir with a wooden spoon to dislodge browned bits from the bottom of the pan. Put the celery into a food processor, along with the chicken stock, and puree; strain through a sieve and return the pureed celery to the pan. Add salt, celery salt, celery seed, bouquet garni, cayenne, and wine to the pan and increase heat to medium-high. Add arrowroot mixture and burnt caramel, stirring, for 2–3 minutes, until the liquid thickens. Return chicken pieces to the pan and simmer, covered, for 1 hour, until chicken is tender.   *Serves 6.*

Per serving: 202 calories / 3 gm fat / 9 gm carbohydrate / 455 mg sodium

～ Chicken with Cream Gravy ～

Another old-timey recipe cooked by Nana. Nana loved chicken but was so wary about other people's preparation of it that she wouldn't eat any but her own. Not Mom's. Not Grandpop's. Not even Grandmom's—her own daughter. The funny thing was that Mom and Grandmom carried forward the same tradition: an insistence on not cooking their chicken until every ounce of yellow fat was removed. I stand guilty, as well.

6 large skinless bone-in chicken breast halves
1 tablespoon lemon juice
1 teaspoon freshly ground white pepper
½ teaspoon paprika
2 teaspoons olive oil
¼ cup flour
1 cup Chicken Stock *(page 81)*

1 teaspoon arrowroot mixed with ¼ cup hot water
2 cups evaporated skim milk, warmed
¼ teaspoon mace
½ teaspoon ground sage
1 teaspoon salt
Pinch of cayenne

Split the halved chicken breasts in half again; place them in a shallow bowl and sprinkle with lemon juice, pepper, and paprika. Toss to mix. In a large nonstick skillet, heat 1 teaspoon oil over medium-high heat. Dredge six chicken pieces in flour, shake off excess, and panfry for 3–5 minutes on each side, until well browned. Remove from pan and repeat with the remaining oil and chicken. Add chicken stock to the pan and stir to loosen the browned bits from the pan. Pour in the arrowroot mixture and continue to stir for 2 minutes more, until mixture thickens. Add milk, mace, sage, salt, and cayenne and reduce heat to low. Return chicken to pan and simmer for 30 minutes, covered, until chicken is tender.   *Serves 6.*

Per serving: 183 calories / 3 gm fat / 10 gm carbohydrate / 484 mg sodium

~9~

Dinner Classics

I call this chapter "Dinner Classics" out of a desire to preserve the atmosphere and ingredients of those memorable dishes of my childhood. These mostly side dishes were featured at our Sunday potlucks, which were held about once every month and functioned as reunions of a sort for the extended family. The cast changed from time to time, but we had our regulars, our stalwart munchers—of which I, of course, was one. I could always be counted on to appear, especially if my favorite dish was being prepared. The supporting cast included Uncle Greg, who always greeted me with our secret code, *Ping-a-Pong-Ping*; jolly Aunt Ruby, a former cover girl who loved to mix gin with Welch's grape juice; Uncle Bay, the finicky eater and lovable instigator; and cousin Rachel, a pro-bowler, who'd been accused more than once of eat-and-run syndrome, a sin among the elders in the family. Our gatherings usually took place at Grandmom and Grandpop Cothran's house, which was easily accessible—besides, as I noted earlier, Grandpop loved to cook. I enjoyed how their dog, Yankee, would have a conniption fit each time someone made an entrance, especially Aunt Penny.

Often, there would be so many guests that Grandmom would have to pull out the card table, place a tablecloth on it, and reserve it for the smallest of the clan, which included me, my younger siblings, and a young cousin. What a day it was when I graduated to the junior table, sitting between my uncle Garry, who knew how to walk on his hands, and Aunt Connie, a small and meticulous lady with an excellent vocabulary. The Big Table in the dining room accommodated the grown-ups, and at the head of that table was her highness—Nana—who was as grand as she was down-to-earth. She didn't drink, but loved the taste of piña coladas, so Mom would make a G-rated version just for her. Festive music was in the background, from Nana's favorite, "C. C. Rider," to Peggy Lee singing Grandmom's favorite, "Fever."

We were never served dinner by the course—every dish was placed on Grandmom's highly polished mahogany buffet table in the dining room. There, we'd scoop up mounds of hot and cold delicacies, whose plates were artfully set upon a variety of crisp, white doilies. What I loved most about these dinners was the unplanned mixture of dishes—how eclectic the spread was, since practically everyone brought a dish with them. Most of these dishes brought a sense of frugality (not that there was much of a choice in the matter) and a high sense of creativity. I wrote some of the recipes as I remember them, and others I've altered to suit my taste, and, I hope, yours.

⁓ Field Greens with Vidalia Onion Vinaigrette ⁓

There was always a big wooden salad bowl in the center of the buffet, loaded with mixed greens. Grandpop always put oranges and onions in his leafy salads. Okay, so he also used iceberg lettuce in those days—didn't everyone? Here, I've made a more contemporary version of his salad.

1 orange
1 head romaine lettuce
1 bunch of dandelion greens
1 bunch of watercress
1 handful of arugula

1 tablespoon chopped chervil
¼ cup Vidalia Onion Vinaigrette
   (recipe follows)
Freshly ground black pepper

Peel orange and break into segments. Separate leaves from romaine, and place in a large basin of clean, cold salted water. Add dandelion greens, watercress, and arugula and swish vigorously around in the water to rinse. Drain and repeat, this time with unsalted cold water. Rinse a final time and dry in a large salad spinner. Put greens in a large bowl and add chervil and orange segments. Pour on vinaigrette and toss. Add freshly ground pepper.   *Serves 4.*

Per serving: 60 calories / 2 gm fat / 7 gm carbohydrate / 63 mg sodium

Vidalia Onion Vinaigrette

The idea here is to chop the onion so fine that it almost looks like a puree. This tends to pull in even those who generally dislike raw onion in their salads. Take it from a reformed raw-onion hater.

1 small Vidalia onion, finely minced	1 cup Chicken Stock *(page 81)* or Vegetable Stock *(page 85)*
1 clove garlic, crushed	2 tablespoons soy sauce
1 teaspoon dry or Dijon mustard	Juice of 1 lemon
¼ cup olive oil	1 teaspoon grated lemon zest
	¼ cup balsamic vinegar

Place onion, garlic, mustard, and oil in jar with a tight-fitting lid. Pour in stock, soy sauce, and lemon juice and zest, and shake vigorously. Add vinegar and shake once more.   *Makes 1 pint.*

Per serving (1 tablespoon): 33 calories / 3 gm fat / 0 gm carbohydrate / 46 mg sodium

∼ Cucumbers in Peppered Vinegar ∼

Sweet simplicity. This is one of Grandmom's hits—I believe she tossed a few onions into her version, but I prefer to let the vinegar take center stage.

**4 cucumbers, peeled and sliced
   crosswise into ultra-thin
   slices**

½ teaspoon salt
¼ cup Peppered Vinegar *(page 15)*

In a shallow bowl, toss cucumber in salt until well mixed. Add vinegar and toss again. Chill and serve.   *Serves 8.*

Per serving: 24 calories / 0 gm fat / 5 gm carbohydrate / 270 mg sodium

∼ Scallop Salad ∼

Grandpop made two salads regularly: Waldorf, and this exquisitely light salad. They were in a dead-heat as my favorites. He used French dressing instead of vinaigrette, which you may substitute if you prefer the authentic work.

**1 pound bay scallops, steamed
   and chilled *(see Glossary for
   instructions on steaming
   fish)***
1 teaspoon lemon juice
**2 Golden Delicious apples, peeled,
   cored, and thinly sliced**

3 stalks celery, sliced ⅛ inch thick
1 teaspoon tarragon, chopped
½ teaspoon salt
Freshly ground white pepper
**¼ cup Vidalia Onion Vinaigrette
   *(page 141)***

Place the scallops in a large bowl and add lemon juice. Slice apples and add to the bowl, along with celery, tarragon, salt and pepper. Toss thoroughly. Add dressing and toss again.   *Serves 4.*

Per serving: 162 calories / 4 gm fat / 10 gm carbohydrate / 424 mg sodium

~ Shrimp Salad ~

Mom encouraged us to experiment, sometimes bringing flavors that were alien to us into usually humdrum dishes. Her encouragement inspired me to take a simple shrimp salad all the way to Japan.

¼ **cup hijiki** *(optional)*
2 **cups water**
2 **pounds shrimp, peeled, deveined, and steamed**
1 **cup chopped scallions**
2 **tablespoons finely grated gingerroot**
1 **teaspoon Lemon Pepper (page 5)**

¼ **teaspoon cayenne**
2 **tablespoons soy sauce**
1 **tablespoon fino or dry sherry**
1 **tablespoon lemon juice**
1 **tablespoon olive oil**
2 **tablespoons reduced-fat mayonnaise**

Soak hijiki in 2 cups water for ½ hour; drain and put aside. Put shrimp and hijiki in a large bowl, add scallions, ginger, lemon pepper, and cayenne, and toss. In a small bowl combine soy sauce, sherry, lemon juice, oil, and mayonnaise, and beat with a wire whisk until well mixed. Pour over shrimp mixture and toss. Refrigerate for at least 1 hour.   *Serves 8.*

NOTE: Hijiki, a form of dried seaweed, can be obtained at most health food stores.

Per serving: 141 calories / 4 gm fat / 1 gm carbohydrate / 366 mg sodium

~ Curried Macaroni Salad ~

Another buffet item that I just couldn't leave alone! I love to balance the high-carbo pasta with loads of vegetables. The curry is very much at home within the dish. I prefer the texture of fusilli or rotelli—the corkscrews seem to retain more flavor in a full-bodied salad such as this one.

1 **pound pasta, cooked and drained**	2 **tablespoons curry powder**
1 **large carrot, grated**	1 **tablespoon pickle relish**
1 **green bell pepper, seeded and chopped**	1 **teaspoon salt**
1 **red bell pepper, seeded and chopped**	1 **tablespoon Lemon Pepper (*page 5*)**
1 **small onion, finely chopped**	2 **7-ounce cans tuna in water**
2 **stalks celery, finely chopped**	2 **tablespoons reduced-fat mayonnaise**
1 **apple, peeled, cored, and finely chopped**	1 **tablespoon olive oil**
	Paprika

Rinse cooked pasta in cold water and put in refrigerator to chill further. In a large bowl, combine carrot, peppers, onion, celery, apples, and curry powder, and toss to mix. Add relish, salt, lemon pepper, tuna, mayonnaise, and oil, and toss again. Sprinkle the top of the salad with paprika. *Makes 8 servings.*

Per serving: 327 calories / 5 gm fat / 50 gm carbohydrate / 518 mg sodium

~ Potato Salad ~

For down-home aficionados, potato salad is not limited to summer picnics. The trick here is to keep the serious flavor without a lot of mayo. Scrub those potatoes really well and leave the skins intact—they carry a lot of good vitamins.

3 pounds small red potatoes
2 hard-boiled egg whites, coarsely chopped
3 small sweet pickles, finely chopped
¼ cup chopped red bell pepper, seeded
2 tablespoons chopped red onion
2 tablespoons chopped chives

1 tablespoon Raspberry Vinegar *(page 14)* or red wine vinegar
1 tablespoon celery seed
1 teaspoon paprika
1 tablespoon dill, chopped
1 teaspoon salt
2 tablespoons reduced-fat mayonnaise
1 tablespoon nonfat sour cream
Freshly ground black pepper

Boil potatoes in their skins for 15 to 20 minutes in water to cover, or until tender. Set aside to cool. In a large mixing bowl, place egg whites, pickles, red bell pepper, onion, and chives. Add vinegar and toss gently. Dice potatoes and add to the mixture, along with the celery seed, paprika, dill, and salt. Toss gently, adding mayonnaise and sour cream a little at a time. Shape into a decorative bowl and cover top with freshly ground pepper. *Makes 8 servings.*

Per serving: 128 calories / 2 gm fat / 25 gm carbohydrate / 384 mg sodium

～ Grandmom's Roasted Chicken with Cornbread Stuffing ～

While Grandpop and Mom were the versatile family gourmets, Grandmom concentrated on perfecting a few good dishes. One of those dishes was chicken and stuffing, food that got right to the point. Grandmom didn't make a big production of it, either—all that was required was a freshly plucked chicken. I've taken the liberty of adding an herb bundle and a cup of wine to her recipe, with hopes that she will understand.

1 **large roasting chicken** **(5 to 7 lbs.)**
2 **lemons, 1 peeled, the other sliced in half**
1 **teaspoon salt**
1 **teaspoon freshly ground pepper**
1 **Bouquet Garni** *(page 7)*

1 **carrot, trimmed**
1 **stalk celery**
25 **cloves garlic, unpeeled**
2 **bay leaves**
1 **onion, peeled**
1 **cup dry white wine** **Cornbread Stuffing** *(recipe follows)*

Preheat the oven to 350 degrees F. Clean chicken thoroughly, removing fat from inside cavity. Rub juice of one of the halved lemons into cavity and sprinkle salt and pepper inside. Place bouquet garni inside, along with carrot, celery, peeled lemon, and 15 cloves of garlic. Place a bay leaf on each breast, beneath the skin. Plug cavity up with the onion and close by crisscrossing legs of bird and binding with two strings. Put chicken into a roasting pan with rack. Sprinkle juice of remaining lemon half and add remaining garlic cloves to the pan. Place a tent of foil atop the chicken and bake for ½ hour. Remove tent and pour wine into pan. Cook for 1 hour more, basting chicken with its juices every 5 minutes. Take chicken from the oven and let stand for 15 minutes. Remove vegetables and bay leaves and discard. Serve with cornbread stuffing on the side.   *Makes 8 servings.*

Per serving: 192 calories / 10 gm fat / 8 gm carbohydrate / 444 mg sodium

Cornbread Stuffing

I prefer to bake the stuffing in a separate pan—it feels more like an accessory to the meal than a by-product of the chicken. Serve it instead of, not along with, mashed potatoes or rice, to prevent carbo-overload.

¼ **cup chopped shallots**
½ **cup chopped celery**
1 **cup chopped mushrooms**
1 **tablespoon olive oil**
4 **cups crumbled cornbread**
½ **cup finely chopped cooked**
   chicken giblets

3 **tablespoons crumbled dried**
   sage
1½ **cups Chicken Stock** *(page 81)*
   or Vegetable Stock *(page 85)*

Preheat the oven to 325 degrees F. Butter a large soufflé dish. Sauté shallots, celery, and mushrooms in oil for 5 minutes, stirring occasionally until cooked but firm. Remove from heat. Put bread crumbs in a large mixing bowl and add giblets, sage, and shallot mixture. Pour in stock and mix well. Pack into the baking dish and bake for 20 minutes, uncovered, until top is well browned.   *Makes 8 servings.*

Per serving: 126 calories / 3 gm fat / 15 gm carbohydrate / 380 mg sodium

～ Smothered Cabbage ～

Ever since I began eating kim-chi, the fiery Korean appetizer of pickled cabbage, I've begun putting lots more pepper in my cabbage dishes. Believe it or not, I've actually edited the quantity of peppers in this dish to half of what I normally use. If you're daring, throw in a bit more. The meek may cut the amount by half.

1 **large head cabbage**
1 **large onion, coarsely chopped**
1 **tablespoon olive oil**
1 **Granny Smith apple, peeled**
   and cored

1 **green bell pepper, seeded and**
   sliced into thin strips
2 **teaspoons crushed red pepper** *(see*
   page 10 for handling instructions)

Shred cabbage coarsely and set aside. In a large skillet or Dutch oven, sauté onion in oil over medium heat for 15 minutes, until light golden. Slice apples thin and add to onions. Toss in cabbage, green bell pepper, and pepper, and cover. Cook for 25 minutes, until cabbage is soft but not wilted, tossing occasionally.   *Serves 8.*

Per serving: 56 calories / 2 gm fat / 9 gm carbohydrate / 223 mg sodium

∼ String Beans with Potatoes ∼

A simple wonder to behold.

1 tablespoon olive oil	1 teaspoon salt
1 whole onion	½ teaspoon grated lemon zest
1 pound green beans, trimmed	1 tablespoon lemon juice
1 pound red new potatoes, quartered	½ teaspoon freshly ground white pepper

Heat olive oil in large heavy skillet. Sauté onion in oil for 15 minutes, until golden. Blanch beans for 5 minutes in boiling water, then plunge into a bowl of ice water. Drain. Add beans to the onion mixture in the skillet, and add potatoes, salt, and lemon zest. Cook over medium heat for 30 minutes, or until potatoes are soft. Add lemon juice and pepper.   *Serves 8.*

Per serving: 81 calories / 1 gm fat / 15 gm carbohydrate / 342 mg sodium

~ Corn Pudding ~

Some people like to eat their foods piping hot, no matter what. I find that quite a few dishes are tastier when served at room temperature, as in the case of this pudding. I generally let it sit for 20 minutes before serving it.

4 ears of fresh corn, kernels removed from the cob
1 teaspoon salt
2 teaspoons ground tapioca
¼ cup chopped red bell pepper, seeded
¼ cup chopped green bell pepper, seeded

1 small jalapeño pepper, seeded and chopped *(see page 10 for handling instructions)*
1½ cups evaporated skim milk
2 egg yolks
1 tablespoon sugar
½ teaspoon nutmeg
½ teaspoon freshly ground white pepper

Preheat the oven to 375 degrees F. Butter a large baking or soufflé dish. Place the corn in a large heat-resistant mixing bowl. Add the salt, tapioca, red and green bell peppers, and jalapeño, and toss to mix. Heat the milk in the top of a double boiler over simmering water. Beat the yolks with the sugar, nutmeg, and pepper, and add milk, by teaspoonfuls, to the eggs, stirring rapidly, until the egg mixture is doubled in volume. Slowly pour the egg mixture into the hot milk in the double boiler and stir for 2 to 3 minutes, until sauce is thick enough to coat a spoon. Pour the hot mixture into the corn mixture and toss to mix.

Spoon into the baking dish and set in a pan of warm water that reaches halfway up the sides of the dish. Bake for 1 hour, until center is firm to the touch of a finger.   *Serves 8.*

Per serving: 139 calories / 2 gm fat / 26 gm carbohydrate / 326 mg sodium

～ Grandpop's Macaroni and Cheese ～

My sister Diana and I split on the issue of macaroni and cheese; she preferred Grandmom's, which was elegant in its own right—but a bit too cheesy—while I leaned toward Grandpop's lighter version. I'm not certain if Grandpop used ricotta cheese, but I find it a pleasurable addition.

4 cups macaroni, cooked al dente
1 cup sliced mushrooms
¼ cup chopped shallots
2 stalks celery, finely chopped
2 teaspoons butter, melted
1½ cups evaporated skim milk
¾ cup part-skim ricotta cheese
1 egg, beaten
1 red bell pepper, seeded and diced
1 tablespoon minced tarragon
1 teaspoon salt
½ teaspoon freshly ground white pepper
1 teaspoon ground tapioca
¼ teaspoon nutmeg
¼ cup grated Parmesan cheese
1 teaspoon grated lemon zest
¼ cup bread crumbs
2 tomatoes

Preheat the oven to 350 degrees F. Butter a large soufflé dish and set aside. Put cooked macaroni in a large mixing bowl. Sauté mushrooms, shallots, and celery in butter over low heat for 5 minutes, until cooked, but firm; add to macaroni and toss. Combine milk, ricotta, egg, bell pepper, tarragon, salt, pepper, tapioca, and nutmeg, and beat until well blended. Pour mixture over the macaroni and transfer macaroni to the soufflé dish. In a small bowl, combine Parmesan, lemon zest, and bread crumbs. Slice tomato thinly and pat dry. Starting from the center, form a spiral across the top of the macaroni with the tomatoes, overlapping if necessary. Sprinkle crumb mixture on top and bake for 35 minutes, until golden brown on top. *Serves 8.*

Per serving: 198 calories / 5 gm fat / 27 gm carbohydrate / 433 mg sodium

～ Cranberry Relish ～

This is another one of those dishes people tend to reserve for large winter holiday meals. I am a cranberry lover—when they're in season I use them in as many dishes as possible.

1 **pound cranberries**	¼ **cup finely ground walnuts**
Zest of 1 orange, cut into thin strips, avoiding bitter white pith	1 **cup orange juice**
	1 **teaspoon allspice**
2 **Granny Smith apples, peeled, cored, and chopped**	½ **cup sugar**

In a 2-quart saucepan, simmer all ingredients, uncovered, over low heat for 45 minutes, stirring often, until cranberries are softened and break up into the liquid. Serve warm or chilled.   *Serves 8.*

Per serving: 126 calories / 2 gm fat / 27 gm carbohydrate / 2 mg sodium

～ Mashed Potatoes ～

If anyone admits to me that they dislike mashed potatoes, I immediately suspect them of being an alien life form. For me, mashed potatoes are probably the most comforting of all comfort foods: fluffy and nurturing, yet so very solid and satisfying. Most mashed potatoes are skinless, loaded with butter and cream, whipped to alpine heights, and served with a pat of butter. I prefer the rugged version, skins intact, lumps, and a little buttermilk and chives to give it more flavor. My secret ingredient (or at least it was a secret until now) is mayo— reduced-fat mayonnaise, that is, which adds a creamy taste and texture to it all.

8 large potatoes, scrubbed
1 tablespoon Garlic Butter
    (page 205) or plain butter
2 tablespoons minced chives
¾ cup 1 percent fat buttermilk,
    warmed

2 tablespoons reduced-fat
    mayonnaise
1 teaspoon salt
    Freshly ground white pepper

Boil potatoes in water to cover for 20 to 25 minutes, or until tender when a fork is inserted. When fairly cool, drain and grate, or put through a potato ricer, including the skins, into a large bowl. Add butter and chives, and mash. With a large fork, whip the potatoes while adding milk. Add mayonnaise, salt, and pepper, and whip again.   *Serves 8.*

Per serving: 119 calories / 2 gm fat / 21 gm carbohydrate / 306 mg sodium

～ Ginger Beans ～

Baked beans were what we had almost every Saturday, and I loved them so much I bartered with my sister Diana, who was always willing to fork over her beans in exchange for my hot dogs. I don't eat baked beans as frequently as I used to, but when I do, I like to spice them up. Try these beans with roasted chicken.

1 large onion, diced
1 tablespoon butter
3 cups vegetarian baked beans
    (two [12-ounce] cans)
2 tablespoons grated gingerroot
1 tablespoon freshly ground
    black pepper

1 teaspoon allspice
½ teaspoon mustard
1 tablespoon maple syrup
1 teaspoon Burnt Caramel
    (page 202)

In a large skillet, sauté the onion in butter over low heat for 10 minutes, until softened. Add beans, ginger, pepper, allspice, mustard, syrup, and Burnt Caramel, and stir to mix. Cover and simmer for 15 minutes.   *Serves 6.*

Per serving: 160 calories / 2 gm fat / 32 gm carbohydrate / 297 mg sodium

~ Mom's Mashed Turnips with Sage Butter ~

Mom gave me this recipe over the phone. I asked her if it was okay to add a little sage butter to her original recipe. She paused, as if to taste it in her head, and finally gave me the go-ahead.

5 pounds turnips	1 teaspoon salt
3 quarts water	1 tablespoon sugar
2 tablespoons butter	1 tablespoon freshly ground
12 leaves of sage	black pepper
2 tablespoons evaporated	
skim milk	

Peel turnips and cut into large cubes. In a large pot, boil turnips in water for 25 minutes, or until tender. Drain and mash. Melt butter in a small saucepan over low heat. When the butter begins to bubble, add sage leaves. Cook sage in butter for 1 minute, until sage becomes crisp. Remove sage and drain on paper towel. Add butter to turnips, along with milk, salt, sugar, and pepper. Fluff with a fork, and just before serving, crumble sage on top of turnips.   *Serves 8.*

Per serving: 100 calories / 3 gm fat / 20 gm carbohydrate / 490 mg sodium

~ Ambrosia ~

I like this dessert in the fall, when the oranges are on their best behavior. Fresh coconut and pineapple make this down-home classic live up to its name.

4 oranges	¼ cup confectioners' sugar
2 bananas	2 tablespoons sweet sherry
1 small pineapple	or kirsch
½ cup freshly grated coconut	
meat	

Peel and segment oranges. Slice the bananas crosswise ¼ inch thick. Peel and core pineapple and cut into ½-inch cubes. Place the oranges, bananas, and pineapple in a large bowl; add coconut, sugar, and sherry, and toss.   *Makes 6 servings.*

Per serving: 255 calories / 3 gm fat / 63 gm carbohydrate / 9 mg sodium

～ Basmati Rice Pudding ～

This recipe started out in the classic mode, with basmati rice a mere substitute, but then I got a bit carried away. . . .

- 6 cups evaporated skim milk
- 12 whole cardamom pods, split open
- 1 cinnamon stick
- ½ cup blanched basmati rice (*see Note*)
- ¼ cup Lemon Sugar (*page 18*)
- 2 tablespoons pistachio nuts, crushed
- ½ cup golden seedless raisins
- ¼ cup freshly grated coconut meat
- 1 tablespoon rosewater

In a large heavy saucepan, bring the milk to a boil. Decrease the heat to low, add the cardamom and cinnamon, and simmer for ½ hour, stirring occasionally, until milk is reduced to two-thirds the amount. Remove cardamom and cinnamon, and discard. Add rice to the milk, along with the sugar, pistachios, raisins, and coconut, and simmer for 30 minutes more. Remove from heat and add rosewater. Chill or serve at room temperature.   *Makes 8 servings.*

NOTE: Basmati rice is blanched by adding rice to 2 cups boiling water for 5 minutes and draining.

Per serving: 334 calories / 3 gm fat / 61 gm carbohydrate / 221 mg sodium

～ Chocolate Chestnut Truffle Cupcakes ～

How's this for retro cuisine? The last cupcake I ate, aside from this recipe, was one that Grandmom Cothran made for me. Her icing was a dense deep chocolate, with a matte finish. Recently, I made some chocolate chestnut truffles from a wonderful low-cal cookbook. After eating one of these delicious truffles I knew I'd rediscovered Grandmom's frosting.

4 tablespoons butter, softened
1 cup sugar
¼ cup unsweetened chestnut puree
1 egg
2 cups all-purpose unbleached flour
1 cup unsweetened cocoa powder

2 teaspoons baking soda
1 teaspoon salt
1½ cups evaporated skim milk
½ cup nonfat sour cream
1 teaspoon vanilla extract
Chocolate Chestnut Truffle Frosting *(recipe follows)*
¼ cup unsweetened cocoa powder

Preheat the oven to 350 degrees F. Butter two 12-cup muffin tins. In a large mixing bowl, cream together the butter, sugar, chestnut puree, and egg. In another large bowl, sift together the flour, cocoa, soda, and salt. Alternating with the milk, blend the sifted ingredients with the chestnut mixture. Add sour cream and vanilla and beat well. Pour batter up to the halfway point in each muffin tin and bake for 12 minutes, until a toothpick inserted into a muffin comes out dry. Cool for 10 minutes and remove from tins.

Per serving: 202 calories / 4 gm fat / 35 gm carbohydrate / 222 mg sodium

Chocolate Chestnut Truffle Frosting

1 cup unsweetened chestnut puree
¾ cup evaporated skim milk
4 ounces semisweet chocolate, grated

1 tablespoon confectioners' sugar
1 teaspoon vanilla extract
1 tablespoon brandy

In a medium saucepan, combine the chestnut puree and milk, and simmer over low heat for 15 minutes, until well blended, stirring occasionally. Add the chocolate and remove from heat, stirring to mix. Put the chocolate mixture and the sugar in a food processor and process until smooth; add the vanilla and brandy and pulse a few times, until mixed. Place the truffle mixture in a bowl and refrigerate for 1 hour, or until firm. Spread a small amount of frosting on each cupcake and sift a little cocoa powder over it.   *Makes 24 cupcakes.*

～ Chocolate Pudding with Hazelnuts ～

Nana knew how to make all kinds of pudding: butterscotch, banana, and chocolate—my favorite. You'd never see instant pudding boxes on her shelf; Nana made it all from scratch.

⅓ cup unsweetened cocoa
   powder
½ cup sugar
   Pinch of salt
2 tablespoons cornstarch

3 cups evaporated skim milk
1 teaspoon vanilla extract
6 teaspoons finely ground
   hazelnuts

In a small bowl, combine chocolate, sugar, salt, and cornstarch. Add ½ cup milk and the vanilla, and stir until well blended. Heat remaining milk in a large saucepan until it reaches a near-boil; slowly add chocolate mixture to the pan and bring to a boil, stirring rapidly at all times for 3 to 4 minutes, until mixture thickens. Pour pudding into 6 ramekins and sprinkle 1 teaspoon of hazelnuts on top of each pudding. Chill for 1 hour.   *Makes 6 servings.*

Per serving: 195 calories / 2 gm fat / 35 gm carbohydrate / 146 mg sodium

~ 10 ~
Nola: Palatable New Orleans

Although the name of the hometown of Early American decadence is mostly pronounced by the locals as N'awlins, I prefer to use the feminine acronym Nola (New Orleans, LA). That's because the city is so like a lady, a good-hearted, strong, sometimes bawdy grande dame. It's a city bursting with celebration, a magical, mystical bayou town that was "multicultural" long before the term was coined. A haven for expatriates, Nola became the first culinary center of North America for a whole host of reasons. Chief among them was the sheer abundance of cultural influences, which pollinated the city with their various customs and cuisines: the native Choctaws, who laid the foundation; the Spaniards, whose contribution of jambalaya (a paella of sorts) will keep them alive forever on the grateful palates of diners; the French exiles, who arrived in waves, beginning in the mid-eighteenth century, and gave the city much of its flair and raciness; and, of course, the Africans, whose highly developed improvisational and culinary skills helped patch together that crazy quilt of savory cuisine called Creole.

Creole, full of terms like *etouffee, café au lait*, and *beignet,* is also derived in large part from the land of Escoffier, which is to say, France. But somebody's got to ask: Just *who* was doing the cooking? Follow the okra and you'll soon find out. Take even a dish as traditionally *français* as bouillabaisse. The name may wear a superior attitude, but the New Orleans version of this wonderful fish chowder is plumped up and thickened with that humble green pod of the Motherland.

Kissing cousin to Creole cooking is that particularly peppery cuisine called Cajun. The two styles are so close that many people lump them together, but they are far from identical. Both originated in Louisiana, but Cajun cooking comes to us from France via a detour through Nova Scotia. The Cajun (Acadian) cooking style is heartier, simpler, and hotter than its older, more sophisticated sister.

Louisiana cookery, like so many of America's best products, is a hybrid form, woven together out of a rainbow of influences. It's one of our tastiest and most classical regional cuisines. That it comes from as funky a place as New Orleans makes it all the more delectable.

∽ Barbecued Shrimp ∾

This is the kind of dish you eat at a casual gathering of friends, with plenty of cold beer and warm laughter. If you absolutely hate to eat with your hands, you may peel the shrimp ahead of time, briskly sauté them in the spice mixture, and serve over rice. Unfortunately, you'll miss out on the finger-licking. Serve with a crisp green salad and crusty bread.

2 pounds shrimp, with shells and heads intact	1 tablespoon chopped basil
1 teaspoon cayenne	1 tablespoon minced rosemary
1 teaspoon freshly ground pepper	1 tablespoon minced oregano
½ teaspoon salt	1 tablespoon Worcestershire sauce
¼ teaspoon nutmeg	2 teaspoons Dijon mustard
1 teaspoon crushed red pepper	½ cup Fish Stock *(page 82)*
1 tablespoon thyme leaves	½ cup beer

| 3 cloves garlic, crushed | 2 tablespoons Roux *(page 201)* |
| 1 tablespoon olive oil | |

Rinse shrimp and set aside. In a small bowl, mix together the cayenne, ground pepper, salt, nutmeg, crushed pepper, thyme, basil, rosemary, and oregano. Mix the Worcestershire sauce with the mustard, stock, and beer. Sauté the garlic in the oil over low heat for 1 minute, until lightly browned. Add the herb and spice mixture to the pan and toss, mixing it all together with the oil. Because of the small amount of oil used, the mixture will appear dry and may stick to the pan slightly. Add a little water if necessary and continue tossing, shaking the pan as you go along. Toss in the shrimp and when a little pink, mix in the roux. Working fast to avoid overcooking the shrimp, toss around for 1 minute, until well mixed with the roux. Add the liquid mixture, smoothing out any lumps as you go along. Add more beer and/or stock if you want a thinner sauce. Remove from heat and let sit for about 5 minutes before serving.   *Serves 6.*

VARIATION: You may eliminate the cayenne through the oregano and use Barbecue Shrimp Seasoning (page 7) instead.

Per serving: 226 calories / 7 gm fat / 5 gm carbohydrate / 459 mg sodium

～ Chicken and Shrimp Jambalaya ～

Jambalaya is derived from paella, a dish of rice, vegetables, herbs, spices, and seafood that falls into the international pilau category. It's credited to the Spaniards, who were one of the first immigrants to Nola. Though it is generally made with andouille, a smoked pork sausage, I find the chicken to be a lean and delicious alternative. Have a frosty pitcher of Wine Punch (page 226) at hand.

1 pound shrimp, peeled and
  deveined
1 pound boneless, skinless
  chicken breasts
3 teaspoons olive oil
5 cloves garlic, minced
½ cup finely chopped shallots
1 small fennel bulb, finely
  chopped
2 carrots, finely chopped
¼ cup chopped scallions
  (green and white parts)
1 red bell pepper, seeded and
  chopped
1 green bell pepper, seeded and
  chopped
4 tomatoes, peeled and chopped

¼ cup minced parsley
2 teaspoons thyme leaves
8 basil leaves, minced
2 bay leaves
1 cup beer
¼ cup tomato paste
2 tablespoons Worcestershire
  sauce
1½ teaspoons salt
1 teaspoon freshly ground
  pepper
¼ teaspoon cayenne
1 teaspoon grated gingerroot
3 cups Shrimp Stock *(page 83)*
  or clam juice
1 cup uncooked long-grain rice
2 teaspoons grated lemon zest

Cut each shrimp into thirds. Pound the chicken thin with a mallet, and cut into thin strips. In a Dutch oven, sauté the shrimp and chicken in 1 teaspoon oil over medium heat for 2 minutes, until shrimp begins to turn pink, tossing to cook evenly. Remove and set aside. Add the remaining oil and cook the garlic for 1 minute, until lightly browned. Add the shallots, fennel, carrots, scallions, and red and green bell peppers to the pan and cook for 5 minutes, until vegetables are cooked but not wilted. Add the tomatoes, parsley, thyme, basil, and bay leaves and simmer, stirring often, for 15 minutes. Mix in beer, tomato paste, Worcestershire, salt, pepper, cayenne, ginger, and 1 cup stock, and cook for 25 minutes more, until it looks like a thick puree. Add the remaining stock and bring all to a boil. Sprinkle in rice and stir to mix evenly. Add zest and simmer, covered, for 15 minutes, until rice is firm, but tender. Mix in the shrimp and chicken and cook for 10 minutes more. Let jambalaya develop for 15 minutes before serving. Remove the bay leaves and discard. *Serves 8.*

Per serving: 361 calories / 4 gm fat / 46 gm carbohydrate / 497 mg sodium

∼ Shrimp Gumbo ∼

Okra is an instant hit in stews because of its neutral flavor and super thickening abilities. In this recipe, I've prepared it in the old style—by cooking the okra down into a paste, and grating the shrimp instead of using them whole. For variation, try eating this dish over Cornbread Stuffing (page 147).

2 large onions, finely chopped
1 tablespoon olive oil
5 cloves garlic, minced
1 pound okra, trimmed of tops
   and tails and sliced into
   ¼-inch rings crosswise
1 teaspoon salt
1 bay leaf
2 pounds shrimp, peeled and
   deveined

1 tablespoon lemon juice
2 tablespoons chopped
   parsley
6 cups Vegetable Stock
   (page 85)
¼ cup tomato paste
1 cup beer
2 teaspoons thyme leaves
2 teaspoons Lemon Cayenne
   (page 5)

In a Dutch oven, sauté onions in oil over medium heat for 20 minutes, until well browned. Add garlic and cook for 3 minutes more. Add okra to the onions, along with the salt and bay leaf. Reduce heat and simmer for 30 minutes, stirring often, until okra has completely broken apart. Meanwhile, steam shrimp until pink and cool to room temperature. Into a bowl, grate shrimp, sprinkle with lemon juice and parsley, and set aside. To the okra mixture add the stock, 1 cup at a time, until well blended. Add tomato paste and beer and cover, simmering for 15 minutes more. Add shrimp, thyme, and lemon cayenne and remove from heat. Stir and let develop for 10 minutes, covered. Remove and discard bay leaf before serving.   *Serves 6.*

Per serving: 211 calories / 4 gm fat / 16 gm carbohydrate / 468 mg sodium

∼ Chicken Oyster Gumbo ∽

I love odd combinations, items that are a little out of sync with the rest of the operation. This recipe appeals to me for that reason as well as others—especially flavor. Although it seems a peculiar match, your palate will tell you otherwise. Serve this with Sweet Potato Cornbread (page 76) and you'll have yourself one very eccentric—and delicious—meal.

12 **large oysters, shucked, reserving oyster liquor** *(see page 186 for preparation)*
2 **large onions, finely chopped**
1 **tablespoon olive oil**
5 **cloves garlic, minced**
1 **pound okra, trimmed of tops and tails and sliced crosswise into ¼-inch rings**
1 **teaspoon salt**
1 **bay leaf**

1 **pound skinless, boneless chicken breasts**
1 **tablespoon lemon juice**
1 **tablespoon Lemon Pepper** *(page 5)*
6 **cups Chicken Stock** *(page 81)*
¼ **cup tomato paste**
1 **cup beer**
2 **teaspoons thyme leaves**
½ **teaspoon cayenne**

In a nonstick skillet, cook oysters over low heat for 2 minutes, until the edges begin to ruffle. Remove from heat, chop coarsely, and set aside. In a Dutch oven, sauté onions in oil over medium heat for 20 minutes, until well browned. Add garlic and cook for 3 minutes more. Add okra to the onions, along with the salt and bay leaf. Reduce heat and simmer for 30 minutes, stirring often, until okra has completely broken apart. Meanwhile, coarsely chop chicken breasts, place in a bowl, sprinkle with lemon juice and lemon pepper, and set aside. To the okra mixture add the stock, 1 cup at a time, until well blended. Add chicken, tomato paste, and beer and cover, simmering for 15 minutes more, until chicken is cooked but tender. Add oysters, thyme, and cayenne and remove from heat. Stir and let develop for 10 minutes, covered. Remove and discard bay leaf before serving.   *Serves 8.*

Per serving: 211 calories / 5 gm fat / 13 gm carbohydrate / 453 mg sodium

~ Shrimp Creole ~

The best shrimp Creole I've had thus far was made by Blanche Tisdale, the mom of one of my friends. I never thought to ask her for the recipe, but was inspired to create my own.

1½ pounds shrimp, peeled and
    deveined
    Juice of 1 lemon
1 teaspoon salt
½ teaspoon cayenne
1 tablespoon olive oil
5 cloves garlic, minced
1 large onion, coarsely chopped
3 stalks celery, seeded and
    coarsely chopped
1 green bell pepper, seeded
    and diced
1 red bell pepper, seeded and
    coarsely chopped
3 large tomatoes, peeled and
    chopped

⅓ cup tomato paste
1 teaspoon sugar
5 sprigs of thyme
2 bay leaves
1 teaspoon Seafood Seasoning
    (page 9) or Old Bay
    Seasoning
3 cups Fish Stock *(page 82)*
2 teaspoons grated lemon zest
1 teaspoon freshly ground
    pepper
½ cup vermouth
3 tablespoons chopped parsley

Place the shrimp in a bowl and sprinkle 1 tablespoon of the lemon juice, just a pinch of the salt, and the cayenne over them. Toss and refrigerate. Heat oil in a large skillet over medium-high heat and sauté garlic for 1 minute, until garlic turns light brown. Add onion and cook for 3 minutes, until onion is slightly wilted. Add celery and bell peppers and cook 10 minutes, until cooked but not wilted. Add tomatoes, tomato paste, remaining salt, sugar, thyme, bay leaves, and seafood seasoning, and cook an additional 10 minutes. Slowly stir in stock, bring to a boil, reduce heat, and simmer for 15 minutes, stirring occasionally as sauce begins to thicken. Add shrimp, grated zest, remaining lemon juice, pepper, vermouth, and parsley and continue cooking for 5 minutes, covered. Remove and discard bay leaves before serving.   *Serves 6.*

Per serving: 257 calories / 6 gm fat / 23 gm carbohydrate / 530 mg sodium

~ Creole Green Beans ~

This savory side dish can upstage quite a few main entrees. Serve it with Onion Pie (page 168), an equally tantalizing dish, for a savory vegetarian dinner.

1 **pound fresh green beans,** trimmed	1 **red bell pepper, seeded and** diced
5 **cloves garlic, minced**	2 **large tomatoes, peeled and** chopped
1 **tablespoon olive oil**	½ **teaspoon salt**
¼ **cup shallots, finely chopped**	¼ **teaspoon cayenne**
2 **stalks celery, sliced ⅛ inch** thick	1 **teaspoon Lemon Pepper (page 5)**

Blanch the beans in boiling water for 3 minutes. Drain. In a large heavy skillet, sauté the garlic in the oil for 1 minute over medium heat, until lightly browned. Add shallots, celery, and red bell pepper, and sauté for 5 minutes, until cooked but not wilted. Decrease heat to low, toss in green beans, and cook, covered, for 20 minutes. Add tomatoes, salt, cayenne, and pepper, and simmer, covered, for 15 more minutes, until green beans are tender but firm.   *Makes 8 servings.*

Per serving: 50 calories / 2 gm fat / 8 gm carbohydrate / 283 mg sodium

～ Creole Scrambled Eggs ～

One Sunday while in New Orleans, a couple of days before Mardi Gras, my friend Cynthia took me to a great restaurant for brunch. The atmosphere was warm and relaxing—in contrast to the festive chaos abroad in the streets—and the smells of the food were intoxicating. Every so often a trumpet from the band would blare, and everyone would rise from their seats and dance around the restaurant. I recall having second thoughts about having to tear myself away from a plate of scrambled eggs topped with this unusually delicious tomato sauce. Here I've tried to re-create the taste I remember.

1 **medium onion, chopped**	1 **teaspoon Lemon Pepper**
1 **teaspoon olive oil**	**(page 5)**
1 **medium green bell pepper,**	1 **teaspoon thyme leaves**
seeded and chopped	1 **tablespoon chopped parsley**
2 **stalks celery, finely chopped**	**Pinch of cayenne**
12 **egg whites**	2 **teaspoons butter**
2 **egg yolks**	½ **cup Creole Sauce (page 200)**
½ **teaspoon salt**	

In a large nonstick skillet, sauté the onion in oil for 20 minutes over medium heat, tossing often, until onion is well browned. Add green bell pepper and celery and cook for 3 minutes more, until vegetables are softened. Remove from heat, put the cooked vegetables on a plate, and set aside. Wipe the skillet clean with a paper towel. In a large bowl, combine eggs, salt, lemon pepper, thyme, parsley, and cayenne, and beat until frothy. In the same skillet, heat the butter over medium heat. When the butter begins to bubble, add the eggs and cook for 2 minutes, stirring occasionally, until the eggs begin to set. Add the vegetable mixture and stir to mix, cooking until eggs are firm, but not runny. Place eggs on a platter and top with Creole Sauce.   *Makes 6 servings.*

Per serving: 82 calories / 3 gm fat / 3 gm carbohydrate / 398 mg sodium

∼ Fancy Mess o' Greens ∼

The formal name for this dish is gombo aux herbes *or* gumbo z'herbes, *but I can't see the logic of using either, since the dish lacks the title ingredient, gumbo (okra). As far as I'm concerned this is just a swankier version of the old healing bowl of greens, often referred to in those days as a mess o'greens. This mixture packs a powerhouse of vitamins: each serving provides more than twice the daily required amount of vitamins A and C, one third the amount of calcium, and nearly half the iron. How's that for a wholesome meal?*

1 pound mustard greens
1 pound collard greens
1 pound spinach
½ pound beet greens
1 pound Swiss chard
1 small cabbage, shredded
1 large bunch of watercress
1 bunch of parsley
3 onions, finely chopped
1 tablespoon olive oil
5 cloves garlic, minced
1 cup scallions, chopped
5 cups Fish Stock *(page 82)* or
    Vegetable Stock *(page 85)*

¼ cup Raspberry Vinegar
    (page 14)
1 cup dry white wine
1 teaspoon salt
½ teaspoon freshly ground
    pepper
½ teaspoon allspice
¼ teaspoon ground cloves
1 teaspoon crushed red pepper
    (see page 10 for handling
    instructions)
1 bay leaf
5 sprigs of thyme
2 sprigs of marjoram

Soak the greens, chard, cabbage, watercress, and parsley in a large pot of cold salted water. Rinse and soak again, this time in clear cold water. Trim the leaves of all stems, and chop finely. In a Dutch oven, sauté the onions in oil over medium heat for 20 minutes, until well browned. Add garlic and scallions, and sauté for 3 minutes more. Decrease heat to low and add all the greens to the onion mixture, tossing well to mix. Add stock, vinegar, wine, salt, pepper, allspice, cloves, crushed pepper, bay leaf, thyme, and marjoram, and simmer, covered, for 45 minutes, until greens are softened but not wilted. Remove and discard bay leaf before serving.   *Serves 12.*

Per serving: 134 calories / 2 gm fat / 20 gm carbohydrate / 482 mg sodium

∼ Red Beans and Rice ∼

I love the compact size of adzuki beans, and what's more, they are chock-full of potassium. Adzuki beans are a Japanese staple, sweetened considerably and eaten in ice cream, in pastes, and in steamed buns. They work well in this classic dish. You may use another type of red bean if you prefer, but allow extra cooking time, as this is much smaller than the kidney bean that is traditionally used.

1 pound adzuki beans (can be obtained at health food stores everywhere)
1 onion, finely chopped
2 cloves garlic, minced
2 stalks celery, sliced ¼ inch thick
1 tablespoon olive oil
5 cups Chicken Stock *(page 81)* or Vegetable Stock *(page 85)*
1 teaspoon salt

1 bay leaf
¼ cup chopped parsley
1 teaspoon chopped thyme
1 tablespoon Worcestershire sauce
1 teaspoon Tabasco sauce
1 teaspoon grated lemon zest
2 tablespoons sugar
4 cups cooked long-grain rice

Soak beans in water to cover for at least 8 hours and drain. In a Dutch oven, sauté onions, garlic, and celery in oil for 3–5 minutes, until celery is cooked but firm. Add beans, stock, salt, bay leaf, parsley, and thyme. Simmer, uncovered, for 1 hour, until beans begin to soften, adding water if beans begin to dry out and stick to the pan. Add Worcestershire, Tabasco, lemon zest, and sugar and continue to simmer for 20–30 more minutes, or until beans are firm yet tender. Serve over rice.   *Serves 6.*

Per serving: 382 calories / 2 gm fat / 68 gm carbohydrate / 448 mg sodium

⌒ Onion Pie ⌒

My friend Lisa brought an onion pie to a gathering and I just couldn't get enough of it. She told me it was an old Creole recipe that had been passed down through the generations. I'm glad she passed it on to me. It's best to use a sweet onion such as Vidalia to make this pie, and slice the onions very thin. A mouthwatering treat.

1 9-inch Piecrust *(page 233)*
1 tablespoon butter
5–6 large onions, chopped finely
1 teaspoon salt
1 egg, beaten
½ cup nonfat sour cream

2 teaspoons tarragon, chopped
1 tablespoon thyme leaves
2 tablespoons chopped chives
1 tablespoon chopped parsley
½ teaspoon freshly ground white pepper
¼ teaspoon nutmeg

Preheat the oven to 325 degrees F. Put the piecrust into the oven for 5 minutes; remove and increase oven temperature to 400 degrees F. In a large skillet, melt the butter and add the onions; cook for 5 minutes over low heat, until onions are soft. Remove from heat, add half the salt, and put into a large mixing bowl. Beat together the egg, sour cream, tarragon, thyme, chives, parsley, remaining salt, pepper, and nutmeg. Pour over onions and mix thoroughly, but gently. Spoon into the piecrust and bake for 15–20 minutes, until crust turns a golden brown.   *Serves 8.*

Per serving: 155 calories / 8 gm fat / 16 gm carbohydrate / 439 mg sodium

∽ Oyster Loaf ∽

This makes an excellent first course.

1 large loaf of French bread
24 oysters, shucked, discarding
     oyster liquor *(see page 186*
     for preparation)
1 tablespoon Garlic Butter
     (page 205)
2 tablespoons very finely
     minced watercress

½ teaspoon salt
⅛ teaspoon cayenne
1 teaspoon lemon juice
⅛ teaspoon anisette or anise
     extract

Warm the bread and slice lengthwise in half. Scrape out the insides and keep the bread warm while preparing the oysters. Melt the butter in a heavy, preferably cast-iron, skillet over low heat. Sauté the oysters in the butter for 2–3 minutes, until edges begin to curl. Add watercress, salt, cayenne, lemon juice, and anisette and remove from heat. Toss to mix and spoon onto the toasted bread.   *Serves 4.*

Per serving: 264 calories / 5 gm fat / 42 gm carbohydrate / 689 mg sodium

∽ Oyster Po' Boy ∽

Normally the oysters in a Po' Boy are breaded and fried. I never could see the point in doing that, since the oysters are already surrounded by so much bread.

6 oysters, shucked, discarding
     oyster liquor *(see page 186*
     for preparation)
1 teaspoon Herb Butter *(page 205)*
1 baguette, gutted and sliced
     lengthwise

1 teaspoon lemon juice
¼ teaspoon salt
¼ cup chopped shallots
1 tomato, sliced ¼ inch thick
6 sprigs of watercress
4 lettuce leaves

In a nonstick skillet, cook the oysters in the butter over medium heat until the oysters begin to curl; remove and place in a row on the upper half of the baguette. Sprinkle with lemon juice and salt. Add shallots to the same skillet and cook for 5 minutes, until softened. Remove from the pan and spread on the bottom half of the bread, followed by the tomato slices, watercress, and lettuce. Bring the two halves together and slice in half, crosswise. *Makes 2 servings.*

Per serving: 114 calories / 3 gm fat / 14 gm carbohydrate / 499 mg sodium

～ Pain Perdu ～

Pain perdu *is French for "lost bread," which refers to bread that has been sitting 1 day too long. Here is an excellent way to find it again. Serve with maple syrup.*

1 cup evaporated skim milk	1 teaspoon brandy
1 egg, beaten	½ teaspoon cinnamon
1 tablespoon orange juice	4 (2-inch) slices day old
½ teaspoon grated orange zest	French bread

Lightly grease a heavy griddle, preferably cast iron, and heat over medium heat. In a large bowl, combine the milk, egg, orange juice, zest, and the brandy. Dip both sides of each slice of bread into the egg mixture. Mop up any leftover egg with the bread slices. Let slices stand for 1 minute. The griddle should be quite hot by this time. Cook the soaked bread for 1 minute on each side, until browned. Transfer each slice to a warm (200 degrees F.) oven, until ready to eat. *Makes 4 servings.*

Per serving: 139 calories / 2 gm fat / 20 gm carbohydrate / 222 mg sodium

~ Creole Bread Pudding ~

Perhaps you've bought more bread than you thought you needed, or maybe you have a half of a large loaf left over. Here is another way to put it to delicious use.

5 cups evaporated skim milk	1 cup golden raisins
1 vanilla bean, split	1 teaspoon grated lemon zest
12 cardamom pods, split open	1¼ cups sugar
1 small loaf of French bread	2 eggs, separated
2 tablespoons butter, softened	¼ cup bourbon
1 teaspoon Pie Spice *(page 9)*	

Preheat the oven to 350 degrees F. Butter an 8-inch-square baking dish and set aside. Pour 4 cups milk into a saucepan and add vanilla bean and cardamom pods. Cook over medium-high heat until near boiling, and remove from heat. Break up bread (including crust) and put into a large mixing bowl. Add butter, pie spice, raisins, zest, and ⅔ cup sugar, and toss until bread is well mixed. Strain the cooled milk and add to the bread mixture. Toss again and pour into the buttered dish. Bake for 20 minutes, until top is browned.

Beat egg whites with ⅓ cup sugar until stiff. Spread the whites on top of cooled pudding. Put back in the oven for 10 minutes, until browned on top.

Put the remaining sugar and the egg yolks in a double boiler over low heat. Stir in the bourbon and continue to stir until well blended. Stirring, pour remaining milk in a thin stream into the hot mixture until mixture thickens, about 3 minutes. Cut pudding into nine squares and pour 2 teaspoons sauce over each square. *Serves 9.*

Per serving: 460 calories / 5 gm fat / 85 gm carbohydrate / 373 mg sodium

~ 11 ~
Gullah:
Sea Island Flavor

Tucked away in the Low Country of Georgia is a people who until recent times lived a life seemingly untouched by the twentieth century. Descended from the slaves on local rice plantations that fell into ruin after the Civil War, they lived on various islands off the coasts of South Carolina and Georgia for years by fishing and farming. They carried with them a precious African matrix of lore, language, and love of community, in pure form.

The first thing that strikes a visitor here is the warmth of the islands—not just the sunshine, but a smile on the face of practically everyone you see. And a sense of progress. During my stay at St. Helena's Island, I visited the Brick church, a historic house of worship, where a ceremony was in progress honoring some of the young parishioners who had just received their advanced degrees. When that was finished, a collection was taken up to help send Natasha Robinson, a local soon-to-be Olympic contender, to Spain.

And then there's food. And what food it is. The laughter and warmth and sun-struck soul of the islands come shining through in the local cooking. Oysters, shrimp, and crab were plentiful in the dishes; rice or grits were served with practically everything I ate—and boy, did I eat everything!

~ Shrimp and Corn Pie ~

One of the great things about eating shrimp in the Low Country is the guarantee of freshness. You're likely to have shrimp for dinner that were caught that very afternoon. Adding to the attraction is the fact that shrimp are less expensive there than what I'm used to shelling out, if you'll pardon the pun. This pie is like a corn pudding, only zestier, and with the addition of shrimp, it graduates from side dish to main course. Serve with a crisp salad.

1 pound shrimp, peeled and deveined	4 ears of corn, grated
1 tablespoon lemon juice	2 egg yolks
1 tablespoon butter	1 teaspoon salt
¼ cup chopped scallions	1 tablespoon powdered tapioca
½ cup chopped red bell pepper, seeded	¼ teaspoon cayenne
1 teaspoon very finely minced marjoram	1 tablespoon grated lemon zest
	¼ teaspoon nutmeg
3 tablespoons chopped parsley	½ teaspoon freshly ground white pepper
2 tablespoons finely chopped dill	1 tablespoon grated Parmesan cheese
	1 cup evaporated skim milk

Preheat the oven to 325 degrees F. Butter a large soufflé dish and set aside. Coarsely chop shrimp. Transfer to a large bowl and sprinkle lemon juice over them. Toss and set aside. Melt butter in a large nonstick skillet and add scallions. Cook for 5 minutes and add red bell pepper, marjoram, parsley, and dill. Add shrimp and cook for 2 to 3 minutes, until the shrimp turns pink. Remove from heat, add corn, and set aside. Combine yolks, salt, tapioca, cayenne, lemon zest, nutmeg, pepper, Parmesan, and milk in a large bowl and beat for a minute or so, until frothy. Pour egg mixture over shrimp mixture and toss gently, but thoroughly. Spoon into soufflé dish and bake for 1 hour.   *Serves 8.*

Per serving: 194 calories / 4 gm fat / 23 gm carbohydrate / 420 mg sodium

～ Shrimp and Grits Gratin ～

I was inspired by Sherry, the chef at the Gullah House restaurant on St. Helena Island, to create a low-fat version of this classic Low Country marriage of shrimp and grits.

1 **recipe Shrimp Marinade** *(page 115)*	1 **teaspoon grated lemon zest**
1 **pound shrimp, shelled and deveined**	2 **tablespoons chopped parsley**
4 **cups cooked grits**	½ **teaspoon salt**
	1 **teaspoon pepper**
	¼ **cup grated Parmesan cheese**

Butter a 2-quart casserole dish and set aside. Pour marinade over shrimp, toss, and let sit in the refrigerator for at least 2 hours. When you are ready to continue the recipe, preheat the oven to 350 degrees F. In a large mixing bowl, mix grits with lemon zest, parsley, salt, pepper, and half of the cheese. Add marinated shrimp, discarding marinade, and toss. Carefully pour the shrimp-grits mixture into the casserole and top with remaining cheese. Bake for 30 minutes.   *Serves 6.*

Per serving: 205 calories / 5 gm fat / 20 gm carbohydrate / 556 mg sodium

～ Shrimp Cakes ～

I was in Lady's Island when I first heard of a shrimp burger. I called every fish house in the phone book to find one that used fresh, not frozen, shrimp. I eventually found my shrimp burger: ground shrimp, deep-fried, on a seeded bun with a dollop of mayonnaise. It was an interesting idea, but I missed the solid texture of the shrimp between my teeth. The bun was not right either—it felt and tasted like the ghost of good bread. It deserved a little more flavor, I decided, so what did I do? I went home and invented one. Please do not put this favorite cake between anything less than two dazzling pieces of bread!

1½ **pounds shrimp, peeled and deveined**	½ **teaspoon Barbecue Shrimp Seasoning *(page* 7) or Old Bay Seasoning**

1 teaspoon minced shallots
½ teaspoon Worcestershire sauce
2 teaspoons Bread Crumbs
(page 16)
1 teaspoon reduced-fat mayonnaise
1 teaspoon Lemon Cayenne *(page 5)*

1 tablespoon chopped chives
1 tablespoon chopped parsley
1 teaspoon grated gingerroot
1 egg, beaten
2 teaspoons butter

Put raw shrimp into a food processor; pulse for just a few seconds, or chop by hand until coarsely ground. In a large bowl, mix together shrimp, barbecue seasoning, shallots, Worcestershire, bread crumbs, mayonnaise, lemon cayenne, chives, parsley, gingerroot, and egg. Shape into eight flattened-out patties and chill in the refrigerator for at least 1 hour. Melt 1 teaspoon butter in a 13-inch nonstick skillet. Put four patties in the pan and cook over medium heat for 4 minutes on each side, until browned. Drain on paper towels and repeat with the remaining patties and butter.   *Makes 8 patties.*

Per serving: 85 calories / 2 gm fat / 1 gm carbohydrate / 261 mg sodium

~ Breakfast Shrimp Gravy ~

Shrimp are so inexpensive in the Sea Islands that the locals eat them for breakfast, unlike myself, who could never quite envision shrimp and sunrise in the same room. It may take a bit of getting used to, and if it's too hard for you to fathom, cut the shrimp to ½ pound —the sauce will hold its own in this mouthwatering breakfast classic. Have a pot of hot grits handy.

1 medium onion, chopped
1 teaspoon olive oil
1 small green bell pepper, seeded
and chopped
2 stalks celery, chopped
2 tablespoons light Roux *(page 201)*
2 cups Vegetable Stock *(page 85)*
1 teaspoon Worcestershire sauce
½ cup stewed tomatoes

1 teaspoon salt
1 teaspoon freshly ground pepper
1 teaspoon ground sage
½ teaspoon Lemon Cayenne
(page 5)
2 teaspoons chopped savory
or thyme
1 pound shrimp, shelled and
deveined

In a large nonstick skillet, sauté the onions in oil over medium heat for 20 minutes, or until well browned. Add green bell pepper and celery and cook for 5 minutes more, until vegetables are softened. Blend in the roux, pour in the vegetable stock, and stir until thickened. Add Worcestershire sauce, tomatoes, salt, pepper, sage, lemon cayenne, and savory. Cover and simmer for 10 minutes, stirring occasionally. Add shrimp and simmer for 5 minutes more, until shrimp begin to lose their translucency. Remove skillet from heat. Let flavors develop for 10 minutes before serving.   Serves 4.

Per serving: 137 calories / 4 gm fat / 8 gm carbohydrate / 350 mg sodium

～ Crab Pie ～

Crabs are cheap; crabmeat, unfortunately, is not. The reason is that the labor that goes into picking the cartilage from the crabmeat is tedious and time-consuming, and, therefore, expensive. Often I'll steam a bunch of crabs the night before making a special dish, and hand-pick the meat out. Whichever method you choose, I'm sure you'll agree that this pie is worth either your money or your time.

1 pound lump crabmeat
2 eggs, beaten
1 tablespoon lemon juice
½ cup evaporated skim milk
1 teaspoon salt
½ teaspoon dry mustard
1 teaspoon Worcestershire sauce
2 teaspoons grated lemon zest
¼ teaspoon cayenne
1 tablespoon chopped parsley

1 tablespoon chopped fresh
   tarragon or 1 teaspoon dried
2 tablespoons snipped fresh
   chives or 2 teaspoons dried
1 teaspoon minced fresh chervil
   or ½ teaspoon dried
½ cup cracker crumbs
1 teaspoon freshly ground
   white pepper

Preheat the oven to 350 degrees F. Butter a 2-quart baking dish and set aside. Pick over the crabmeat to remove cartilage and put in a large bowl. In another bowl, blend the eggs, lemon juice, milk, salt, mustard, Worcestershire sauce, 1 teaspoon lemon zest, cayenne, parsley, tarragon, chives, and chervil, and half of the cracker crumbs. Pour the egg mixture over the crabmeat and toss gently until well mixed. Spoon the crab mixture evenly into the baking dish. In a small bowl, combine the remaining cracker crumbs with the remaining lemon zest and pepper, and sprinkle over the crabmeat mixture. Bake for 30 minutes, until browned on top.   *Makes 8 servings.*

Per serving: 131 calories / 3 gm fat / 10 gm carbohydrate / 413 mg sodium

~ Deviled Crab ~

This dish only needs to be matched with a side dish of equal subtlety, such as String Beans with Potatoes (page 148) or Field Greens with Vidalia Onion Vinaigrette (page 140).

1 pound lump crabmeat	1 egg, beaten
1 clove garlic, minced	1 teaspoon lemon juice
2 teaspoons chopped shallots	1 teaspoon grated lemon zest
1 tablespoon butter	2 teaspoons finely chopped
½ teaspoon cayenne	parsley
½ teaspoon mustard	1 teaspoon paprika
½ teaspoon salt	

Preheat the oven to 350 degrees F. Butter a large gratin dish and set aside. Pick over crabmeat to remove cartilage. In a small skillet, sauté the garlic and shallots in butter over medium heat for 3 minutes, until softened. In a large mixing bowl, gently toss the crabmeat with cayenne, mustard, salt, egg, lemon juice, zest, and parsley. Add the garlic mixture to the crabmeat. Spoon into the gratin dish and sprinkle with paprika. Bake for 20 minutes, until browned on top.   *Makes 6 servings.*

Per serving: 99 calories / 3 gm fat / 1 gm carbohydrate / 435 mg sodium

⌒ She-Crab Soup ⌒

Because I am not that fond of cream-based soups, I almost overlooked this culinary heirloom. I modified the creamy richness by incorporating equal portions of stock with evaporated skim milk, which has twice the density of whole milk without an ounce of fat.

1 tablespoon butter	¼ teaspoon cayenne
3 tablespoons flour	1 tablespoon chopped parsley
3 cups evaporated skim milk	½ teaspoon chopped tarragon
2 cups Fish Stock *(page 82)*	1 teaspoon minced chives
½ teaspoon salt	1 teaspoon grated lemon zest
¼ teaspoon ground sage	1 pound lump crabmeat,
¼ teaspoon nutmeg	cartilage removed
¼ teaspoon paprika	¼ cup dry sherry

Melt the butter in a Dutch oven over low heat and add flour, cooking for 1 to 2 minutes, until flour browns. Slowly add milk, stirring rapidly until liquid has thickened, about 3 minutes. Add stock, salt, sage, nutmeg, paprika, cayenne, parsley, tarragon, chives, and lemon zest, and simmer for 5 minutes. Flake in crabmeat and stir to mix. Pour in sherry and serve immediately.   *Serves 6.*

Per serving: 233 calories / 3 gm fat / 21 gm carbohydrate / 467 mg sodium

Quail

Like shrimp, quail was once abundant and therefore accessible to those without much money. In the past, the Gullah people ate wild quail regularly, and prepared it with much creativity. Today, quail is being raised and sold to many specialty stores, but can be a little expensive for serving at large gatherings. For information on obtaining quail through the mail, see List of Mail-Order Resources on page 268.

～ Braised Quail with Brown Onions ～

I like quail without all the fancy spices; it's so refined a bird, I simply want to savor the firm but delicate flesh. The bird really holds its own among the onions.

4 quail
1 teaspoon lemon juice
1 teaspoon salt
½ teaspoon freshly ground
   pepper
4 onions, sliced ⅛ inch thick

1 tablespoon olive oil
½ cup dry vermouth
1 teaspoon Dried Herbs Mix
   (page 8) or fines herbes
¼ cup evaporated skim milk

With a sharp knife, split the quail down the backbone. Press down on the quail with the palm of your hand to flatten each side out. Sprinkle with lemon juice, ½ teaspoon salt, and pepper and set aside. In a large nonstick skillet, sauté the onions in oil over medium heat for 25 minutes, tossing often, until onions are reddish-brown in color. Remove onions from pan, add remaining salt to onions, and place quail in the pan, breast side down, and cook for 7 minutes, until quail is browned. Turn quail over and cook for 4 minutes more. Remove quail from pan and add vermouth, stirring to dislodge the browned bits. Add herbs and milk and decrease heat to low, while continuing to stir. Return the onions to the pan and lay the quail atop the bed of onions. Cover and simmer for 30 minutes, until flesh is tender but firm.   *Serves 4.*

NOTE: Fines herbes can be obtained at almost any supermarket.

Per serving: 329 calories / 14 gm fat / 10 gm carbohydrate / 341 mg sodium

∽ Smothered Quail over Savory French Toast ∾

Quail over toast was once a popular dish in the Low Country. But unless I'm using fresh-baked bread, the combination doesn't quite do it for me. The exception is when I make an evening version of the classic French Toast to complement the quail.

4 quail
1 teaspoon salt
1 tablespoon butter
2 tablespoons chopped chives
1 teaspoon very finely minced tarragon
2 cups Chicken Stock *(page 81)*

2 teaspoons arrowroot mixed with ¼ cup water
1 teaspoon Burnt Caramel *(page 202)*
2 tablespoons dry sherry
4 triangles of Savory French Toast *(recipe follows)*

Clip the wings of each quail. Split the quail down the backbone with a sharp knife. Flatten out each side with the palm of the hand. Sprinkle the quail inside and out with salt. In a large nonstick skillet melt the butter over medium heat until butter begins to foam. Arrange all the quail in the pan, breast side down, and cook each side for 7 minutes, until evenly browned. Remove quail from pan. Add chives, tarragon, and stock to the skillet; increase heat and bring to a boil. Add arrowroot mixture and stir for 2 to 3 minutes, until thickened. Stir in burnt caramel and sherry and remove from heat.

Return quail to the skillet and simmer over low heat, covered, for 25 minutes, until flesh is tender. Place each quail on four points of savory French toast and spoon gravy over all.   *Serves 4.*

Per serving: 293 calories / 13 gm fat / 3 gm carbohydrate / 376 mg sodium

Savory French Toast

1 egg

1 cup evaporated skim milk

½ teaspoon salt

½ teaspoon freshly ground
white pepper

1 teaspoon grated lemon zest

½ teaspoon ground sage

¼ teaspoon cayenne

1 tablespoon brandy

4 slices of bread

Oil a large nonstick griddle and heat over medium-high heat. In a large shallow bowl, combine egg, milk, salt, pepper, lemon zest, sage, and cayenne, and beat until frothy. Pour in brandy and beat for a few seconds more. Mop the egg mixture up with both sides of the bread slices and place the bread on the hot griddle. Cook for 2 minutes on each side, until well browned. Cut each slice four ways, into points.   *Serves 4.*

Per serving: 138 calories / 2 gm fat / 20 gm carbohydrate / 223 mg sodium

～ Grilled Quail with
Oyster Bread Pudding ～

Here's a great dish for an intimate holiday gathering. The oyster bread pudding is a good match for the understated quail. Brown Sherry Gravy (page 203) is a great accompaniment.

4 quail

1 recipe Poultry Marinade
(page 126)

Oyster Bread Pudding
(recipe follows)

Split quail down the backbone and press flat with the palm of the hand. Pour marinade over the quail and let sit in the refrigerator for at least 4 hours. Preheat the broiler. Place quail, breast side up, on a rack on the lowest rung of the broiler, and grill between 10 and 15 minutes (depending on the position of the rack), until evenly browned. Turn over and grill for 10 minutes more, until brown. Serve alongside a square of oyster bread pudding.   *Serves 4.*

Per serving: 241 calories / 12 gm fat / 1 gm carbohydrate / 56 mg sodium

Oyster Bread Pudding

12 oysters, shucked, reserving
    oyster liquor *(see page 186
    for preparation)*
4 cups evaporated skim milk
1 loaf of stale French bread,
    broken up
2 tablespoons butter, softened
2 teaspoons Brown Onions
    (page 12)

1 stalk celery, finely chopped
1 teaspoon very finely minced
    tarragon
1 egg
1 teaspoon salt
1 teaspoon Pernod or
    ¼ teaspoon anise extract
Pinch of cayenne

Place oysters in a large skillet. Cook over low heat for 3 minutes, just until the edges begin to curl, and remove from heat. Chop coarsely and set aside. Preheat the oven to 350 degrees F. Butter an 8-inch-square baking dish and set aside. Pour milk into a saucepan and heat until near boiling and remove from heat. Put bread, butter, onions, celery, and tarragon into a large mixing bowl and gently toss until well mixed. Strain the cooled milk and beat into it the oyster liquor, egg, salt, Pernod, and cayenne. Pour into the bread mixture. Add the oysters and gently toss until well mixed. Pour into the buttered dish and bake for 20 minutes, until golden on top. Cut into squares.   *Makes 9 squares.*

Per serving: 269 calories / 5 gm fat / 40 gm carbohydrate / 431 mg sodium

～ Brown Oyster Stew with Mushrooms ～

This stew is simple to prepare, yet it has the depth of an intricate dish. Serve it with Sweet Potato Cornbread (page 76) and Herbed Rice (page 107).

18 oysters shucked, reserving
    liquor *(see page 186 for
    preparation)*
1 teaspoon olive oil
¼ cup finely chopped onion

1 cup thinly sliced mushrooms
2 tablespoons Roux *(page 201)*
2 cups Shrimp Stock *(page 83)*
    or clam juice
1 cup water

1 teaspoon salt
1 teaspoon freshly ground
     pepper
  Pinch of cayenne
1 teaspoon finely minced
     marjoram

2 tablespoons finely minced
     parsley
3 tablespoons dry sherry
1 teaspoon Burnt Caramel
     (page 202)

In a large, heavy, preferably cast-iron pot, cook the oysters over medium heat for 2 minutes, until the edges begin to curl. Remove oysters from pot and set aside. In the same pan, add oil and sauté the onion and mushrooms for 10 minutes, until softened. Add roux, along with the stock, and cook for 2–3 minutes, occasionally stirring while the liquid thickens. Continuing to stir, add reserved oyster liquor and water to the pot, and add salt, pepper, cayenne, marjoram, and parsley. Let simmer for 10 minutes, covered, until thick enough to coat a spoon. Add oysters, sherry, and burnt caramel, and let flavors develop for 5 minutes off the stove. *Serves 6.*

Per serving: 87 calories / 3 gm fat / 4 gm carbohydrate / 290 mg sodium

～ Oyster Purlo ～

This dish looks uninteresting, but it's a sleeper—whenever I serve it, it is the last thing that people put on their plates and the first to go.

12 oysters, shucked, reserving
     liquor *(see page 186 for
     preparation)*
1 medium onion, finely chopped
1 tablespoon olive oil
3 cloves garlic, minced

1 teaspoon thyme leaves
1 cup uncooked long-grain rice
1 teaspoon salt
1 teaspoon freshly ground pepper
1 teaspoon grated lemon zest
2 cups Vegetable Stock *(page 85)*

In a large nonstick skillet, cook the oysters over low heat until the edges begin to curl. Remove oysters from pan, chop coarsely, and set aside. In the same pan, sauté onion in oil over medium-high heat for 20 minutes, until golden brown. Add garlic and thyme, mixing thoroughly for 5 minutes. Toss in rice, salt, pepper, and lemon zest, tossing rice thoroughly with the onion mixture. Pour in reserved oyster liquor and stock, and cover. Simmer for 20 minutes, until rice is tender.   *Serves 4.*

Per serving: 199 calories / 4 gm fat / 34 gm carbohydrate / 447 mg sodium

～ Gullah Rice ～

There are so many variations of this rice, I'm not sure which is the authentic one—but I had plenty of fun creating my own version.

¼ **cup pistachio nuts**	3 **cups water**
½ **cup chopped celery**	1 **teaspoon salt**
½ **cup chopped carrots**	1 **tablespoon thyme leaves**
1 **teaspoon butter**	1 **cup uncooked long-grain rice**

In a 2-quart saucepan, sauté the nuts, celery, and carrots in butter for 5 minutes over medium heat, until vegetables are softened. Add water and salt, and bring to a boil. Add thyme and rice and bring to a second boil. Reduce heat and cover, simmering for 20 minutes, or until rice is cooked.   *Serves 6.*

Per serving: 126 calories / 3 gm fat / 23 gm carbohydrate / 378 mg sodium

~ 12 ~

Oyster House

Now, for all those newcomers wondering—How does the oyster fit into the down-home category?—I'll tell you a couple of ways. Way back when, in the late 1800s when oysters were plentiful and cheap, there were societies of Africans who devoted themselves to the art of oyster cultivation, primarily as shuckers and tongers (rakers) for the oyster houses in various small towns. Like the position of a sharecropper, it was a thankless job, tedious and low paying, with no chance for advancement. Had these oystermen had the cash to open their own oyster houses, they could have dominated the industry, for they had a monopoly on their special skill. A few took their abilities elsewhere and managed to open oyster houses along the Southern coast, but many had no more than a muscular torso to show for all their hard work.

Oysters were also a large part of the Gullah culture, and were used in stews and mixed with rice to make an incredible pilau. The Creole culture embraced the tasty mollusks as well, roasting them, stuffing them into French bread, and tossing a bunch in a hot pot of gumbo at the last minute. And who can go south without sampling the taste of an oyster in a crispy corn-meal crust?

I can remember being quite traumatized by my first experience with oysters. It was on a sunny fall afternoon, right after Labor Day, and we were having our final summer outing, with a lot of unexpected family members showing up. Abundance was key at these events, and so there were crabs, clams, sweet corn on the cob, apple and peach pies, and—the topper—a Brown Cow, custom-made by Mom: foamy root beer, with a giant scoop of vanilla ice cream on top. The adults were playing pinochle and Pokeno®, and Fats Domino's "Blueberry Hill" was spinning on the record player. Grandpop Carey, Nana's first husband (Nana was on speaking terms with all her ex-husbands), had popped in from Harlem with a small bushel of raw oysters. Grandpop Carey brandished his bushel sack and, knowing I'd never tried one before, offered me the staggering sum of a dollar for every oyster I ate. With everyone watching, Grandpop Carey shucked an oyster, dabbed it with a spot of Creole sauce, and squirted on a little lemon. I gulped, but was determined to go through with it. In a flash the oyster was in my mouth; just as quickly, that same oyster was lying relatively unscathed on our neighbor's, Miss Peanut's, lap. "I can't do it," I said. "It tastes too much like baloney dipped in seawater!" I got the dollar for my bravado, but didn't touch an oyster for 15 years after that. As I look back at the years I missed out on oysters I say to myself, "What a loss!" How could I have rejected that velvety texture, the briny aftertaste? Believe me, I've tried to make up for it.

I'm amused by the mysteries surrounding the oyster: their midlife sex-change; the alleged aphrodisiacal effect they have on people; the theory about eating oysters only in the *R* months (you can eat them anytime; however, they usually become soft and fatty during the summer months when they are spawning; they are in their prime in the fall); the danger of eating them raw (incidentally, a little Tabasco sauce helps to kill much of the bacteria that thrives in raw oysters). I love oysters in all shapes and forms, raw, cooked, plain, or dolled up in a dish, and I enjoy the entire process of eating them, from the first shuck to the last drop of salty liquor.

If this is your first time with oysters, you might want to have them pre-shucked. Buy them fresh at your local market and ask to have them shucked. It shouldn't cost any more to do that and if it does, you're in the wrong store. You may want to ask the shucker to leave a couple unshucked and practice at home.

To prepare and shuck oysters, scrub the shells clean with a vegetable brush. Take a potholder or a tea towel and put it in your left hand (right, if you are a lefty). Place the oyster, cupped side facing downward, in the palm of your hand, with the hinged edge facing away from you. Keep your hand level so that once the oyster is opened, the liquor doesn't spill over. Using a knife with a broad pointed blade, carefully force the blade into the shell at the hinge, twisting it slightly to ease penetration of the knife into the shell. The top shell should relax. Place the knife along the inside of the upper shell and cut the muscle attached to the shell. Do the same along the bottom shell. Pour the juice of the oyster, which is most often referred to as liquor, into a cup and *voilà!* Once you learn to shuck your own oysters, you'll never return to the preshucked. Eat as many as you like, for they are high in calcium, niacin, iron, and protein. Now that we've got those oysters open, let's find something to do with them!

~ Oysters on the Half-Shell with Three Sauces ~

There was a time when oysters on the half-shell before dinner were all the rage. Now, a lot of people are cautious about eating them because of bacterial diseases linked to raw seafood. Recently we've been given evidence that Louisiana hot sauce destroys certain bacteria that thrive in raw oysters. Except for the most cautious, people are delighted when you bring out a skillfully arranged tray of fresh oysters with homemade sauces. Try it sometime, and make sure you have plenty of hot sauce on hand.

36 oysters *(see page 186 for preparation)*	**Hot Herb Broth *(recipe follows)***
Fresh seaweed or lettuce	**Chili-Lemon Butter *(recipe follows)***
3 lemons	
Bloody Mary Sauce *(recipe follows)*	

Shuck oysters and leave them in their bottom shells, along with their liquor. Place them on a large platter that has been garnished with shaved ice and the fresh seaweed. Cut the lemons into thin wedges and place them in a small dish. Squirt oysters with lemon juice just before applying individual sauces.   *Makes 6 servings.*

NOTE: Fresh seaweed can be bought at Asian groceries.

Per serving: 67 calories / 2 gm fat / 9 gm carbohydrate / 182 mg sodium

Bloody Mary Sauce

1 pound tomatoes
1 teaspoon tomato paste
1 chili pepper *(see page 10 for handling instructions)*
2 tablespoons vodka, iced
1 tablespoon chopped shallots
1 tablespoon chopped scallions

1 tablespoon chopped celery
2 tablespoons freshly grated horseradish
1 teaspoon salt
1 teaspoon Lemon Pepper *(page 5)*

In a food processor, puree the tomatoes, tomato paste, pepper, and vodka. Transfer to a medium-sized bowl and add shallots, scallions, celery, horseradish, salt, and lemon pepper. Toss and chill.   *Makes 1 cup.*

Per serving (1 tablespoon): 13 calories / 0 gm fat / 2 gm carbohydrate / 139 mg sodium

Hot Herb Broth

2 tablespoons chopped shallots
4 cloves garlic, crushed
1 teaspoon butter
1 teaspoon very finely minced marjoram

2 tablespoons finely chopped basil leaves
3 tablespoons chopped parsley
1 cup Shrimp Stock *(page 83)*
¼ cup dry white wine

In a small nonstick skillet, sauté shallots and garlic in butter for 5 minutes over low heat, until shallots are translucent; add herbs and remove from heat. In a small saucepan, bring stock to a rapid boil; reduce heat to medium, add wine, and cook for 2–3 minutes more, until bubbles form around the edges of the pan. Pour boiling stock into garlic-herb mixture and stir. Place in a small heatproof dish.   *Makes 1 cup.*

Per serving (2 tablespoons): 22 calories / 0 gm fat / 1 gm carbohydrate / 15 mg sodium

Chili-Lemon Butter

¼ cup butter
Juice of 3 lemons

1 small chili pepper, seeded and diced *(see page 10 for handling instructions)*

Melt butter in a small saucepan over low heat; add juice and pepper and cook for 1 minute more.   *Makes ⅓ cup.*

Per serving (1 teaspoon): 26 calories / 2 gm fat / 0 gm carbohydrate / 29 mg sodium

～ Oyster Roast ～

Oyster roasts were once a community occasion, as much of a public event as the ever-popular fish fry. People would gather around a big grill, watch bushels of oysters being thrown into a large steel pan above the coals, and just wait, salivating, for the shells to pop open. Everywhere would be sounds of the shells cracking open, the supping of the oyster liquor, and the groans of delight.

36 oysters
2 lemons, cut into 8 wedges

Creole Sauce *(page 200)*

Preheat grill for 15 minutes. Put oysters in a large roasting pan and place on the grill, about 5 inches away from the coals. Roast for 15 minutes, or until shells begin to open. Serve with lemon wedges and Creole sauce.   *Serves 6.*

Per serving: 64 calories / 1 gm fat / 7 gm carbohydrate / 181 mg sodium

~ Pickled Oysters ~

For centuries pickling was one of the main ways of preserving foods, since there were no fridges or freezers around in those days. Today people pickle as a hobby, to stock up for the winter, or just because they love the tartness of pickled foods. Oysters bring their own brininess to the already briny pickling liquid.

½ cup Brown Onions *(page 12)*
24 oysters, shucked, reserving liquor *(see page 186 for preparation)*
1 teaspoon fennel seed
1 teaspoon freshly ground black pepper

2 cups white vinegar
1 cup beer
1 teaspoon salt
Zest of 1 lemon, avoiding bitter white pith
12 allspice berries

Put onions, oysters and reserved liquor, fennel seed, and pepper in a 1-quart Mason-type jar. In a 2-quart saucepan, combine vinegar, beer, salt, lemon zest, and allspice berries, and bring to a boil. Pour vinegar mixture into oyster jar, filling to about 1 inch from the top. Seal tightly and store. Eat within the week, or see instructions for canning (page 207). *Serves 4.*

Per serving: 126 calories / 3 gm fat / 24 gm carbohydrate / 363 mg sodium

~ Baked Oysters ~

For those who are still gun-shy about eating raw oysters, this is a pleasant alternative.

2 teaspoons butter
2 cloves garlic
2 tablespoons minced shallots
1 cup Cornbread Crumbs *(page 17)* or regular bread crumbs
¼ teaspoon cayenne

½ teaspoon salt
1 teaspoon finely minced tarragon
½ cup dry vermouth
½ cup Shrimp Stock *(page 83)*
36 oysters, shucked, reserving liquor *(see page 186 for preparation)*

Preheat the oven to 450 degrees F. Butter a large gratin dish or 6 rame-kins. In a heavy saucepan, melt butter over low heat. Add garlic and shallots, and sauté for 5 minutes, until garlic is lightly browned. In a medium mixing bowl, combine cornbread crumbs, cayenne, salt, tarragon, vermouth, stock, and reserved oyster liquor, and toss until well mixed. Pour in the butter mix-ture and continue tossing. Put oysters into baking dish or ramekins and spoon bread crumb mixture on top. Bake for 25 minutes, until cornbread is well browned.   *Serves 6.*

Per serving: 134 calories / 3 gm fat / 11 gm carbohydrate / 499 mg sodium

∼ Deviled Oysters ∼

Don't be deceived by the title—this dish is heaven-sent.

2 **stalks celery, finely chopped**	½ **teaspoon salt**
1 **teaspoon butter**	¼ **teaspoon cayenne**
24 **oysters, shucked, reserving liquor *(see page 186 for preparation)***	1 **teaspoon grated lemon zest**
	2 **tablespoons chopped parsley**
1 **cup finely chopped Brown Onions *(page 12)***	1 **cup Cornbread Crumbs *(page 17)***
1 **teaspoon Worcestershire sauce**	

Preheat the oven to 325 degrees F. Butter a 2-quart baking dish and set aside. In a large nonstick skillet, sauté celery in butter over low heat for 15 minutes, or until browned. Add oysters and cook for 2 minutes, just until the edges of the oysters begin to curl, and remove from heat. Add reserved oyster liquor, onions, Worcestershire, salt, cayenne, lemon zest, parsley, and half the cornbread crumbs, and toss gently to mix. Spoon the mixture into the baking dish and sprinkle the remaining crumbs over. Bake for 30 minutes, until top is browned.   *Makes 8 servings.*

Per serving: 61 calories / 2 gm fat / 7 gm carbohydrate / 333 mg sodium

～ Creamed Oysters over Toast ～

This is my partner Eli's favorite breakfast treat. On those rare weekends that we're home alone, I'll occasionally make him breakfast in bed, which involves squeezing a half-dozen oranges into juice, and serving a generous helping of this.

18 oysters, shucked, reserving
   liquor *(see page 186 for
   preparation)*
2 tablespoons light Roux
   (page 201)
¼ cup chopped shallots
1½ cups evaporated skim milk
1 teaspoon salt
½ teaspoon freshly ground
   white pepper

¼ teaspoon cayenne
½ teaspoon paprika
2 tablespoons chopped parsley
1 teaspoon grated gingerroot
½ teaspoon grated lemon zest
3 very finely minced basil leaves
2 tablespoons dry sherry
4 pieces toast sliced into
   quarters

Put the oysters in a medium saucepan and cook for 2 minutes, until they begin to curl. Remove oysters from pan, chop coarsely, and set aside. Heat the roux in a heavy skillet over medium heat and add shallots, tossing to mix. Add oyster liquid and milk in increments, stirring briskly with a wooden spoon. Stir in the salt, pepper, cayenne, paprika, parsley, ginger, lemon zest, and basil leaves and simmer over low heat for 4 to 5 minutes, until thickened. Remove from heat and add sherry and oysters. Serve on toast points.   *Makes 4 servings.*

Per serving: 181 calories / 4 gm fat / 24 gm carbohydrate / 478 mg sodium

～ Oysters in Cornmeal Crust ～

This savory classic has been revised so that we can enjoy this unusual treat without having to deep-fry.

18 large oysters, shucked *(see page 186 for preparation)*
½ cup cornmeal
1 teaspoon freshly ground pepper
¼ teaspoon cayenne
½ teaspoon ground sage
½ teaspoon salt
3 to 4 teaspoons olive oil

Drain oysters and discard liquor. In a shallow bowl, combine cornmeal, pepper, cayenne, sage, and salt and mix well. Dredge the oysters in cornmeal mixture and refrigerate for at least ½ hour. Heat 1 teaspoon oil in a large non-stick skillet over medium-high heat for 3 minutes, occasionally spreading the oil around the pan with a pastry brush. Carefully place oysters in pan, and cook for 1 minute, until golden brown. Turn over and cook for an additional minute, to brown the other side. Remove and drain on paper towels. Remove excess crumbs from pan and add an additional teaspoon of oil. Repeat until all oysters are cooked.   *Makes 6 servings.*

Per serving: 101 calories / 4 gm fat / 11 gm carbohydrate / 298 mg sodium

~ Oyster Pie ~

This is an excellent winter holiday appetizer, preceding Braised Quail with Brown Onions (page 179), Stewed Greens with Cornmeal Dumplings (page 43), Sweet-Hot Yams (page 53), Yeast Rolls (page 65), Persimmon Custard (page 245), and Syllabub (page 227).

24 oysters, shucked, reserving liquor *(see page 186 for preparation)*
1 cup grated cooked shrimp
½ cup finely chopped cooked mushrooms
2 cups cracker crumbs
½ cup chopped shallots
1 tablespoon butter
½ cup dry white wine

2 tablespoons chopped parsley
½ teaspoon fennel seed, crushed
1 teaspoon finely minced marjoram
2 cups evaporated skim milk
2 eggs
1 teaspoon salt
2 teaspoons ground tapioca
⅛ teaspoon cayenne

Preheat the oven to 325 degrees F. Butter a 2-quart baking dish. In a large skillet, cook oysters in their liquor over medium heat for 2 minutes, until the edges begin to ruffle; remove oysters from pan and discard any oyster liquor that remains. Place oysters in a large bowl and toss with shrimp, mushrooms, and cracker crumbs. In a medium skillet, sauté the shallots in butter over medium heat for 8 minutes, or until shallots begin to turn brown. Add wine to the pan and stir to mix. Toss in parsley, fennel, and marjoram and remove from heat. Add shallot mixture to oyster mixture and toss gently. Beat milk, eggs, salt, tapioca, and cayenne together and pour over oysters. Spoon into baking dish and bake for 1 hour, until puffed and brown on top. *Makes 8 servings.*

Per serving: 188 calories / 5 gm fat / 23 gm carbohydrate / 436 mg sodium

∼ Oyster Omelet ∼

This one takes a little more time and effort than the average omelet, but I promise you it's worth it.

3 large oysters, shucked, reserving liquor *(see page 186 for preparation)*
2 tablespoons chopped onion
1 teaspoon olive oil
1 clove garlic, crushed
2 tablespoons minced celery
2 tablespoons very finely minced green bell pepper
1 teaspoon brandy
¼ cup evaporated skim milk

1 teaspoon very finely minced marjoram
1 teaspoon butter
6 egg whites
⅛ teaspoon salt
½ teaspoon freshly ground white pepper
¼ teaspoon ground sage
¼ teaspoon Lemon Cayenne *(page 5)*

In a small nonstick sauté pan, cook oysters over low heat for 2 minutes, until edges begin to curl; remove from pan, and set aside. In the same pan sauté onion in olive oil for 5 minutes, until transparent; add garlic and cook for 1 minute, until garlic is lightly browned. Increase heat to medium high, toss in celery and pepper, and pour in brandy. Add milk and marjoram and stir to mix. Add oysters and reserved liquor and remove from heat. Melt butter in a 9-inch nonstick omelet pan over medium heat.

In a small mixing bowl, combine egg whites, salt, pepper, sage, and lemon cayenne. Whip until frothy and pour into the hot pan. Increase heat to medium-high and cook for 3 minutes, until bottom begins to brown. Flip the omelet over and place the oyster filling on one side. Cook for 1 minute more, until set, and fold omelet in half, covering all the filling. Serve immediately. *Makes 2 servings.*

Per serving: 146 calories / 5 gm fat / 9 gm carbohydrate / 273 mg sodium

~ Oyster Mush ~

This is one of those comfort dishes, like mashed potatoes, that I like to eat when it's rainy outside or when I'm just not feeling up to par.

12 oysters, shucked, reserving
    liquor *(see page 186*
    for preparation)
3 cups water
⅛ teaspoon anise extract
1 teaspoon salt

1 clove garlic, crushed
1 cup cornmeal
½ teaspoon grated lemon zest
¼ teaspoon crushed red pepper
1 tablespoon olive oil

In a large cast-iron skillet, cook oysters for 2 minutes over medium heat, until edges ruffle; remove from pan, chop coarsely, and set aside. Wipe the skillet clean and season with a little oil. In a 2-quart saucepan, combine water, anise, salt, garlic, and cornmeal and bring to a boil. Decrease heat to medium and cook for 15 minutes, constantly stirring, until cornmeal begins to pull from the bottom. Remove from heat and add oysters, reserved liquor, lemon zest, and crushed pepper. Heat the oil in the cast-iron skillet over medium-high heat. When the skillet is hot enough to make a drop of water sizzle, pour the meal mixture into the skillet and reduce the heat to low. Cook without stirring for 5 to 8 minutes, until a crust forms on the bottom. Scrape the crust into the rest of the mush and repeat the process of cooking and scraping until most of the cornmeal mixture is browned. *Makes 6 servings.*

Per serving: 124 calories / 2 gm fat / 19 gm carbohydrate / 436 mg sodium

～ Oyster-Cornbread Stuffing ～

This is an excellent stuffing for large fish.

1 tablespoon butter	½ cup chopped shallots
12 large oysters, shucked, reserving liquor *(see page 186 for preparation)*	4 cups crumbled cornbread
	1½ cups Shrimp Stock *(page 83)*
	1 teaspoon salt
1 cup chopped celery	½ teaspoon freshly ground
3 tablespoons chopped parsley	black pepper

In a large skillet, melt the butter and sauté the oysters for 2 minutes over low heat, until the edges begin to curl. Remove oysters, chop coarsely, and put into a large mixing bowl. Preheat oven to 325 degrees F. Butter a large soufflé dish and set aside. Sauté the celery, parsley, and shallots for 5 minutes over low heat, until softened. Place in the mixing bowl with the oysters and add the crumbled cornbread, reserved oyster liquor, stock, salt, and pepper; toss thoroughly to mix. Pack into the buttered dish and bake for 20 to 25 minutes, until browned on top.   *Serves 8.*

Per serving: 134 calories / 3 gm fat / 16 gm carbohydrate / 545 mg sodium

~ 13 ~

Extraordinary Extras

I have a high regard for "the extras," those enhancers whose function in the culinary theater is to make the leading lights shine more brightly. Their supporting role should not be underestimated. Where, after all, would Grilled Quail with Oyster Bread Pudding be without the crucial addition of Brown Sherry Gravy? And what makes this good gravy but a properly nurtured Roux and a dash of Burnt Caramel to deepen the color? And yes, I could simply grill my chicken over hot coals—but why, when I've got a delightful Barbecue Sauce to marinate it in?

Sometimes these extras will lend a single, all-important aha! to a dish. Other times they'll simply add contrast to an already complete blend of flavors. Some of the extras are appetizers, and do just as the word implies: whet the taste buds for what's to follow. Here's to the value of bit players, the special significance of their task.

~ Barbecue Sauce ~

Barbecue sauce can be easily bought at your local grocer at a reasonable price, but have you taken the time to read the ingredient labels on the back of some of those bottles? Some of them sound like a spill at a poison gas plant. Of course you can spend a bit more to get one that has been made with "natural" ingredients, but since they are bottled without preservatives they spoil pretty easily. My solution is to go to the cupboard. Most likely, you'll find there all the ingredients you need to make a robust and tangy sauce of your own. Marinate the chicken (or fish) overnight in it and you'll have a juicy item on your hands.

1 small onion, minced
3 cloves garlic, crushed
1 tablespoon butter
1 tablespoon finely minced
    gingerroot
¼ cup dark brown sugar
½ cup tomato puree
2 tablespoons tomato paste
½ cup red wine
½ cup dark beer
1 tablespoon Worcestershire
    sauce

2 tablespoons balsamic vinegar
1 teaspoon Dijon mustard
1 teaspoon salt
1 teaspoon ground sage
1 teaspoon Lemon Pepper
    (page 5)
3 sprigs of thyme
1 hot chili pepper, seeded and
    finely chopped *(see page 10 for
    handling instructions)*
½ teaspoon ground cumin

In a 2-quart saucepan, sauté onion and garlic in butter over medium heat. Add remaining ingredients, increase heat to high, and bring to a boil. Reduce heat to low and simmer for 25 minutes, until thickened.   *Makes 2 cups.*

Per serving (1 tablespoon): 11 calories / 1 gm fat / 1 gm carbohydrate / 96 mg sodium

~ Creole Sauce ~

This sauce is used in New Orleans the way most people use ketchup. Use it to accent the flavor of cooked fish and chicken, dunk an oyster in it, or just have it on the side of the plate for those flavor emergencies.

1 large tomato, peeled, seeded, and coarsely chopped
1 red bell pepper, seeded and coarsely chopped
1 hot chili pepper, seeded *(see page 10 for handling instructions)*

2 cloves garlic, crushed
¼ cup chopped shallots
1 teaspoon grated lemon zest
2 tablespoons lime juice
1 tablespoon dry sherry
2 tablespoons chopped parsley

Puree the tomato, red bell pepper, and chili pepper in a food processor until smooth; transfer to a medium mixing bowl. Add garlic, shallots, lemon zest, lime juice, sherry, and parsley and toss until well mixed. Serve cold.   *Makes ½ cup.*

Per serving (1 tablespoon): 16 calories / 0 gm fat / 3 gm carbohydrate / 3 mg sodium

~ Peppered Rum ~

This power-packed sauce can bring new life to a bowl of greens. But use with caution.

1 Scotch bonnet pepper, seeded *(see page 10 for handling instructions)*

2 cups dark rum

Make slits in the sides of the pepper and place it in a tightly lidded jar. Pour the rum over the pepper and let it sit in a cool dark place for 24 hours. Strain and refrigerate, for up to a month.   *Makes 1 pint.*

Per serving (1 tablespoon): 18 calories / 0 gm fat / 0 gm carbohydrate / 1 mg sodium

～ Rhubarb Applesauce ～

The sweet-tartness of this dish makes it a good partner for spicy foods, such as Barbecued Shrimp (page 158). It also makes a good topping for vanilla ice cream or frozen yogurt.

4 cups apple juice	½ teaspoon allspice
2 pounds Golden Delicious apples, cored and peeled, about 5 or 6	½ teaspoon cinnamon
	¼ teaspoon nutmeg
	12 stalks rhubarb, coarsely chopped

Cook the apple juice over medium-high heat until it is the consistency of syrup, about 8 to 10 minutes, watching constantly so that it doesn't brown. Quarter apples and place in a heavy, lidded pot. Pour in apple juice, add allspice, cinnamon, and nutmeg, and cook for 15 minutes, until the apples begin to break down. Add the rhubarb and cook, covered, for 20 minutes over low heat until the apples and rhubarb blend together into a mush. Continue to cook for another 10 minutes, until pinkish in color, stirring occasionally. Serve at room temperature.   *Makes 6 servings.*

Per serving: 356 calories / 2 gm fat / 85 gm carbohydrate / 39 mg sodium

～ Light or Dark Roux ～

There are two main grades of roux: light and dark. Light roux is better for thickening, since its starch granules —the swelling agent—aren't as damaged by high heat. Dark roux is better used for giving sauces additional flavor. I keep a bit of each around the kitchen. Since I use only 1 or 2 tablespoons of roux at a time, I freeze roux in an ice cube tray and pop one or two cubes out as I need it.

1 cup olive oil	1 cup flour

Heat the oil in a heavy skillet over medium heat. When the oil is hot, add the flour, whisking briskly to prevent lumps. If lumps do form, smooth them out with the back of a wooden spoon. Reduce heat to very low. Cook for at least 45 minutes, stirring often. For a dark roux, cook for an additional 10 minutes. If roux burns, discard and try again. When roux is cooked, immediately pour it into a heat-resistant bowl and whisk for 10 minutes. Refrigerate for up to 3 days, or freeze.   *Makes 1 cup.*

Per serving (1 tablespoon): 98 calories / 9 gm fat / 4 gm carbohydrate / 0 mg sodium

~ Burnt Caramel ~

People often buy a bottle of "instant color" from the supermarket to turn their pallid homemade gravy or sauce into a rich brown hue, when the same effect can be achieved with just minutes at the stove—and for a few pennies less. Just a small amount of this caramel will turn your gravy a deep, deep brown.

1 cup packed dark brown sugar	**½ cup boiling water**

In a 1-quart saucepan, melt sugar over medium heat for 15 minutes, stirring often, until it becomes deep brown in color. Stir in boiling water and let cool. Pour into a heavy jar with a tight-fitting lid, and store in the refrigerator, for up to a month.   *Makes 1 cup.*

Per serving (1 tablespoon): 25 calories / 0 gm fat / 6 gm carbohydrate / 2 mg sodium

～ Brown Sherry Gravy ～

Try a little of this on top of a hot stack of Oyster-Corn Griddle Cakes (page 32).

2 tablespoons light Roux
    (page 201)
2 cups Chicken Stock *(page 81)*
    or Vegetable Stock *(page 85)*
¼ cup dry sherry
1 teaspoon Burnt Caramel
    (page 202)

½ teaspoon salt
½ teaspoon freshly ground
    black pepper
2 tablespoons chopped parsley

In a large nonstick skillet, heat roux over medium heat, stirring, for 1 minute, or until melted. Slowly pour in the stock, sherry, and burnt caramel and cook for 5 minutes, stirring, until gravy begins to thicken. Add salt, pepper, and parsley and serve.   *Makes 1 pint.*

Per serving (2 tablespoons): 24 calories / 1 gm fat / 1 gm carbohydrate / 82 mg sodium

～ Red Pepper Gravy ～

This gravy mixes sweet and hot red peppers to deepen the flavor base. Perfect on Rice and Shrimp Waffles (page 30) and great over any type of grits.

2 teaspoons olive oil
¼ cup chopped shallots
2 sweet red peppers, seeded
    and finely chopped
1 red chili pepper, seeded
    and finely chopped *(see
    page 10 for handling
    instructions)*
½ cup red wine
2 cups Chicken Stock *(page 81)*
    or Vegetable Stock *(page 85)*

1 bay leaf
3 sprigs of thyme
2 teaspoons arrowroot mixed
    with ¼ cup water
½ teaspoon salt
1 teaspoon freshly ground
    pepper
    Pinch of cayenne
4 tablespoons chopped parsley

Heat oil in a large skillet over medium heat. Add shallots, red peppers, and chili pepper, and sauté for 5 minutes, until vegetables are cooked but not wilted. Transfer to a food processor, add wine, and puree; return to the skillet. Pour in stock and add bay leaf and thyme. Cover and simmer for 15 minutes. Remove bay leaf and increase heat to medium-high. Add arrowroot mixture, stirring until gravy begins to thicken, about 3 minutes. Add salt, pepper, cayenne, and parsley and remove from heat.   *Makes 3 cups.*

Per serving (2 tablespoons): 20 calories / 1 gm fat / 2 gm carbohydrate / 56 mg sodium

～ Sawmill Gravy ～

This classic gravy is great for stretching leftover poultry into a dish with the feel of lovingly prepared food. Nana used to make it after she'd roasted a bird. She'd meticulously pick all the leftover meat from the carcass, wrap the carcass up, and put it in the icebox for stock, and then make a rich gravy that she poured over Sage Biscuits (page 73).

2 tablespoons light Roux
  (page 201)
¼ cup chopped shallots
1 cup evaporated skim milk
2 cups Chicken Stock *(page 81)*
1 cup finely shredded cooked
  chicken (leftover meat from
  a roasted chicken works well)

½ teaspoon salt
½ teaspoon grated lemon zest
½ teaspoon freshly ground white
  pepper
Pinch of cayenne
½ teaspoon savory or thyme
  leaves

In a large skillet, heat roux over medium heat, stirring, for 1 minute, or until melted. Add shallots, and stir for 1 minute, until coated with roux. Slowly pour in milk, while continuing to stir, and follow with stock, until gravy begins to thicken, about 3 minutes. Add the chicken, salt, lemon zest, pepper, cayenne, and savory and remove from heat. Serve at once.   *Makes 1 quart.*

Per serving (2 tablespoons): 24 calories / 0 gm fat / 1 gm carbohydrate / 52 mg sodium

~ Herb Butter ~

Though I am not a butter worshiper, I do use it sparingly on a few foods. One that comes to mind is corn on the cob. I can't imagine a hot roasted ear without a dab of this tasty butter.

½ cup butter, softened	1 tablespoon chopped parsley
1 teaspoon minced dill	½ teaspoon minced tarragon
½ teaspoon thyme leaves	

Put butter in a small mixing bowl. Add herbs; whip until fluffy and refrigerate. Use within the week or freeze for future use.   *Makes ½ cup.*

Per serving (1 teaspoon): 33 calories / 3 gm fat / 0 gm carbohydrate / 39 mg sodium

~ Garlic Butter ~

This butter adds flair to the flavor of mashed potatoes, string beans, and baked fish, to name a few.

1 head garlic	½ cup butter, softened

Preheat the oven to 325 degrees F. Rub whole head of garlic with olive oil and place in oven on a baking sheet. Bake for 35–45 minutes, or until garlic becomes soft to the touch. Remove from oven and let cool for 15 minutes. With a sharp knife, remove the top of the garlic. From the bottom, squeeze the head until all the garlic is released. Mix the garlic paste with the butter and chill. Use within the week or freeze for future use.   *Makes ½ cup.*

Per serving (1 teaspoon): 33 calories / 3 gm fat / 10 gm carbohydrate / 39 mg sodium

∽ Cinnamon-Orange Butter ∼

Try a dab of this on hot Sweet Potato Waffles (page 54).

½ cup sweet butter, softened   1 tablespoon grated orange zest
2 tablespoons superfine sugar   1 tablespoon orange juice
1 tablespoon cinnamon

Cream the butter with the sugar and cinnamon. Add orange zest and orange juice and whip until fluffy. Use within the week or freeze for future use.   *Makes ½ cup.*

Per serving (1 teaspoon): 37 calories / 3 gm fat / 10 gm carbohydrate / 1 mg sodium

∽ Raspberry Butter ∼

Don't be afraid to try this on Raspberry Pancakes (page 32). The double raspberry taste is intensely good!

½ cup butter, softened   1 cup fresh raspberries
¼ cup maple syrup   1 teaspoon allspice

In a mixing bowl, combine the butter with the honey and whip until fluffy. Fold in raspberries and allspice and chill. Use within the week or freeze for future use.   *Makes 1 cup.*

Per serving (1 teaspoon): 17 calories / 1 gm fat / 1 gm carbohydrate / 16 mg sodium

～ Lemon Curd ～

In the mornings, when I'm all alone in the kitchen, I spread lemon curd on Strawberry Biscuits (page 74), brew myself a pot of tea, watch the sun rise, and give thanks for these small pleasures. Lemon curd is equally at home on top of a square of warm Gingerbread (page 241).

2 lemons	**1 cup sugar**
¼ cup butter	**2 eggs, beaten**

Grate peel from the lemons, avoiding bitter white pith. Into a bowl, squeeze juice from both lemons. Melt the butter in the top half of a double boiler over simmering water. Add lemon juice, grated zest, and sugar and whip with a wire whisk for 2 to 3 minutes, until sugar is dissolved. Slowly add the eggs, stirring until mixture is considerably thickened. Remove from heat and serve at room temperature.   *Makes 1 cup.*

Per serving (1 teaspoon): 23 calories / 1 gm fat / 3 gm carbohydrate / 12 mg sodium

NOTES ON PRESERVING

Canning is simple, yet technical. You must take your time and follow the proper procedures if you want to prolong the shelf life of your foods. There are two main types of canning: the open-kettle method and the hot water bath method, which is open-kettle canning taken a step further. The first method, open kettle, is used for high sugar or acidic foods that will be stored in the refrigerator or freezer. It is a simple method of sterilizing the jars beforehand. The other method, hot water bath, is also used for foods high in acid and/or sugar content, but it is for foods that will be stored at room temperature. It involves sterilization of the jars, and once the food is sealed in the jars, placing the jars in a large pot of boiling water for 20 minutes.

Equipment (see List of Mail-Order Resources on page 268 for information on obtaining equipment)

Mason-type jars (3-piece), including a sealing compound (rubber-lined underside) and a screw band

Large stockpot with lid

Round cake rack that fits in the pot

Jar funnel

Jar lifter

Rubber spatula

To sterilize the jars, place a cake rack or a round cloth pot holder in the bottom of a large stockpot. Check around the rim of the jars for cracks. Wash the jars in hot sudsy water, rinse well, and set them upright in the pot, making sure they do not touch the sides of the pot or each other. Fill the jars to the brim with hot water, and fill the pot up to cover the jars by an inch. Cover the pot and bring to a boil. Reduce heat to medium-high and continue boiling for 15 minutes. Let the jars remain in the water until you are ready to fill them.

To remove a jar from the pot, grip it below the rim with a jar lifter—not a pair of standard tongs. Drain the jars of their water and stand them upright on a layer of cloth to dry. Using the funnel, fill the jars while they are still hot, within ½ inch from the top of the rim. Insert a rubber spatula around the inside of the jar, and jog it up and down until all the air bubbles have risen. Wipe the upper rim of the jar clean and place the inner lid (with the sealing compound facing down) on the top of the jar. Place the screw band on and tighten it until you begin to feel resistance. And then turn it a slight bit more.

For hot water bath, with your tongs, place the filled jars back in the pot, on top of the rack. Add water, if necessary, to the pot so that it is 1 inch above the top of the jars. Bring the water to a gentle boil and maintain it for 20 minutes. Remove the jars with the jar lifter and place jars on a clean cloth or newspaper in a draft-free area for 12 to 24 hours. Do not place the hot jars on a cold surface, as they may crack. After 12 to 24 hours, remove the outer screw band. Press the middle of the lid with your finger. If the lid springs up when you withdraw your finger, the lid has been improperly sealed. Do not try to reseal; remove the contents and start over.

~ Fig Chutney ~

Chutneys are used a lot in Indian cuisine, and are gaining popularity here thanks to our newly curious and eclectic palates. In the same way that salsa has supplanted ketchup for certain foods, chutney can often take the place of a sweet mustard. For example, this chutney is divine on a turkey sandwich but just as wonderful beside Chicken and Shrimp Jambalaya (page 160).

2 pounds fresh figs	2 tablespoons grated gingerroot
½ to 1 Scotch bonnet pepper, seeded *(see page 10 for handling instructions)*	2 tablespoons lemon juice
	1½ cups malt vinegar
1 cup dried cranberries	1 cup sugar
2 teaspoons grated lemon zest	½ teaspoon salt

Puree the figs, pepper, and cranberries in a food processor; transfer to a 3-quart saucepan. Add zest, gingerroot, lemon juice, vinegar, sugar, and salt and cook over low heat, stirring often, for 30 minutes. Place in two sterilized (see page 208) pint jars and follow procedure for hot water bath (see page 208). Let develop for 1 month, at room temperature.   *Makes 2 pints.*

Per serving (1 tablespoon): 11 calories / 0 gm fat / 3 gm carbohydrate / 0 mg sodium

～ Corn Relish ～

Grandpop makes great corn relish: full of sweet freshly hulled corn and loads of hot peppers that give it that inimitable sweet-hot taste.

1 sweet red bell pepper, seeded and chopped

1 green bell pepper, seeded and chopped

2 hot chili peppers, seeded and chopped *(see page 10 for handling instructions)*

¼ cup chopped shallots

1 teaspoon grated gingerroot

1 carrot, finely chopped

1 stalk celery, finely chopped

Juice of 1 lemon

1 cup white wine vinegar

1 tablespoon sugar

3 ears of corn, kernels scraped from the cob

1 teaspoon Lemon Pepper *(page 5)*

1 tablespoon finely minced cilantro

½ teaspoon paprika

Combine the peppers, shallots, gingerroot, carrot, celery, lemon juice, vinegar, and sugar in a 2-quart saucepan and simmer over low heat for 3 minutes, until softened. Add the corn and cook for 5 minutes more, until corn is cooked but firm. Add lemon pepper, cilantro, and paprika, and toss well. Serve cold. This dish can be eaten right away or canned, using the hot water bath (page 208).   *Makes 8 servings.*

Per serving (1 tablespoon): 78 calories / 0 gm fat / 18 gm carbohydrate / 19 mg sodium

～ Cowpea Chow Chow ～

Whenever I am at a loss for what to serve as an appetizer, I turn to this old standby. Excellent with warm nacho chips.

1 onion
1 green bell pepper, seeded and chopped
1 red bell pepper, seeded and chopped
2 hot chili peppers, seeded and chopped *(see page 10 for handling instructions)*
2 large tomatoes, seeded and chopped

2 cups cooked black-eyed peas *(see page 46 for preparation)*
¼ cup chopped cilantro
Juice of 1 lime
1 garlic clove, crushed
2 tablespoons white vinegar
1 teaspoon salt
½ teaspoon freshly ground pepper

Cut up onion and peppers and put in food processor; pulse until mixture is almost liquefied. Put in a bowl. Put the tomatoes in the processor and pulse until finely chopped; strain and add to onion mixture. Add peas, cilantro, lime juice, garlic, vinegar, salt, and pepper, and toss well. Refrigerate for at least 1 hour before serving. This recipe may also be preserved, using the hot water bath (page 208).   *Makes 20 servings.*

Per serving (2 tablespoons): 23 calories / 0 gm fat / 4 gm carbohydrate / 25 mg sodium

～ Pepper Relish ～

This trusty condiment works well with Codfish Cakes (page 119) and Crab Cakes (page 120).

2 red bell peppers, seeded and
  chopped finely
2 green bell peppers, seeded and
  chopped finely
2 yellow bell peppers, seeded
  and chopped finely
½ to 1 Scotch bonnet pepper,
  seeded and minced *(see
  page 10 for handling
  instructions)*

1 small onion, minced
1 cup boiling water
½ cup cider vinegar
½ cup sugar
1 teaspoon salt

Combine peppers and onion in a large mixing bowl. Pour boiling water over all and let stand 15 minutes. Put the pepper mixture in a colander, set the colander over a large bowl to catch the liquid, and let stand overnight in the refrigerator. Discard the liquid. In a 3-quart saucepan, combine the pepper mixture with the vinegar, sugar, and salt. Bring to a boil, lower heat, and simmer for 20 minutes, until peppers have broken down. Pour into 2 sterilized pint jars (see page 208) and follow procedure for hot water bath (see page 208). *Makes 2 pints.*

Per serving (1 tablespoon): 18 calories / 0 gm fat / 4 gm carbohydrate / 18 mg sodium

∼ Pepper Jam ∼

Spread this jam over a Sweet Potato Biscuit (page 72) and you'll have something to talk about the whole day. The word is "scrumptious."

6 cups apple juice	3 sweet red bell peppers,
12 red hot chili peppers, seeded	seeded and chopped
and chopped *(see page 10*	1 cup white vinegar
for handling instructions)	Juice of 1 lemon

In a 2-quart saucepan, boil apple juice over medium heat for 8 to 10 minutes, until a thick syrup is formed, and remove from heat before it begins to darken. Puree chili and sweet peppers in a food processor; transfer to a 3-quart stainless steel saucepan, and add vinegar, lemon juice, and the apple syrup. Simmer for 35 minutes, until mixture thickens. Remove from heat and put into one sterilized pint jar (see page 208). Follow procedure for hot water method (see page 208).   *Makes 1 pint.*

Per serving (1 tablespoon): 18 calories / 0 gm fat / 4 gm carbohydrate / 18 mg sodium

∼ Pickled Okra ∼

This is one of the rare instances where okra makes a solo appearance and succeeds.

2½ pounds okra pods	3 teaspoons white peppercorns
3 garlic cloves, peeled	3 teaspoons grated lemon zest
3 small chili peppers, seeded	3 teaspoons grated gingerroot
and chopped *(see page 10*	3 teaspoons salt
for handling instructions)	3 cups white vinegar
6 tablespoons chopped dill	1 cup water
3 teaspoons dill seed	

Rinse and drain okra. Snip off a small portion of the tail, but leave the head intact. Pack the okra firmly into three sterilized pint-sized Mason jars (see page 208). Drop 1 garlic clove, 1 chili pepper, 2 tablespoons dill, 1 teaspoon each dill seed, peppercorns, lemon zest, and gingerroot into each jar. In a 2-quart saucepan, combine the salt, vinegar, and water and bring to a boil. Pour equal amounts of the vinegar mixture over the okra to cover, leaving an inch of space at the mouth of each jar. Screw the lids on tightly and refrigerate. If storing in a dry pantry, follow the procedure for hot water bath method (see page 208).   *Makes 6 servings.*

Per serving: 50 calories / 0 gm fat / 12 gm carbohydrate / 544 mg sodium

∼ Pickled Shrimp ∼

This dish redefines the classic meaning of the word appetizer*: to stimulate the desire to eat. You didn't know shrimp could fly? Put them on the table and watch!*

2 **pounds shrimp, shelled, deveined, and slightly cooked**
½ **to 1 Scotch bonnet or habanero pepper, seeded and chopped (*see page 10 for handling instructions*)**
12 **allspice berries**
2 **tablespoons tarragon leaves**

1 **large onion, finely chopped**
1 **tablespoon olive oil**
1 **tablespoon grated lemon zest**
4 **cups white vinegar**
1 **teaspoon salt**
2 **tablespoons lemon juice**

Put shrimp in a large bowl, along with pepper, allspice berries, and tarragon leaves. In a 3-quart saucepan, sauté onion in oil for 5 minutes over low heat, until translucent. Add lemon zest, vinegar, salt, and lemon juice and bring to a boil. Pour hot mixture over shrimp, cover, and let sit until cooled. Put the shrimp into 2 sterilized pint-sized jars (see page 208) and fill with the vinegar mixture. Follow the hot water bath method (page 208).   *Makes 6 servings.*

Per serving: 226 calories / 3 gm fat / 21 gm carbohydrate / 340 mg sodium

∽ Watermelon Rind Pickles ∽

An unlikely-sounding combination that works wonderfully.

4 cups cubed watermelon, red
　　flesh and green rind peeled,
　　leaving white part of the rind
¾ cup cider vinegar
1 cup sugar
½ cup water

Juice of 1 lemon
Zest of 1 lemon, avoiding
　　bitter white pith
3 whole cloves
12 allspice berries
1 cinnamon stick

Soak rind overnight in a pan of salted water. Drain and rinse rind and put in a 3-quart saucepan. Cover rind with water and bring to a boil. Decrease heat and simmer, covered, for 8 minutes. Remove from heat. Drain and put rind back into saucepan. In another large saucepan, combine vinegar, sugar, water, lemon juice, lemon zest, cloves, allspice berries, and cinnamon stick and bring to a boil; decrease heat to low and simmer for 25 minutes. Strain vinegar mixture and pour over rind. Simmer for 10 minutes, until a slight glaze forms over the pickles, and cool. Put into two sterilized 1-pint jars (see page 208) and follow hot water bath method (page 208). *Makes 16 servings.*

Per serving: 60 calories / 0 gm fat / 16 gm carbohydrate / 356 mg sodium

∽ Hot Pickled Lemons ∽

I adore lemons, and rarely throw any part of them away. This Moroccan-inspired condiment is great in spicy fish and chicken dishes, as well as in seasoning pastes.

8 lemons
2 cups water
½ cup kosher salt
½ cup lemon juice

½ to 1 Scotch bonnet pepper, seeded
　　and chopped *(see page 10 for
　　handling instructions)*

Cut each lemon lengthwise into four wedges. In a 1-quart saucepan bring 2 cups water to a boil. Reduce heat to a simmer and drop in the lemons. Simmer for 4 minutes, until lemons are softened, and drain. Combine the salt and lemon juice, and pour into a sterilized (see page 207) 1-pint jar. Add the lemons and pepper, and seal tightly. Let stand for at least 7 days, at room temperature, shaking the jar each day to redistribute the salt mixture. Rinse lemons before using. Refrigerate after opening. Will keep for 1 month after opening.   *Makes 32 slices.*

Per serving: 6 calories / 0 gm fat / 3 gm carbohydrate / 411 mg sodium

～14～

Beverages

What exactly does one drink with down-home cooking? A fragrant full-bodied Bordeaux? A fruity Gewürztraminer? An icy dark lager perhaps, or a cold sweet glass of lemonade? The answer is simple: whatever you please. Flexibility is the soul of down-home cuisine, and the beverages sipped along with it depend entirely on the preferences of the diner.

I especially love iced teas, fruit infusions, and lemonades. Is there anything better on a broiling summer day than the tangy, come-hither aroma of a glass of cold peppermint tea? And what could be more refreshing than the freshly squeezed wake-up call of a good lemonade?

The down-home drinks that follow are long on fruit and herbs, and short on sugar, although obviously you can sweeten to taste. They take their inspiration from a variety of sources, historical and personal, with one thing in common: they taste great. I encourage you to make your drinks for the sake of the drink, and not just to accessorize your meal. A toast to your health!

～ Sweetwater ～

This is a good summertime item to have on hand for sweetening cold drinks without the bother of waiting for sugar to dissolve. Keep sweetwater in your fridge and that gritty sugar-swirl on the bottom of lemonade will be a thing of the past. The ginger gives it a tang, but feel free to omit it.

1 cup water	1 (¼-inch-thick) slice
2 cups sugar	gingerroot

In a 1-quart saucepan, combine water, sugar, and ginger. Boil until sugar dissolves. Pour into a jar with a tight-fitting lid and refrigerate up to 2 months.   *Makes 1 pint.*

Per serving (1 tablespoon): 45 calories / 0 gm fat / 12 gm carbohydrate / 0 mg sodium

～ Sweet Tea with Lemon Ice Cubes ～

A classic summer drink—thirst-quenching and light.

2 tablespoons loose black tea	Lemon Ice Cubes (recipe
4 cups boiling water	follows)
¼ cup sugar	8 mint leaves

Put the tea into a large teapot or bowl. Pour water over the tea and let steep for 4–5 minutes. Strain tea into another pot and add sugar. Stir and pour into a 2-quart pitcher filled with Lemon Ice Cubes. Garnish each glass with a mint leaf.   *Makes 1 quart.*

Per serving (½ cup): 23 calories / 0 gm fat / 6 gm carbohydrate / 4 mg sodium

Lemon Ice Cubes

Juice of 3 lemons　　　　**15 allspice berries**
1½ cups water

Mix lemons with water; pour into an ice cube tray. Drop a berry into each compartment and freeze.   *Makes 12 cubes.*

～ Iced Peppermint Tea ～

A good pick-me-up on a sweltering day.

1 cup fresh peppermint leaves,　　　**2 tablespoons honey**
　　chopped, or ⅛ cup dried　　　　**1 lime, thinly sliced**
4 cups boiling water

Place peppermint leaves in a large teapot. Pour in the boiling water and let steep for 10 minutes. Strain into a large heat-proof pitcher and add the honey, stirring until fully dissolved. Let cool. Refrigerate for at least 1 hour. Pour into tall glasses and garnish with a slice of lime.   *Makes 1 quart.*

Per serving (1 cup): 51 calories / 0 gm fat / 13 gm carbohydrate / 8 mg sodium

～ Rose Hips Iced Tea ～

This thirst-quencher, made with vitamin C–packed rose hips, has a refreshing citrusy taste.

2 tablespoons dried rose hips　　　**2 tablespoons honey**
4 cups boiling water　　　　　　　**2 cups cold water**

Place rose hips in a teapot. Add boiling water; let steep for 1 hour, and strain into a 6-cup measuring pitcher. Add honey and cold water, and stir. Pour into tall glasses filled with ice.   *Makes 1½ quarts.*

Per serving (1 cup): 11 calories / 0 gm fat / 3 gm carbohydrate / 5 mg sodium

~ Black Currant Iced Tea ~

Black currant tea has a rich, intoxicating fragrance and a fruity taste.

> 2 tablespoons black currant tea leaves
> 4 cups boiling water
>
> 2 tablespoons honey
> 2 cups ice cubes

Place tea leaves in large teapot; pour boiling water over leaves; let steep for 4–5 minutes, and strain. Pour into a large pitcher and add honey. Stir until honey is dissolved. Add ice and serve.   *Makes 1½ quarts.*

Per serving (1 cup): 16 calories / 0 gm fat / 4 gm carbohydrate / 8 mg sodium

~ Lemonade with Mint Ice Cubes ~

Everybody has their own way of making lemonade; some like it real sweet, others prefer it lip-puckering tart. The mix of cayenne and allspice in this version provides a depth of flavor that enriches the classic.

> 3 lemons
> 4 cups water
> ½ cup Sweetwater *(page 218)*
> 2 cups crushed ice
>
> Pinch of allspice
> Pinch of cayenne
> Mint Ice Cubes *(recipe follows)*

Squeeze the lemons into a large jar. Coarsely chop the lemons with a sharp knife and add to the jar with the water and sweetwater. Shake vigorously for 1 minute. Add ice, allspice, and cayenne and shake for another minute. Strain and serve in tall glasses filled with Mint Ice Cubes. *Makes 1½ quarts.*

Per serving (1 cup): 17 calories / 0 gm fat / 7 gm carbohydrate / 4 mg sodium

Mint Ice Cubes

24 peppermint leaves

Place one peppermint leaf in each of two ice cube tray compartments and fill with water. Freeze until set. *Makes 24 cubes.*

～ Strawberry Limeade ～

I like to use a juice extractor for the strawberries; it presses them so fine that they don't need to be strained.

⅔ cup Sweetwater *(page 218)*   **1 pint hulled strawberries**
½ teaspoon allspice   **6 limes**
4 cups boiling water

In a large, temperature-resistant measuring pitcher, mix sweetwater and allspice with the water. Liquefy strawberries in a blender, strain, and add to sweetwater mixture. Juice the limes and cut the rind into quarters. Add both to liquid and let sit, covered, for ½ hour. Strain through a fine sieve, and pour into a large pitcher filled with ice. *Makes 1½ quarts.*

Per serving (1 cup): 66 calories / 0 gm fat / 18 gm carbohydrate / 2 mg sodium

～ Grandpop's Fruit Punch ～

There was a special drink in our family's archives; it was fruit punch. And, of course, there was someone in the family who made the punch memorable. That person was Grandpop. It pleased me to know that while other kids drank Kool-Aid with their dinner, we had the privilege of drinking this delicious, vitamin-rich beverage.

1 cup orange juice	1 cup apple juice
1 cup pineapple juice	1 cup grape juice
Juice of 1 lime	1 pint water
Juice of 1 lemon	½ cup Sweetwater *(page 218)*
1 cup peach nectar	1 quart ginger ale

Mix all the juices together in one large bowl. Add water and sweetwater and chill for at least 1 hour. When ready to serve, pour into a punch bowl and add the ginger ale.   *Makes 3 quarts.*

Per serving (1 cup): 88 calories / 0 gm fat / 22 gm carbohydrate / 9 mg sodium

～ Gingerade ～

The cayenne in this drink really gives it a punch.

¼ cup grated gingerroot	½ cup sugar
6 cups boiling water	Pinch of cayenne
2 lemons	

Add the ginger to the boiling water in a large saucepan and bring to a second boil. Remove from heat. Squeeze juice from lemons and add to ginger mixture, along with a few slices of the peel. Stir in sugar and cayenne, and refrigerate. Once completely chilled, strain and serve.   *Makes 1½ quarts.*

Per serving (¾ cup): 59 calories / 0 gm fat / 16 gm carbohydrate / 7 mg sodium

~ Ginger Beer ~

I fell in love with homemade ginger beer the moment I tasted it. It was nothing like the harsh bottled stuff that I'd tried out as a child. I had it in Jamaica, made by one of the local women selling it at a stand—and it was the very essence of down-home.

1½ cups peeled and grated gingerroot	¾ cup lime juice
1½ cups sugar	6 cups boiling water
	1 teaspoon dry yeast

Place the ginger in a large bowl. Add sugar, lime juice, boiling water, and yeast and cover with plastic wrap. Store in a warm place for 48 hours. Strain and pour into large bottle or jug. Chill thoroughly.   *Makes ½ gallon.*

Per serving (1 cup): 145 calories / 0 gm fat / 41 gm carbohydrate / 6 mg sodium

~ Ginger Tea ~

This is a medicinal tea, good for settling the stomach.

¼ cup grated gingerroot	3½ cups water
Juice of 1 lime	1 tablespoon honey

In a large saucepan, combine grated ginger, lime juice, and water. Bring to a boil. Lower heat and simmer, covered, for 10 minutes. Mix in honey and serve.   *Makes 4 cups.*

Per serving (1 cup): 12 calories / 0 gm fat / 4 gm carbohydrate / 0 mg sodium

~ Spice Tea ~

This is an Indian tea, calming and delightful. Apu, son of my dear friend Kinnu, makes it for me whenever I visit them. Its rich, sweet swirl of flavors is like an entire spice garden in a cup.

3 cups water	12 whole cloves
1 tablespoon minced gingerroot	12 whole cardamom pods
1 cinnamon stick	1⅓ cups evaporated skim milk
¼ teaspoon freshly ground pepper	4 tablespoons sugar
	2 tablespoons loose black tea

Put water in saucepan. Add gingerroot, cinnamon stick, pepper, cloves, and cardamom pods and bring to a boil. Lower heat, cover, and simmer for 10 minutes. Add milk and sugar and simmer, covered, for 10 more minutes. Add tea and steep for 3 minutes. Strain and serve.   *Makes 6 cups.*

Per serving (1 cup): 117 calories / 1 gm fat / 24 gm carbohydrate / 68 mg sodium

~ Plum Wine ~

Mom is the family wine maker. She makes just about every kind of wine imaginable: peach, grape, cherry—she even makes sake! Often a lucky visitor leaves with a bottle of Mom's private label.

3 quarts plums, pitted and chopped	1 pound sugar

In a large mixing bowl, combine plums with sugar. Place plums in a 1-gallon jug and fill to 5 inches from the top with water. Cork the jug with a fermentation lock (can be purchased at a wine-making supply store) and monitor the fermentation process (approximately 3–4 weeks) with the aid of a hydrometer (see List of Mail-Order Resources on page 268). Do not rush this process, as wine that is still fermenting when you cork it will often explode. When fermentation is complete, strain the wine through cheesecloth and bottle. Best if stored in a cool dry place for at least 6 months.   *Makes 1 gallon.*

Per serving (1 cup): 60 calories / 0 gm fat / 15 gm carbohydrate / 0 mg sodium

~ Honeysuckle Wine ~

If you're lucky enough to have sweet honeysuckle blossoms growing in your garden, make use of them by making this wine. I love honeysuckle, whose blossoms, to me, have the bouquet of deep summer itself.

4 cups packed honeysuckle blossoms	1 teaspoon yeast nutrient *(can be purchased at a wine-maker store; see resources guide for information)*
4 cups water	
2 cups sugar	
¾ cup white grape juice	2 cups orange juice, brought to room temperature
Juice of 3 lemons	
1 package dry yeast	1 tablespoon strong tea

Wash the honeysuckle blossoms in a large bowl of cold water. Drain. Put the flowers, water, 1 cup sugar, and grape and lemon juices in a 2-gallon plastic jug with a lid. Let the mixture sit for 1 week. Meanwhile, in another lidded jug, combine the yeast with the nutrient and the orange juice. Cover and shake until well mixed. Let stand for 2 to 3 hours, until frothy. Add the tea, cover loosely, and let the mixture stand for a week. Pour honeysuckle mixture into yeast mixture and strain the liquid into a 1-gallon jug, allowing 5 inches headspace. Cork the jug with a fermentation lock (can be purchased at a wine-making supply store) and monitor the fermentation process (approximately 3–4 weeks) with the aid of a hydrometer (see List of Mail-Order Resources on page 268). Once the hydrometer indicates that the wine has finished fermenting, strain the fermented wine through a cheesecloth bag and place in the cork. (Do not rush this process, because the wine will continue to ferment when you place the final cork and it may explode.) Store in a cool dry place for at least 6 months.   *Makes 1 gallon.*

Per serving (1 cup): 54 calories / 0 gm fat / 14 gm carbohydrate / 0 mg sodium

～ Rosemary Wine ～

This is really a simple infusion; all it takes is a little patience. This wine is great with fish.

¾ cup rosemary leaves   **1 (750-ml) bottle dry white wine**

Put rosemary into a bottle of newly opened white wine and recork. Set in a cool place for 3 days. Strain and decant. Serve chilled.   *Makes 750 ml.*

Per serving (¾ cup): 24 calories / 0 gm fat / 3 gm carbohydrate / 3 mg sodium

～ Wine Punch ～

Mom is a great maker of wine punch, which she carries to family barbecues and picnics. Somewhat like a sangria, this is a great alternative to beer.

2 cups orange juice   **1 cup dry white wine**
  Juice of 1 lime   **1 cup ginger beer or ginger ale**
1 teaspoon grenadine

Mix together the orange juice, lime juice, grenadine, and the wine. Add ginger beer. Pour into tall glasses filled with ice cubes.   *Makes 1 quart.*

Per serving (1 cup): 114 calories / 0 gm fat / 18 gm carbohydrate / 6 mg sodium

∼ Eggnog ∼

Since most of us drink eggnog only once a year, I decided to add a couple of egg yolks. But be cautious—although the fat content still remains relatively low, the sugar in the alcohol makes this a highly caloric drink.

2 egg yolks
½ cup sugar
1 teaspoon vanilla extract
1 cup rum
1 cup cognac

1 cup bourbon
4 cups evaporated skim milk
8 egg whites
Nutmeg

In a large mixing bowl, beat the egg yolks with sugar, vanilla, rum, cognac, bourbon, and milk until smooth. Chill. When ready to serve, put the refrigerated rum mixture into a punch bowl. Beat the egg whites until stiff and fold them into the rum mixture. Sprinkle nutmeg on top.   *Makes ½ gallon.*

Per serving (½ cup): 154 calories / 1 gm fat / 13 gm carbohydrate / 101 mg sodium

∼ Syllabub ∼

I've updated this Old World drink by taking out the heavy cream and cutting back on the egg yolks. Similar to eggnog, this holiday punch disguises the taste of the alcohol very well, so be careful!

2 eggs, separated
¼ cup confectioners' sugar
1 cup brandy

½ cup sweet sherry
2 cups evaporated skim milk
1 teaspoon grated lemon zest

Beat egg yolks with sugar until frothy. Add brandy and sherry and continue beating until well blended. Beat egg whites until stiff and fold into yolk mixture. Add milk and lemon zest and gently beat. Serve chilled.   *Makes 1 quart.*

Per serving (½ cup): 145 calories / 1 gm fat / 7 gm carbohydrate / 48 mg sodium

～ Cool Peach ～

My brother Robert loves to play bartender at our family gatherings. This drink is consistently a hit.

1 **peach, pitted**	¼ **cup vodka**
2 **tablespoons Peach Schnapps**	2 **cups crushed ice**
2 **tablespoons peach nectar**	

Put peach in blender and liquefy for 1 minute. Add schnapps, peach nectar, and vodka and pulse five or six times more. Add ice and whirl until smooth. Serve in tall glasses.   *Serves 2.*

Per serving: 119 calories / 0 gm fat / 12 gm carbohydrate / 5 mg sodium

～ Blue Velvet ～

I got this recipe from a friend, Linda, who swore I'd go crazy for it once I tried it. She was right.

3 **quarts fresh blueberries**	1 **quart vodka**

Wash berries and place in a gallon jug. Fill with vodka. Cork and let it sit in a cool dark place for 6 months. Strain and chill.   *Makes 2 quarts.*

Per serving (¼ cup): 94 calories / 0 gm fat / 7 gm carbohydrate / 4 mg sodium

∼ Mint Julep ∼

Not many of these were being drunk by my ancestors. By and large, those ancestors were busy making them for others to drink. A toast to the changing times!

7 **sprigs of mint**	**crushed ice**
1 **tablespoon Sweetwater**	**¼ cup bourbon**
(page 218)	

Place six of the mint sprigs in a cocktail glass. Add sweetwater and bruise the sprigs with a spoon (the handle of a wooden spoon works quite well), until the syrup looks a little greenish in color. Fill glass with crushed ice and add the bourbon. Stir well and garnish with the final sprig of mint.   *Makes 1 drink.*

Per serving: 161 calories / 0 gm fat / 4 gm carbohydrate / 2 mg sodium

∼ Hot Buttered Rum ∼

This drink conjures up images of popcorn, a fireplace, and fuzzy slippers.

2 **tablespoons dark rum**	**⅔ cup boiling water**
1 **sugar cube**	1 **teaspoon butter**

Pour rum into a mug and drop the sugar cube in. Pour boiling water on top. Add butter and stir until butter melts.   *Makes 1 drink.*

Per serving: 124 calories / 3 gm fat / 7 gm carbohydrate / 44 mg sodium

~ Hot Spiced Cider ~

Another great drink to warm the soul.

4 cinnamon sticks, broken   1 quart apple cider
1 teaspoon allspice berries   1 cup rum
1 teaspoon whole cloves
1 tablespoon chopped gingerroot

In a large saucepan combine cinnamon, allspice, cloves, gingerroot, and apple cider. Bring to a near-boil over medium-high heat. Lower heat and simmer, covered, for 15 minutes. Pour in rum.   *Makes 5 cups.*

Per serving (1 cup): 160 calories / 0.5 gm fat / 27 gm carbohydrate / 8 mg sodium

— 15 —

Just Desserts

The way I see it, dessert is an earned pleasure, appropriately assigned at the end of a day's good eating, crossing the line into a course reserved purely for taste. Our reward for a sensible diet is a little—*underlined little*—splurge. For some, a piece of fruit can satisfy as the close to a good meal. Others require something a little bit more sweet and calorific. And then there are those who want an insulin-shocking portion of sweetness and goo as a reward for having gotten through their dinner. Imagine the combined fat intake of breakfast, lunch, and dinner clocking in at a sensible 45 grams, then being swamped by an 80-fat-gram motherlode of a dessert. What a bust to the system, not to mention the seams of your clothes! Dessert, though an epicurean right, must be modified to remain in proportion with our current dietary knowledge. I enjoy decadence as much as the next one, but not even your local clergyman can pardon a banana split every day.

The desserts I have chosen are a combination of family favorites, down-home classics, and a few of my own variations on both. I've managed to keep the fat level at or below 10 grams per serving, by toning down the butter and sugar and replacing heavy cream with evaporated skim milk. Fresh fruit desserts predominate, and I've made do with pies that require only one crust. More than anything, I've relied on simplicity of preparation in the desserts that follow, though you won't know it from the richness of the taste.

∽ Deep-Dish Apple Pie ∽

This down-home classic is not as American as its reputation suggests. It's actually of British origin, though down-home cooks baked it so wonderfully that it is recognized as the quintessence of American comfort food. This recipe calls for tart apples, such as Granny Smith, Pippin, Winesap, or McIntosh—which, in my opinion, make a more interesting pie. If you choose a sweeter apple (Golden Delicious, Braeburn, or Jonathan), cut the sugar by ¼ cup.

10 large tart apples	1 teaspoon finely chopped
Juice of 1 lemon	crystallized ginger
¾ cup sugar	2 tablespoons ground tapioca
2 tablespoons Pie Spice	3 teaspoons butter
(page 9)	1 9-inch Piecrust (page 233)
½ teaspoon grated lemon zest	Milk

Preheat the oven to 325 degrees F. Butter a 9-inch deep-dish pie plate and set aside. Peel, core, and quarter the apples. Slice the apples ⅛ inch thick and place them in a large bowl of water mixed with the lemon juice. In a small bowl, combine the sugar, pie spice, zest, ginger, and tapioca. Divide into three parts. Drain the apples and divide into thirds. Place the first layer of apples in the baking dish, overlapping the apples if necessary. Sprinkle one third of the spice mixture evenly over the apples and top with 1 teaspoon butter. Repeat with a second and third layer. Cover with the piecrust dough. Crimp the edges with a fork dipped in milk, and cut three slits in the top. Bake for 40 minutes, until golden brown on top. Let come to room temperature before slicing. *Serves 8.*

Per serving: 289 calories / 8 gm fat / 55 gm carbohydrate / 159 mg sodium

∼ 9-inch Piecrust ∼

A good crust is the foundation of a good pie. This crust is a classic—light and flaky.

1 cup all-purpose unbleached flour	¼ cup sweet butter, chilled
½ teaspoon salt	3 tablespoons nonfat sour cream, or 1 percent fat buttermilk, chilled
1 teaspoon sugar	1 teaspoon ice water

Sift the flour, salt, and sugar into a large mixing bowl. Cut the butter into small chunks and, using your fingers, briskly rub the butter into the flour. (This step requires a bit of speed; otherwise, you'll end up with an oily crust.) When the mixture resembles coarse meal, add the sour cream. Using a fork, work the sour cream into the meal. Add ice water and pull the mixture together to form a ball. Knead the dough lightly two to three times. Reshape the dough into a ball again, wrap in plastic, and refrigerate for at least 1 hour. Turn the ball out onto a lightly floured surface and roll out to the desired diameter (9 inches).

NOTE: For a prebaked pie shell, preheat the oven to 375 degrees F. Prick the crust with a fork and bake for 10 to 12 minutes, until golden. Cool.

Per serving: 105 calories / 5 gm fat / 12 gm carbohydrate / 139 mg sodium

∼ Deep-Dish Cherry Pie ∼

I cannot tell a lie: I've had many cherry pies in my day, and only a few were made with freshly pitted cherries. The difference is phenomenal. My question to anyone who takes the shortcut, using canned cherries instead of fresh, is: Why bother making it at all? If cherry pitting is too tedious a job, invest in a cherry pitter (see List of Mail-Order Resources on page 268).

1 teaspoon butter
6 cups tart cherries, pitted and
    halved
1 cup sugar
2 teaspoons Pie Spice *(page 9)*

¼ cup ground tapioca
¼ teaspoon almond extract
1 9-inch Piecrust *(page 233)*
Milk

Preheat the oven to 325 degrees F. Butter a 9-inch deep-dish pie plate and set aside. Melt butter in a 3-quart saucepan over medium heat. Add cherries, sugar, pie spice, and tapioca, and bring to a boil, stirring as it thickens, about 5 minutes. Remove from heat and stir in the almond extract. Pour cherry mixture into the baking dish. Place piecrust over cherries and crimp edges with a fork dipped in milk. Make three slits in the crust and bake for 30 minutes, until browned evenly on top. Serve at room temperature.   *Serves 8.*

Per serving: 272 calories / 7 gm fat / 54 gm carbohydrate / 146 mg sodium

～ Buttermilk Pie ～

When I told our friends that we were having buttermilk pie for dessert, I got polite smiles that I read as disappointment. I don't blame the uninitiated: really, who could imagine that a delicious sweet is produced from sour whey? But the look that flashed across their faces as they bit into their first velvety slice told me that buttermilk pie had converted yet another set of doubters.

1 tablespoon butter
2 tablespoons flour
⅔ cup sugar
⅛ teaspoon salt
½ teaspoon grated lemon zest

2 eggs
1 teaspoon vanilla extract
¾ cup 1 percent fat buttermilk
1 9-inch Piecrust *(page 233)*
Nutmeg

Preheat the oven to 375 degrees F. Melt the butter over low heat and pour into a large mixing bowl. Mix in the flour, sugar, salt, and lemon zest with a wooden spoon. (Add a teaspoon or two of water if mixture is too dry.) Beat the eggs into the mixture; add vanilla and buttermilk. Pour into an unbaked piecrust shell and sprinkle the top with nutmeg. Bake for 45 minutes, until pie is lightly browned. Chill for 1 hour.   *Serves 8.*

Per serving: 213 calories / 8 gm fat / 31 gm carbohydrate / 214 mg sodium

～ Nana's Graham Cracker Pie ～

I always considered this a custard pie, but Nana was adamant about calling it a graham cracker pie, for the simple reason that it's topped with graham crackers. In any event, I remember Nana using this pie for many a bribe.

4 **cups evaporated skim milk**	1 **recipe Graham Cracker Crust**
1 **vanilla bean, split**	**(recipe follows)**
3 **eggs, separated**	¼ **cup graham cracker crumbs**
¾ **cup Vanilla Sugar** *(page 18)*	

Preheat the oven to 350 degrees F. In the top portion of a large double boiler over simmering water, cook milk and vanilla bean over low heat. In a small mixing bowl, beat egg yolks with ½ cup vanilla sugar until cream-colored. Combine egg and milk mixtures by stirring the hot milk into the egg mixture 1 teaspoon at a time, until the egg mixture has doubled in volume. Pour the egg mixture into the remaining milk and continue stirring with a wooden spoon until mixture thickens just enough to coat a spoon, about 5–8 minutes. Remove vanilla bean, scrape the seeds into the custard, and stir to blend. When mixture comes to room temperature, pour into pie shell. Whip egg whites with the remaining sugar until stiff. Spread onto custard and swirl to create peaks. Sprinkle on the cracker crumbs and bake for 15–20 minutes, until visible parts of the meringue turn golden brown. Chill for 1 hour.   *Serves 8.*

Per serving: 332 calories / 9 gm fat / 50 gm carbohydrate / 322 mg sodium

⌒ Graham Cracker Crust ⌒

1¼ cups graham cracker crumbs   **¼ cup butter, melted**
¼ cup sugar

Combine all ingredients in a mixing bowl. Pile the mixture into a 9-inch pie plate. Using the back of a wooden spoon, firmly press the mixture in the bottom and along the sides of the plate. Chill or bake according to recipe.   *Makes 1 (9-inch) piecrust.*

Per serving: 128 calories / 7 gm fat / 16 gm carbohydrate / 137 mg sodium

⌒ Coconut Pie ⌒

The almond extract really brings out the taste of the coconut, and the egg whites add lightness to this delectable pie. I prefer this to the custard-based version.

¾ cup sugar
2 tablespoons flour
1 teaspoon grated lemon zest
¾ cup evaporated skim milk
¼ teaspoon almond extract

1 tablespoon butter, melted
1 cup finely grated coconut meat
2 egg whites
1 9-inch Piecrust *(page 233)*

Preheat the oven to 350 degrees F. In a large mixing bowl, combine the sugar, flour, and lemon zest. Pour in milk and beat until smooth. Add almond extract, butter, and coconut and beat well. Whip egg whites until stiff and fold into coconut mixture. Spoon into the piecrust shell and bake for 45 minutes, until well browned and springy to the touch.   *Serves 8.*

Per serving: 257 calories / 10 gm fat / 36 gm carbohydrate / 196 mg sodium

~ Nana's Lemon Meringue Pie ~

Whenever I ate Nana's lemon meringue pie, I thought to myself: This is what it must be like to eat sunshine and clouds.

3 lemons	1 tablespoon arrowroot
2 tablespoons butter	3 eggs, separated
1 cup water	1 9-inch Piecrust, prebaked
1¼ cups sugar	*(page 233)*

Preheat the oven to 350 degrees F. Grate peel from the lemons, avoiding bitter white pith. Squeeze the juice from the lemons and set aside. Melt the butter in the upper portion of a double boiler over simmering water. Combine water, lemon juice, lemon zest, 1 cup sugar, and arrowroot, and add to the butter. Stir with a wire whisk until sugar is dissolved, about 3 to 5 minutes. Slowly add the egg yolks, and continue beating until mixture is the consistency of pudding, about 3 minutes. Pour into baked pie shell and set aside. Whip the egg whites with the remaining ¼ cup sugar until stiff. Spread onto lemon filling and bake for 10–15 minutes, until meringue begins to brown. Chill for at least 1 hour.   *Serves 8.*

Per serving: 289 calories / 10 gm fat / 48 gm carbohydrate / 193 mg sodium

~ Pinto Bean Pie ~

This is an old Southern favorite that's as nutritious as it is delicious.

4 cups pinto beans, cooked	½ teaspoon grated gingerroot
1 tablespoon butter, melted	¼ cup orange juice
1 cup evaporated skim milk	1 egg
½ cup packed dark brown sugar	1 9-inch Piecrust *(page 233)*
2 teaspoons Pie Spice *(page 9)*	

Preheat the oven to 375 degrees F. In a large mixing bowl, mash the beans and force them through a mill or sieve. Combine the beans, butter, milk, sugar, pie spice, gingerroot, orange juice, and the egg in a large bowl and beat until well mixed and creamy. Pour the bean mixture into unbaked piecrust and bake for 35 minutes, or until well browned. Chill or serve at room temperature.   *Serves 8.*

Per serving: 327 calories / 8 gm fat / 53 gm carbohydrate / 202 mg sodium

∾ Sweet Potato Pie ∾

Of all the sweet potato pies I've had, none come close to the one my sister Diana makes: dense yet wholesome, with the wonderful perky flavor of lime and coconut throughout.

1 **9-inch Piecrust** *(page 233)*	2 **tablespoons bourbon**
6 **large sweet potatoes, boiled in**	2 **teaspoons Pie Spice** *(page 9)*
skins	¼ **cup freshly grated coconut**
½ **cup packed dark brown sugar**	**meat**
½ **cup evaporated skim milk**	½ **teaspoon salt**
2 **tablespoons lime juice**	2 **egg whites**

Preheat the oven 375 degrees F. Put piecrust in the oven for 5 minutes to brown slightly and remove. Peel and mash sweet potatoes, and put into a large mixing bowl. Add sugar, milk, lime juice, bourbon, pie spice, coconut, and salt. Whip egg whites until stiff and fold into potato mixture. Pour into the pie shell and bake for 40 minutes, or until well browned. Serve chilled or at room temperature.   *Serves 8.*

Per serving: 297 calories / 7 gm fat / 61 gm carbohydrate / 318 mg sodium

∽ Burnt Cream Pie ∽

Actually, the "cream" is evaporated skim milk, but that doesn't take anything away from the flavor. Let this pie chill thoroughly before cutting, or you'll have trouble slicing through the caramelized topping.

4 **cups evaporated skim milk**	1 **9-inch Piecrust, prebaked**
1 **vanilla bean, split**	**(page 233)**
3 **egg yolks**	¼ **cup packed dark brown sugar**
½ **cup sugar**	

Preheat the oven to 300 degrees F. Heat milk and vanilla bean in the upper portion of a double boiler over simmering water. Remove and split bean and scrape seeds into the milk. Beat egg yolks and sugar together until cream-colored and incorporate warm milk into the egg mixture 1 tablespoon at a time, until cream has doubled in volume. Pour the egg mixture into the pan and stir until mixture is thick enough to coat a spoon. Remove from heat and force the mixture through a fine sieve. Loosely cover the rim of the piecrust with aluminum foil and pour in the custard. Bake for 30 minutes, until browned on top. Cool. Sift brown sugar over the top of the pie. Preheat the broiler. Keeping the foil intact, place the pie under the broiler for 15 seconds, or until sugar is well browned and crackling. Chill for 1 hour.   *Serves 8.*

Per serving: 323 calories / 8 gm fat / 53 gm carbohydrate / 292 mg sodium

∼ Fig Cake ∼

My sister Kim is the cake baker in the family. Whenever there is a special event, she can be counted on to bring an elaborate production. This is one of her most memorable cakes.

Cake:

¼ cup butter, softened

1 cup sugar

1 egg

2 cups all-purpose
   unbleached flour

½ teaspoon salt

2 teaspoons baking powder

1 cup evaporated skim milk

1 teaspoon vanilla extract

¼ teaspoon almond extract

1 cup chopped stemmed
   fresh figs

Filling:

2 cups chopped stemmed
   fresh figs

¼ cup packed dark brown sugar

¼ cup water

1 tablespoon lemon juice

Preheat the oven to 350 degrees F. Butter two 8-inch round cake pans. In a large mixing bowl, cream butter with the sugar until fluffy. Add egg and beat well. Into a bowl, sift together flour, salt, and baking powder and add to the butter alternately with the milk. Fold in vanilla and almond extracts and chopped figs. Pour batter into cake pans. Bake for 30 minutes, or until a straw inserted in the center comes out dry. Cool before filling.

Combine all filling ingredients in a saucepan and bring to a boil. Reduce heat to medium. Cook until thickened, about 20 minutes. Spread thinly between layers of cake and on top.   *Serves 8.*

Per serving: 345 calories / 7 gm fat / 71 gm carbohydrate / 219 mg sodium

~ Gingerbread ~

Whenever it rained, Mom would bake: cookies, pies, and one of my favorite cakes, gingerbread. Often she'd recruit our help in sifting the flour (what a mess I always made of myself!) or cracking an egg. And after the batter was poured into the pan, Diana and I would have our reward: the gooey, tangy-sweet remnants left in the bowl and on the spoon. To me, this was better than ice cream.

¼ cup butter
⅓ cup packed dark brown sugar
1 egg
⅓ cup sorghum molasses
¼ cup grated gingerroot
2 tablespoons finely chopped
    crystallized ginger
¼ cup hot water

1 teaspoon baking soda
1¼ cups all-purpose unbleached
    flour
1 teaspoon ground ginger
1 teaspoon cinnamon
½ teaspoon allspice
½ cup 1 percent fat buttermilk

Preheat the oven to 375 degrees F. Butter a 9-inch-square baking dish and set aside. In a large mixing bowl, cream the butter with the sugar. Beat in the egg, sorghum, and the grated and crystallized ginger. In a cup, combine the water and baking soda; add to ginger mixture. Sift together the flour, ginger, cinnamon, and allspice. Add to the batter, a little at a time, until batter is smooth. Beat in the buttermilk, and pour the batter into baking pan. Bake for 25 minutes, until a toothpick inserted in the middle comes out clean.   *Makes 9 squares.*

Per serving: 187 calories / 6 gm fat / 28 gm carbohydrate / 278 mg sodium

~ Oat Cookies with Dried Cranberries ~

This is a variation of a classic oatmeal cookie. I found that using long-cooking Irish oats instead of instant oats produces nuttiness without adding the fat of walnuts. Cranberries are a refreshing change from the usual raisins. If you decide to use instant oats instead of long-cooking Irish oats, eliminate the presoaking process.

1½ cups Irish oats	1 teaspoon baking powder
1 cup evaporated skim milk	½ teaspoon salt
1 tablespoon butter, softened	2 teaspoons Pie Spice *(page 9)*
¾ cup Vanilla Sugar *(page 18)*	1 cup dried cranberries
1 egg	½ teaspoon grated lemon zest
¼ teaspoon almond extract	
1½ cups all-purpose unbleached flour	

Place oats in a shallow pan and pour ½ cup milk over them. Soak for 1 hour and drain, discarding the milk. Preheat the oven to 375 degrees F. Butter two large baking sheets and set aside. In a large mixing bowl, cream butter with the sugar and add egg and almond extract. In another bowl, sift together flour, baking powder, salt, and pie spice and add to the creamed mixture alternately with the remaining milk. Add drained oats, cranberries, and lemon zest, and continue beating until well mixed. Drop by teaspoonfuls, 2 inches apart, on the baking sheets, and bake for 12 minutes, until the edges have browned. Immediately remove with a spatula and cool on a wire rack.   *Makes 1 dozen cookies.*

Per serving: 146 calories / 2 gm fat / 29 gm carbohydrate / 147 mg sodium

~ Strawberry Shortcake ~

This summertime delight has undergone a couple of changes: the biscuit has been enriched with a bit of cornmeal, which lends an interesting crunchiness to the texture, and the strawberries are soaked Romanoff-style, in orange juice and vodka. What would have been 30 grams of fat in the original version for the whipped cream alone has been reduced here to a mere 5 grams of fat per serving.

5 cups fresh strawberries	¼ teaspoon baking soda
1 tablespoon vodka	2 teaspoons baking powder
2 tablespoons orange juice	¼ teaspoon salt
¼ cup red currant jam	3 tablespoons butter
1¾ cups all-purpose unbleached flour	¾ cup 1 percent fat buttermilk
¼ cup cornmeal	¼ cup 1 percent fat milk
¼ cup plus 2 tablespoons superfine sugar	1 cup Nonfat Whipped Cream *(page 21)*

Reserve 6 whole strawberries and set aside. Slice remaining strawberries in half and put in a large bowl; sprinkle vodka over them and let sit for 1 hour. Preheat the oven to 450 degrees F. Combine orange juice and jam in a small saucepan; cook over medium heat until jam liquefies. Let cool and add to strawberries; toss until well mixed.

Sift together flour, cornmeal, ¼ cup sugar, baking soda, baking powder, and salt into a large mixing bowl. Briskly rub the butter into the flour mixture until it resembles coarse meal. Add buttermilk and stir until mixture gathers together in a mass. Turn dough out onto a lightly floured board and knead five times. Roll out to ½-inch thickness and cut out 6 2-inch rounds with a biscuit cutter. Place on an ungreased baking sheet and brush the tops with milk. Sprinkle tops with remaining sugar and bake for 12 minutes, until golden brown.

Split biscuits in half and spoon ½ cup strawberry mixture onto the bottom half; place top half of biscuit over strawberry mixture. Garnish with a dollop of whipped cream and a whole strawberry.   *Serves 6.*

Per serving: 353 calories / 6 gm fat / 70 gm carbohydrate / 278 mg sodium

～ Caramelized Banana Pudding ～

This is a high-tech version of the one that Grandmom Cothran used to make.

15 ladyfingers	1 vanilla bean, split
1 teaspoon butter	2 eggs, separated
¾ cup plus 2 tablespoons sugar	¼ cup sweet sherry
3 very ripe bananas, sliced ½" thick	½ teaspoon cream of tartar
3¼ cups evaporated skim milk, warmed	⅛ teaspoon salt

Preheat the oven to 350 degrees F. Put ladyfingers on a baking sheet and place in the oven for 5 minutes, until browned. Butter an 8-inch-square baking dish and line with five of the ladyfingers. In a large nonstick skillet, melt butter and ½ cup sugar and cook over low heat for 5 minutes, until sugar begins to liquefy and turn golden brown. Add bananas and toss about until well coated. Pour in ¼ cup milk and stir until well blended. Put the banana-caramel mixture in the refrigerator until cooled.

Heat remaining milk and vanilla bean over low heat. In a small mixing bowl beat egg yolks with ¼ cup sugar until cream-colored. Blend eggs with milk mixture by stirring some of the hot milk into the egg mixture 1 teaspoon at a time, until the egg mixture has doubled in volume. Pour the egg mixture into the remaining milk and continue stirring with a wooden spoon until mixture thickens just enough to coat a spoon, about 5 to 8 minutes. Remove and split the vanilla bean, scrape the seeds into the custard, and stir to blend.

Sprinkle one third of the sherry onto the ladyfingers that were placed in the baking dish and follow with one third of the bananas and a third of the pudding mixture. Repeat with the ladyfingers, sherry, bananas, and custard until layering is complete. Whip egg whites with the remaining sugar until stiff. Add cream of tartar and salt and whip for a moment more. Spread whites on top of pudding and bake for 25 minutes.   *Makes 8 servings.*

Per serving: 296 calories / 4 gm fat / 53 gm carbohydrate / 203 mg sodium

～ Persimmon Custard ～

When persimmons were in season, Nana kept them around the house. I found these heart-shaped fruits festive but a little too intense for my taste. Still, I could never get enough of the custard she'd often make with them.

3 very ripe persimmons, peeled, seeded, and coarsely chopped	**1 vanilla bean**
	3 eggs
	⅔ cup sugar
3 cups evaporated skim milk	**¼ teaspoon salt**

Preheat the oven to 325 degrees F. In a 1-quart saucepan, cook persimmons over medium heat, stirring occasionally, for 5 minutes. Puree the persimmons in a food processor, then press the puree through a sieve and set aside. Scald the milk with the vanilla bean. Remove the bean, scrape the seeds into the milk, and set aside.

In a medium bowl, combine the eggs, sugar, and salt. Slowly add only enough of the milk mixture, while stirring, to warm the eggs. Then pour the egg mixture into the remaining milk mixture. Fold in the pureed fruit. Pour into a 2-quart baking dish and set into a larger pan. Fill the pan with water until it reaches halfway up the sides of the custard dish and set on the middle rack of the oven. Bake for 35 minutes, or until a toothpick inserted in the center comes out clean. Let the custard cool and refrigerate for 2 hours. *Makes 8 servings.*

Per serving: 231 calories / 2 gm fat / 40 gm carbohydrate / 265 mg sodium

～ Lemon-Brandy Peaches ～

A simple but elegant dessert. Best served cold.

4 **large peaches**	**Zest of 1 lemon, avoiding bitter**
½ **cup sugar**	**white pith, cut into thin strips**
⅛ **cup water**	2 **tablespoons brandy**

Peel and pit the peaches and cut in half. In a large skillet, cook the sugar with the water over high heat until it begins to boil. Add the zest and cook until the sugar begins to caramelize, about 5 minutes. Place the peaches in the pan, cut side down, and cook for 10 to 12 minutes. Remove with a slotted spoon and place on a serving dish. Add the brandy to the sauce and spoon over the peaches.　*Makes 4 servings.*

Per serving: 144 calories / 0 gm fat / 33 gm carbohydrate / 0 mg sodium

~ Peach Cobbler ~

A cobbler is a low-fat alternative to a fruit pie. You get the fruit and a bit of crunch, without the richness of all that shortening-based crust. My sister Kim makes one that will secure a permanent place for her in the Down-Home Hall of Fame.

8 large peaches, peeled, pitted, and sliced 1 inch thick
¾ cup plus 2 tablespoons sugar
1 tablespoon brandy
1 teaspoon allspice
2 tablespoons arrowroot
⅓ cup all-purpose unbleached flour
¼ teaspoon salt
½ teaspoon nutmeg
½ teaspoon baking soda
½ teaspoon baking powder
1 egg
1 teaspoon grated lemon zest
½ cup nonfat sour cream
¼ teaspoon almond extract
⅔ cup finely ground walnuts
1 tablespoon butter, melted

Preheat the oven to 375 degrees F. Butter a medium round baking dish and set aside. In a large mixing bowl, combine the peaches, ½ cup sugar, brandy, allspice, and arrowroot. Toss gently to mix and pour the mixture into the buttered dish. Into a bowl, sift together flour, salt, ¼ cup sugar, nutmeg, baking soda, and baking powder. In another bowl, combine the egg, lemon zest, sour cream, almond extract, walnuts, and butter, and add to the dry ingredients, stirring to mix. Drop the batter by tablespoons onto the peach mixture and sprinkle with remaining sugar. Bake for 40 minutes, until crust is golden brown.   *Makes 8 servings.*

Per serving: 239 calories / 8 gm fat / 39 gm carbohydrate / 153 mg sodium

∼ Raspberry Cobbler ∼

Since I always have an abundance of raspberries in the summertime, I make as many desserts as I can before the birds, bees, and beetles beat me to the crop. This cobbler is very tart, the way I like raspberry desserts.

2 pints fresh raspberries	½ teaspoon nutmeg
1 cup plus 2 tablespoons sugar	½ teaspoon baking soda
1 tablespoon dark rum	½ teaspoon baking powder
1 teaspoon allspice	1 egg
2 tablespoons arrowroot	1 teaspoon grated lemon zest
1 cup all-purpose unbleached flour	½ cup plain low-fat yogurt
	¼ teaspoon almond extract
¼ teaspoon salt	1 tablespoon butter, melted

Preheat the oven to 375 degrees F. Butter a 2-quart baking dish and set aside. In a large mixing bowl, combine the raspberries, ¾ cup sugar, rum, allspice, and arrowroot. Toss gently to mix and pour the mixture into the buttered dish. Into a large bowl, sift flour with ¼ cup sugar, salt, nutmeg, baking soda, and baking powder. In another bowl, combine the egg, lemon zest, yogurt, almond extract, and melted butter, and add to the dry ingredients, stirring to mix. Drop the batter by the tablespoon onto the raspberry mixture. Sprinkle remaining sugar on top of the batter and bake for 30 minutes, or until crust is golden brown.   *Makes 8 servings.*

Per serving: 225 calories / 2 gm fat / 49 gm carbohydrate / 152 mg sodium

∼ Rhubarb-Ginger Cobbler ∼

Rhubarb and ginger are as good a pair as Fred and Ginger. Here, the ginger-bread shares equal billing with the fruit.

4 cups coarsely chopped rhubarb	2 tablespoons grated gingerroot
1 cup sugar	1 teaspoon ground ginger
1 teaspoon allspice	½ teaspoon cinnamon
¼ cup butter	⅛ teaspoon dry mustard
¼ cup tightly packed dark brown sugar	1 teaspoon baking soda
1 egg	1¼ cups sifted all purpose unbleached flour
⅓ cup sorghum molasses	
1 tablespoon crystallized ginger, minced	½ cup 1 percent fat buttermilk

Put rhubarb in a bowl. Pour 1 cup sugar over and toss well to mix. Let stand in refrigerator for an hour. Drain rhubarb and discard all but ¼ cup juice. Return to its bowl, sprinkle with allspice, and toss.

Preheat the oven to 350 degrees F. Butter a large rectangular baking dish. In a large mixing bowl, cream butter with the brown sugar. Beat the egg into the creamed mixture and add the sorghum, crystallized ginger, and the gingerroot. In a small bowl, mix together the ground ginger, cinnamon, mustard, baking soda, and the flour. Add in increments to the batter, stirring as you go along. Add the buttermilk and beat until smooth. Pour the rhubarb mixture into the bottom of the pan. Drop the ginger mixture by the teaspoonful on top. Bake for 30 minutes and then turn the oven temperature down to 325 degrees. Bake for another 15 minutes, until cake is well browned. *Makes 8 servings.*

Per serving: 217 calories / 7 gm fat / 34 gm carbohydrate / 189 mg sodium

~ Blueberry Pear Cobbler ~

I use a bit of cornmeal in the topping here, and very little sugar—just a sprinkling on top. This cobbler has a few interesting flavors coming at you.

4 ripe bosc pears, peeled and
   cored
½ cup plus 2 tablespoons sugar
1 vanilla bean
1 cinnamon stick
1 tablespoon crystallized
   ginger, minced
1 cup water
½ cup sauterne
¾ cup all-purpose unbleached
   flour
½ cup cornmeal
½ teaspoon baking powder
½ teaspoon baking soda
½ teaspoon salt
¼ teaspoon nutmeg
1 teaspoon grated lemon zest
1 egg
½ cup 1 percent fat buttermilk
¼ cup evaporated skim milk
1 tablespoon butter, melted
1½ pints fresh blueberries
¼ cup maple syrup

Preheat the oven to 350 degrees F. Butter a large baking dish and set aside. Slice each pear into eighths. Put ½ cup sugar, vanilla bean, cinnamon, and ginger in a large skillet and heat until sugar caramelizes, about 5 to 8 minutes. Add water and wine and bring to a boil. Reduce heat to low and put pears in the pan. Simmer, covered, for 25 minutes, until pears are tender. Meanwhile, in a large bowl, combine flour, cornmeal, baking powder, baking soda, salt, nutmeg, and lemon zest. In a small bowl, beat the egg with buttermilk and evaporated milk and pour into the dry mixture. Add butter, blend until smooth, and put aside. Rinse the blueberries and drain. Add blueberries to the skillet and pour on maple syrup. Toss gently and pour into buttered dish. Drop cobbler batter by the tablespoon onto fruit and sprinkle top with remaining sugar. Bake for 30 minutes, until batter is golden brown. *Makes 8 servings.*

Per serving: 261 calories / 3 gm fat / 55 gm carbohydrate / 230 mg sodium

~ 16 ~

Body and Soul

Having properly addressed our appetite and quenched our thirst, let's for a moment direct ourselves to the inner body, and the place it lives. About once a week, I take a special kind of evening for myself. It's an evening where I simply relish the quiet time: I play my favorite music, I sip a glass of tawny port, and if it's winter, I stoke a blazing fire in the fireplace. It's a time to let the innermost thoughts drift out in the safe haven of a very private atmosphere. And sooner or later, it all ends up in the bath.

Yes, the bath. Your bathtub can be a porcelain spa, a summer meadow in a room, a secret indulgence which restores and refreshes the soul. We're not referring to toy ducks and Mr. Bubble, we're talking about a tub surrounded by beeswax candles and aromatic soaps. Add to this bath treatment bowls of fragrant potpourri, herbal hair and skin treatments—and well, you get the idea. I take my baths very seriously. And if you've got the time, nothing beats a long, lovingly prepared soak.

To make things even better, there's the fact that nearly all the goodies I just mentioned can be made in your own kitchen. I used to spend lots of money on these products but I've since learned how much money can be saved by making many of them yourself. All that you need is some herbs and plants, some essential oils, and items you probably already have in your kitchen. Most other items can be obtained through the mail at a very low price (see List of Mail-Order Resources on page 268) or at a health food store.

∾ Bathroom Potpourri ∾

Bathrooms, like kitchens, need their own scent; I like mine to carry the scent of lavender and eucalyptus.

3 cups dried lavender flowers	**½ cup witch hazel bark**
1 cup eucalyptus leaves, dried	**½ teaspoon lemon oil**

Put the lavender, eucalyptus, and witch hazel bark in a bowl; sprinkle oil over and toss.

∾ Bath Milk ∾

Milk baths have been around for almost as long as civilization itself and for good reasons: their skin-softening and moisturizing properties, their calming effects, and their sheer luxury. In the ancient world, baths were considered a true sybaritic luxury, and a milk bath consisted of the fresh sweet milk of a cow, sometimes with a few rose petals thrown in, and very little, if any, water. Most of us today are not gifted with our own cows, so the powdered milk will have to suffice. My advice for milk bathers: shower thoroughly first.

½ cup almonds, ground into a	**½ cup baking soda**
fine powder	**1 cup Epsom salts**
4 cups powdered milk	

Put almonds, milk, baking soda, and Epsom salts in a jar with a tight-fitting lid and shake. Fill bathtub up with very warm water and pour in 1 cup of the milk mixture. *Makes 6 1-cup portions.*

∽ Bath Salts ∽

At the end of a hard day, a bath full of salts is almost as good as a full-body massage. This antiseptic formula is excellent for muscle aches.

½ cup dried eucalyptus leaves
½ cup hops
⅛ cup sage, dried

⅛ cup thyme, dried
⅛ cup lavender, dried
1 cup Epsom salts

Crush eucalyptus and put into a small cheesecloth sack, along with the hops, sage, thyme, and lavender. Tie to the bath faucet so that the hot water runs directly on it. When tub is filled, add Epsom salts. *Makes enough for 1 bath.*

∽ After-Bath Toner ∽

The bath tonic, although not as popular as it once was, is a refreshing pick-me-up for after-shower as well.

1 bunch of mint
15 sprigs of lavender
20 sprigs of lemon balm

12 sprigs of rosemary
1 quart witch hazel

Put the mint, lavender, lemon balm, and rosemary in a large bottle with a cap. Pour in the witch hazel. Set in the sun for 2 weeks, stirring daily. Strain into a decorative bottle. *Makes 1 quart.*

～ Dusting Powder ～

A veil of silken delicacy to slip over the just-bathed body.

1 cup cornstarch
¼ cup powdered rosebuds
2 tablespoons powdered
   slippery elm bark

1 teaspoon powdered myrrh
1 tablespoon orrisroot
½ teaspoon French lavender oil

Combine the cornstarch, rosebuds, slippery elm, myrrh, and orrisroot in a dry, moisture-proof container, and shake to mix. Add oil to mixture and shake again.   *Makes 1½ cups.*

～ Foot Bath ～

What a great way to treat your tootsies after a nice hike through the park or woods (or a day spent pounding the city streets).

3 tablespoons dried chamomile
1 tablespoon dried mint
1 tablespoon dried marjoram

1 tablespoon dried rosemary
½ tablespoon dried thyme

Mix all ingredients and store in a small jar with a tight-fitting lid. When ready to use, add 2 teaspoons to 1½ quarts of water. Boil 5 minutes, remove from heat, and let cool to desired temperature. Pour into a small tub and soak feet.   *Makes ⅓ cup.*

∽ Fennel Facial Masque ∾

It's a wonder that cosmetic companies profit so greatly from facial masques, when some of our best treatments are sitting either in the cupboard or the refrigerator. Mostly these items are preservative-free and can be made for pennies.

½ **cup fennel seed**	1 **egg white**
⅛ **cup boiling water**	2 **tablespoons chickpea flour**
2 **tablespoons honey**	1 **tablespoon plain yogurt**

Put the fennel in a shallow dish; pour boiling water over the seeds, and let sit until cooled. In a small bowl, mix the honey with the egg white, flour, and yogurt and add the fennel mixture. Blend well and apply to a clean face. Leave on for 15 minutes and rinse off.   *Makes enough for one masque.*

∽ Peppermint Facial Steam ∾

What better way to unclog the pores than with peppermint-scented vapors? Your well-toned face will tingle for hours.

¾ **cup fresh peppermint leaves**   1 **quart boiling water**

Put the peppermint leaves into a large bowl; pour boiling water over the leaves and tent a large towel over the bowl and your head. Keep your face under the tent for at least 10 minutes.

∾ Sage Facial Toner ∾

1 cup dried sage leaves   **2 cups witch hazel**

Put leaves in a large clear bottle with a cap; pour witch hazel over leaves and let sit in the sun for 3 weeks. Strain.   *Makes 1 pint.*

∾ Rosemary Hair Oil ∾

Rosemary is reputed to stimulate hair growth, while wheat germ oil strengthens hair. It is best if heated before applying to hair and rinsed out ½ hour later with a mild shampoo.

1 cup fresh rosemary leaves   **⅛ teaspoon oil of lemon**
2 cups wheat germ oil

Place dry rosemary leaves in a bottle with a cap. Pour both oils over leaves and let sit for 3 weeks in a warm place. Strain. Use ¼ cup for each treatment, a little more for long or thick hair.   *Makes 1 pint.*

∾ Cinnamon-Mint Mouth Rinse ∾

I love a good mouth rinse in the morning—before I brush, before my first drink of water, before I put anything else in my mouth. But it must not make me think I'm drinking the cloudy water that drips off the roof. This rinse has the refreshing taste of cinnamon and mint.

½ teaspoon star anise   **¼ teaspoon peppermint oil**
¼ teaspoon ground cloves   **⅛ teaspoon cinnamon oil**
¼ teaspoon ground cinnamon   **1½ cups water**
½ teaspoon 60 percent ethyl
**   alcohol**

In a jar, combine spices with the alcohol. Let sit for 1 week, then strain. Mix the oils with the alcohol. Add water and decant into a bottle with lid.   *Makes 1½ cups.*

∼ Orange-Clove Mouth Rinse ∼

Another great taste for the morning.

¼ teaspoon orange oil	½ cup 60 percent ethyl alcohol
⅛ teaspoon clove oil	2 cups water

Dissolve the oils in the alcohol; add water and decant.   *Makes 1 pint.*

∼ Warm Sage Gargle ∼

For sore throats and other cold-related maladies, sage is one of nature's de-congestants.

¼ cup dried sage	1 cup boiling water

Put sage in a small teapot and pour boiling water over the leaves. Let steep for 15 minutes. Strain and let sit for 5 minutes, until tepid enough to gargle with.   *Makes 1 cup.*

∽ Kitchen Potpourri ∽

We come full circle to the kitchen. There was a time when I would keep coffee and bananas around so the aroma would remind me of Nana's kitchen. When I decided to give my kitchen its own personality, I came up with this combination of ingredients, which has a light, understated smell of spices—a scent to complement the aromas of cooking.

1 cup sunflower petals, dried
1 cup lemon verbena leaves, dried
1 cup dried orange peel
1 cup cinnamon chips
⅛ cup whole cloves
1 vanilla bean, split and chopped
½ teaspoon clove oil

Put the sunflower petals, verbena leaves, orange peel, cinnamon chips, cloves, and vanilla bean in a large shallow bowl. Sprinkle on the oil and toss about.

Suggested Menus

～ The Cocktail Hour ～

Thank goodness for small pleasures. And what person who imbibes from time to time doesn't like the designated cocktail or "happy hour," that space in time when the day gives way to evening and the cares of life fall from our hands like an olive—splash!—into a dry martini. Music, munchies, good chat, sherry, wine, or stronger if you dare are the vital ingredients for this long-upheld and wonderful tradition.

Rosemary Wine

———

Oysters on the Half-Shell with Three Sauces:
Bloody Mary Sauce
Hot Herb Broth
Chili-Lemon Butter

———

Cowpea Chow Chow
Pickled Shrimp

∽ Down-Home Comforts ∽

When something goes awry between the world and ourselves, we often seek solace in the foods that evoke memories of better times, or foods that were prepared by those who have cared so deeply for us. Here are a few of my tried-and-true comforts.

Hot Spiced Cider

Chicken Hash
Stewed Greens with Cornmeal Dumplings
Sweet Potato Waffles
Cowpea Stew

Caramelized Banana Pudding

∽ Winter Brunch Buffet ∽

Nothing beats a cold winter day better than a spread of down-home breakfast delicacies.

Watermelon Mimosa
Hot Cocoa

Baked Apple Rings
Poached Plums

Cornmeal Biscuits with
Sawmill Gravy
Breakfast Shrimp Gravy over
Green Onion and Cheese Grits
Gingerbread Waffles
Oyster Omelet
Home Fries with Rosemary and Garlic

∽ Intimate Holiday Dinner ∽

Often, holiday dinners are large and very public affairs. This meal is sized especially for a smaller number of diners, be it the immediate family, close friends, or your favorite couple.

Pickled Okra
She-Crab Soup

Grilled Quail with Oyster Bread Pudding and
Brown Sherry Gravy
Sautéed Mixed Greens
Sweet Potato Pone
Corn Pudding
Cranberry Relish

Sweet Potato Buns

Blueberry Pear Cobbler

∽ Christmas Eve ∽

Deck the Halls! This menu is a compilation of my favorite dishes by my favorite people cooked during my favorite time of year.

Syllabub

Creamed Oysters over Toast

Grandmom's Roasted Chicken with Cornbread Stuffing
Grandpop's Macaroni and Cheese
Mom's Mashed Turnips with Sage Butter
Okra Curry
String Beans with Potatoes

Nana's Graham Cracker Pie

∽ Low Country Feast ∼

A simple but elegant feast, Southern style.

Brown Oyster Stew with Mushrooms
Baked Collards with Smoked Hen
Rice and Shrimp Waffles with
Red Pepper Gravy
Sweet-Hot Yams
Spoonbread

———

Persimmon Custard

———

∽ Creole Vegetarian ∼

These days, you don't have to be a full-fledged vegetarian to enjoy a meatless dinner. Here are a few tasty concoctions that will leave you full and satisfied, not longing for flesh.

Onion Pie

———

Fancy Mess o' Greens
Red Beans and Rice
Baked Gingered Yams

———

Lemon-Brandy Peaches

———

~ Fish Friday ~

Fish on Friday had nothing especially religious about it at our house, though you might have thought so, given how faithfully we ate our fish. On the other hand, with such an avid fishermom in the kitchen, what else could you expect?

Steamed Shrimp

Catfish with Cornmeal Crust
Lemon-Garlic Grits
Okra, Corn, and Tomatoes

Red and Green Pepper Cornbread

Nana's Lemon Meringue Pie

~ Backyard Barbecue ~

There's nothing like the backyard barbecue: a great mix of sunshine and charcoal smoke, food and laughter, where a family can let down its hair, eat off paper plates—and troop indoors to wash off!

Lemonade with Mint Ice Cubes

Barbecued Shrimp
Steamed Crabs
Grilled Barbecued Chicken
Roasted Corn in the Husk
Ginger Beans
Potato Salad
Cucumbers in Peppered Vinegar

Deep-Dish Cherry Pie
Rhubarb-Ginger Cobbler

∽ Picnic ∽

A proper picnic meal should be a mix of convenience and good eating. This one qualifies on both counts.

Strawberry Limeade

Skinless Fried Chicken
Curried Macaroni Salad
Corn Relish
Field Greens with Vidalia Onion Vinaigrette

Deep-Dish Apple Pie

∽ Bath Box ∽

For those friends of yours who relish time spent soaking and dreaming in the tub, this is the perfect gift. It's pretty, fragrant, economical, and, best of all, homemade!

Bathroom Potpourri
Bath Milk
Foot Bath
After-Bath Toner
Dusting Powder

∼ Host Package ∼

If you're ever at a loss as to what to bring your favorite host, here is a sample idea.

Kitchen Potpourri
Dried Herbs Mix
Six-Pepper Oil
Lemon Cayenne
Peppered Rum
Pie Spice
Shellfish Boil
Oat Cookies with Dried Cranberries

Glossary of Cooking Terms and Techniques

Here are a few terms that I use frequently throughout the book.

blanching—this retains and, in some cases, brightens the color of fresh vegetables. I tend to blanch all of my green vegetables, as they have a tendency to turn greenish gray when cooked. *To blanch:* Boil water in a pot large enough to comfortably contain the vegetables. Immerse the vegetables in the pot of water for 1 to 3 minutes. Drain vegetables and immediately shock them by plunging them into a large bowl of ice water. Cook as the recipe directs.

bruise—to slightly crush an ingredient, such as mint or garlic, in order to release its flavor.

caramelize—to cook sugar over relatively high heat until it liquefies and turns a golden brown. You can also *caramelize* foods that contain sugar by cooking until the sugar is released and produces a dark brown glaze.

deglaze—to add a liquid, most often wine, stock, or vinegar, to the pan after food, usually meat, has been cooking in it. The liquid dislodges the browned particles of food and acts as a base for a sauce.

develop—simply means to let your cooked foods sit, covered, off the heat to allow the flavors to settle. Ever notice how much better leftover food tastes the day after? This is because the flavors have been allowed to *de-*

velop overnight in the refrigerator. For a more intense taste, it's preferable to cook stews at least an hour before serving time, or cook them the day before and refrigerate overnight.

dredge—the act of lightly coating food with flour, cornmeal, bread crumbs, or seeds, before frying or baking.

flake—to use a fork or a similar utensil to break off small sections of food.

fold—to gently combine a light mixture (egg whites, for example) with a heavier base, such as batter or pureed fruit. The lighter mixture is folded into the base. A rubber spatula is used to cut down through the mixture, across the base of the bowl, and up the side so as to turn the mixtures over each other. Concurrently, the bowl should be rotated slightly with each series of strokes to combine mixtures evenly.

reduce—to cook liquid uncovered over high heat in order to thicken and to concentrate the flavor.

scald—to heat a liquid until just below the boiling point; used in earlier days to pasteurize milk.

sear—to brown meat by exposing it to very high heat in a skillet or broiler in a relatively short amount of time. The idea is to seal in the meat's juices. This is good for meats that are going to be stewing for a while.

steam—fish: put fresh fish into a steamer basket or a small colander that will fit comfortably into your pan. Pour 1 cup water or wine into the steamer pot. Place the steamer basket in the pot and secure with a lid. Cook over medium-high heat for at least 3 minutes. Turn the fish over and cook until fish flakes with a fork (the cooking time varies with the type of fish you use).

List of Mail-Order Resources

Each mail-order source will provide a catalog upon request. Places marked with an asterisk (*) are available 24 hours a day.

The Baker's Catalogue*
P.O. Box 876
Norwich, VT 05055-0876
800 827-6836
(natural sugar, bakeware,
high gluten flour [yeast breads],
low gluten pastry flour [biscuits])

Beer Wine and Hobby
180 New Boston Street
Woburn, MA 08101
800-523-5423 (to order)
617-933-8829 (consultation)
(wine-making supplies, hydrometer,
fermentation lock)

International Home Cooking
305 Mallory Street
Rocky Mountain, NC 27801

800 237-7423
(game birds, quail, dried fruits and
berries)

No Common Scents, Inc.
Kings Yard
220 Xenia
Yellow Springs, OH 45387
800 686-0012
(potpourri ingredients, essential oils)

Rafel Spice Company
2521 Russell
Detroit, MI 48207
800 228-4276 (to order)
313 259-6373 (for inquiries)
(powdered rosebuds, dried herbs, and
spices)

Shepherd's Garden Seeds
30 Irene Street
Torrington, CT 06790
203-482-3638
(seeds and seedlings for growing
vegetables and herbs)

Sur La Table*
84 Pine Street
Pike Place Farmer's Market

Seattle, WA 98101
800-243-0852
(cookware, garlic mandoline)

Williams-Sonoma*
P.O. Box 7456
San Francisco, CA 94120-7456
800-541-2233
("atmospheric" items, cherry pitter,
canning equipment)

Selected Bibliography

Bivins, Thomas
The Southern Cookbook
Press of the Hampton Institute 1912
Hampton, VA

Burns, LaMont
Down Home Southern Cooking
Doubleday 1986 Garden City, NY

Campbell, Tunis G.
Hotel Keepers, Head Waiters and Housekeepers' Guide
Coolidge and Wiley 1848 Boston, MA

Copage, Eric V.
Kwanzaa: An African-American Celebration of Culture and Cooking
William Morrow and Company 1991
New York

Darden, Norma Jean and Carole
Spoonbread and Strawberry Wine
Anchor Press 1978 New York

Egerton, John
Southern Food: At Home, on the Road, in History
Alfred A. Knopf 1987 New York

Ferguson, Sheila
Soul Food: Classic Cuisine from the South
Weidenfeld & Nicolson 1989 New York

Genovese, Eugene D.
Roll, Jordan, Roll
Vintage Books 1976 New York

Harris, Jessica B.
Iron Pots and Wooden Spoons
Atheneum 1989 New York

Jones, Evan
American Food: The Gastronomic Story
E. P. Dutton 1975 New York

Lewis, Edna
In Pursuit of Flavor
Knopf 1988 New York

Mendes, Helen
The African Heritage Cookbook
Macmillan 1971 New York

Neal, Bill
Biscuits, Spoonbread and Sweet Potato Pie
Alfred A. Knopf 1991 New York

Roberts, Leonard E.
The Negro Chef Cookbook
Vantage Press 1969 New York

Roberts, Robert
The House Servants Directory
Munroe and Francis 1828 Boston, MA

Root, Waverly, and De Rochemont, Richard
Eating in America
The Ecco Press 1981 New York

Schneider, Sally
The Art of Low Calorie Cooking
Stewart, Tabori & Chang 1990 New York

Smart-Grosvenor, Vertamae
Vibration Cooking, or the Travel Notes of a Geechee Girl
Ballantine Books 1970 New York

Wilson, Ellen Gibson
A West African Cookbook
Lippincott 1971 Philadelphia

Index

• A NOTE ON THE TYPE •

The typeface used in this book is one of many versions of Garamond, a modern homage to—rather than, strictly speaking, revival of—the celebrated fonts of Claude Garamond (c.1480–1561), the first founder to produce type on a large scale. Garamond's type was inspired by Francesco Griffo's *De Ætna* type (cut in the 1490s for Venetian printer Aldus Manutius and revived in the 1920s as Bembo), but its letter forms were cleaner and the fit between pieces of type improved. It therefore gave text a more harmonious overall appearance than its predecessors had, becoming the basis of all romans created on the continent for the next two hundred years; it was itself still in use through the eighteenth century. Besides the many "Garamonds" in use today, other typefaces derived from his fonts are Granjon and Sabon (despite their being named after other printers).